CHARLES
ALCOCK
& THE
LITTLE
TIN
IDOL

(150 YEARS OF THE FA CUP)
1871-72 TO 2021-22

1st Edition: 16th October 2021

ISBN: 9798479058967

www.chesfoxbooks.com

'Centre- FOREWORD'

Firstly, let me begin by saying that this book is not intended to be an historical tome, dedicated to the facts, figures and minutiae of the first FA Cup and the evolution of the 'beautiful game'. Rather, it is an attempt to use the historical information of the time to paint a picture of what it is was like to play the game at its conception in Victorian society.

There are many splendid books that detail the history of the game and the FA Cup and I have listed some of these in the bibliography which can be found at the back of this book.

I have tried to stick to the facts as accurately as possible, but I implore your forgiveness if I have embellished some of them in order to convey the atmosphere of the Victorian age and bring to life the key figures and places of the greatest Cup competition in the world.

The paragraphs written in *italics* are extracts from Victorian newspapers and books and as such reflect the language of the time.

To avoid interrupting the flow of the narrative the author's notes are annotated in the text with a Roman numeral and then listed at the end of each chapter.

Ian Chester
Warwickshire
October 2021

DEDICATION

For Colleen, my wife, who has had to put up with me talking football
bollocks for far too long.

ACKNOWLEDGEMENTS

To Chris Gedge, my excellent proof reader. A member of the apostrophe
police, who has reported me for crimes committed against punctuation.

To Jane Kennedy, Ian Hudson and Richard Hawker, the 'typo' detectives,
who have corrected my many errors and inconsistencies.

To Phil Martin, whose telephone conversations and email exchanges have
kept this book on the correct historic track. (Not in Seddon.)

To Peter Hamersley, whose research into Upton Park FC and football in the
East End of London added greatly to this section of the book.

To Mark Smith of Maidenhead United Football Club, whose detailed
research into the 150-year history of his club was invaluable.

To Terry Staines. Chairman of Marlow Football Club, for his time and
hospitality on what was a busy 150th anniversary FA Cup Day.

To David Chapman, whose detailed information on the Forest Club enabled
me to piece together the birth of the Alcock's first football club.

To Peter Manning whose book 'Palace at the Palace' and email exchanges
guided me through the early days of football in this magical place.

To Frank McCrossan of Queen's Park Football Club, who quite correctly
opened my eyes to the importance of this amateur Scottish club in the
development of the game we know and love today.

To Anthony Brown and the wonderful team at Hitchin Football Club, who
are so rightly proud of their roots and their 150-year-old history.

To Major Glen Lishman of the Royal Engineers who allowed me to visit the
Brompton Barracks in Chatham and who helped fill in the missing gaps of the
Sappers history.

To Keith Richards, who has compiled a database of all the early Victorian
football matches and helped me to fill a few gaps with regard to the Royal
Engineers and Reigate Priory.

To Martin Westby (R.I.P.) whose painstaking research into the early English
football clubs and in particular the influence of football in Sheffield allowed this
book to be written.

CONTENTS

1.   Well, the Numbers to Watch out for are…...
2.   Fancy a Kickabout? - Shrove Tuesday Football (1840).
3.   Made of Steel – The Creation of Sheffield FC (1857)
4.   Cock of the North 'Cock House' Cup Final, Harrow (1858)
5.   On the Origin of Species: The Forest Football Club (1859)
6.   All the President's Men - Formation of the FA (1863)
7.   North versus South - London versus Sheffield (1866)
8.   The Youdan Cup: First Football Cup Competition (1867)
9.   Look, No Hands! England versus Scotland (1870)
10.   The Little Tin Idol is Born

THE FIRST FA CUP 1871-72

11.   The Fifteen Teams
12.   The first FA Cup Game?
13.   Oarsmen v. The Admiralty
14.   The Battle of the Brewers
15.   The First FA Cup Goal?
16.   Clapham Rovers are not Common at all
17.   This Pitch isn't Big Enough for the Both of Us!
18.   Brothers in Arms
19.   Who Let the Dogs Out?
20.   A Royal Hitch for Hitchin
21.   Cuthbert John Ottaway, I Presume?
22.   Heathens Sapped of Strength
23.   A Day for Thanksgiving
24.   Enter John Brown and the Scots
25.   Who'd be a Goalkeeper?
26.   Please Do Not Strain the Ropes!

***

27.   Where are They Now? 150 Years Later (2021-22)
28.   Charles Alcock & The Little Tin Idol

APPENDICES:

1.   Rules of Harrow Football (1858)
2.   Rules of the Forest Club (1861)
3.   Rules & Regulations for the Government of Sheffield FC (1857)
4.   Sheffield Playing Rules (October 1858)
5.   The Laws of the Game (December 1863)
6.   Football in Battersea Park by the Rules of the London Association (Jan. 1864)
7.   The Laws of the Game (1871)
8.   1871-1872 FA Cup Round by Round
9.   The Anniversary programmes 1922, 1972, 2022?

Chapter 1: "Well, the Numbers to Watch out for are…..."

"Number 2 – Arsenal of course, who have the record number of FA Cup wins. Mikel Arteta was successful last season in an epic final against Chelsea, who are ball number 12. Tottenham, currently the Premier League leaders, are number 39. Manchester United, 24, who are looking to close the gap that Arsenal have when it comes to the record number of FA Cup successes. Liverpool, the reigning Premier League champions, are at number 21. Leicester City, number 20. Stockport, 49. Chorley of course, have made it through and they're number 53, Marine are 58 and Canvey Island, who are in the eighth tier of English football, are drawn number 60 if they can overcome Boreham Wood. It will be a fascinating Third Round draw, coming up very shortly indeed. Well, those are the most important numbers."

54 sets of watching supporters of the other teams shake their heads at the TV in disapproval. Their team is the most important number in the draw and they want to know what it is.

"Shall we start the draw?"

"Yes, we shall."

"Make sure they all go in - Give it a check."

Ex-player and TV pundit, Robbie Savage, picks up the velvet bag containing 64 shiny black porcelain balls each inscribed with a bright white number, representing the teams that will compete in this year's FA Cup Third Round. Robbie carefully tips the balls into the glass globe from which the draw will be made.

"Oooooooh!"

A tense moment. One of the balls gets stuck in the bag and Robbie has to squeeze it from top to bottom to make sure all the balls are correctly in the glass globe.

The draw commences.

All over the land players and supporters sit, hoping and praying that their sides get the most exciting tie.

"The first team out of the bag and they will play at their home ground is..

Number 18 – Huddersfield Town, 13th in the Championship, Carlos Corberán is in charge of them.

Against Number 50 – Plymouth Argyle. Ryan Lowe's side, 11th in League One."

Robbie Savage is probably the best suited TV pundit to do the FA Cup draw. His childish enthusiasm and excitement cannot be contained. He swirls the balls around in the glass globe and picks out the next team.

"Number 53… is Chorley, the National League North side, who have already seen off Wigan and Peterborough. In the Third Round for the first time ever and you've given them a home tie, Robbie."

Robbie rubs his hands with glee. "C'mon!"

The next ball comes out of the globe. Robbie takes a quick sideways look at the list of numbered teams that remain in the draw before revealing the ball to the camera.

"Ooooh 15."

"15 - Derby County, bottom of the Championship. Wayne Rooney now in sole charge of your old team."

"Aaaaah!"

The next number out of the pot is '58'.

"Number 58 is Marine, just the second eighth tier side to get to the Third Round. What a story they are! You've drawn them at home as well."

"My friend, Paddy McKewell, is a massive Marine fan. C'mon!"

Football supporters, all over the country, hope and pray the minnows of Marine (The Mariners) from Crosby on Merseyside can hook themselves a 'big fish'. After another swirl of the black balls Robbie turns the chosen ball to the camera to reveal the fateful number.

"Against 39."

"39 – TOTTENHAM HOTSPUR! The Premier League leaders out of the hat to play Marine. What a tie that is!"

Robbie can't contain his excitement and punches the air as if he's just scored the winning goal in this year's FA Cup Final.

"WO-O-O-O-OW!"

Over the years the draw for the FA Cup Third Round is always eagerly anticipated as this is the round when the top ranked clubs enter the competition. The draw itself has gone through various guises from its origins in 1871 when the results of the draw would be communicated in the National Press. In the early days of radio in the 1920s players and fans would gather around their Bakelite wireless radios listening with nervous anticipation to find out who their team would draw. By the 1960s, wireless radios had developed into portable transistor radios which could be carried into Clubs' board rooms or even changing rooms for players to listen to the draw.

Billy Shankly of Preston North End tunes into the FA Cup draw to discover who his team will play in the semi-final of 1938.

Soon the British public would witness the advent of television and the broadcasting of football through the BBC. The draw often took place in the FA's offices in Lancaster Gate where a dour procedure took place in front of the oak panelled walls of the FA's boardroom. The draw would be made by the Chairman of the Challenge Cup Committee and the Chairman of the Football Association. A velvet bag would be passed between the two seated gentlemen by an FA official and a non-committed neutral expression would be adopted by both as each team was drawn out. Contrast that to today's draw which is a half an hour programme, held in a football team's clubhouse or bar featuring interviews with the players and managers of the lowest ranked teams. A football celebrity or two are then drafted in to make the draw for the home and away teams. Robbie Savage's performance on this occasion was TV gold.

Of course, the Third Round Draw isn't the start of the FA Cup and the Marine Association Football Club had already played six ties before reaching the Third Round stage of the competition. The current FA Cup usually starts in the summer month of August with an extra-preliminary round and then a preliminary round, before going through four regional qualifying rounds to get to the First Round Proper in November.

In the season 2019-20, 736 teams took part with 644 playing in the qualifying rounds and 124 in the main competition. This year's competition featured teams such as Hashtag United, a team formed on the internet, that became a social media sensation by showing highlights of their matches on YouTube, Twitter and Instagram. Other teams to enter the competition were Newport Flowserve, Pontefract Collieries and a personal favourite of mine, the New Salamis.

The New Salamis were formed in 1971 by fans of the Cypriot club 'Nea Salamis Famagusta' with the Cyprus-based club acting as a parent club. Playing in the KOPA League, a British Cypriot league, the club won the 2016 FA Sunday Cup following a penalty shoot-out win against Barnes AFC at Selhurst Park.

In what seems to be an amazing coincidence, Barnes Football Club just happen to be one of the teams that entered the first-ever FA Cup 150 years ago. Things were very different in those days and in 1871 there were just fifty members of the Football Association, (today there are over 40,000), who were invited to play in the inaugural FA Challenge Cup competition.

To understand more we need to go back in time.

Chapter 2: 'Fancy a Kickabout?'
Shrove Tuesday Football
Richmond-upon-Thames
(Tuesday 3rd March 1840)

John Newman sat at the large wooden farmhouse kitchen table and tucked into his breakfast consisting of a bowl of flour, butter and water (porridge?) followed by a piece of bacon and two thick slices of farmhouse bread. He ate his breakfast with gusto this morning as he knew he was going to need all of his strength today. This was his first day off work in what seemed like ages. His job as a farm labourer didn't give him a lot of time for recreational pursuits but today was a day he had been looking forward to for months.

In fact, he was more excited today than he been a couple of weeks ago when Queen Victoria and Prince Albert had passed near his home town of Isleworth in their royal carriages. It was the day of their wedding and the happy couple had passed along the road from Brentford to Hounslow on the way to Windsor from St. James' Palace. It being a Monday, John had to work in the fields with his father tending the livestock and preparing the land for this season's planting of crops. As they toiled they could hear the church bells ringing out repeatedly across the open fields and then in the afternoon they could hear the cheers of the local dignitaries and school children as the royal procession passed through their towns and villages. However, today was Shrove Tuesday, a day off work and time for a game of football.

After washing down his breakfast with a small pitcher of beer, John retired to his room to get ready for the day's proceedings. Instead of his normal working uniform of a farmer's smock and breeches, the nineteen-year-old John donned a thick cotton, wide-cut shirt complete with neckerchief. He then pulled on a waistcoat and stepped into his full-length trousers. To complete his outfit, he wore a thick jacket and a cloth cap. Stooping down to put on his leather boots, he double checked that the buttons and laces were secure and with a twirl of his moustache, he stepped out onto the pavement and headed for the main street.

Living in Isleworth, on the banks of the River Thames, John was meeting up with a couple of his pals and heading down towards Richmond Bridge to complete the short walk across to Richmond-upon-Thames where the match was to take place. As they approached the bridge the crowd began to thicken and John reached into his jacket pocket to pull out the halfpenny piece required to pass through the tollbooth and onto the bridge itself. Crossing the bridge, they could hear the boatmen shouting out encouragement from the waterfront below, as they loaded their passengers onto the skiffs and punts for a short pleasure ride on the Thames.

"C'mon lads, today's the day!"

Everybody was headed for Richmond Green, the meeting place for the throwing up of the balls. As they approached the wide expanse of grass, they could see groups of lads huddling around in clusters. It was a cold and fresh Spring morning and you could make out the mist of conversational breath as the men whispered to one another.

"Have you heard what they're trying to do?"

"No, what's happening?"

"Well, some of the lads who have come down from the town have said that they're going to stop us from playing football this year and the local residents have asked the police to step in and break up the match!"

"What, I don't believe it! It's fine for them to undertake their sports and row in their regattas on the Thames. We can't afford to play sports like cricket or go shooting and fishing. This is all we've got."

"Yeah, and it's a tradition that's worth fighting for. It's only once a year and we've been playing man and boy for as long as I can remember."

"I've heard that they've already stopped the match in Twickenham from going ahead and they're going to move it onto a meadow under the supervision of some sportsman."

"Well, they tried to ban it five years ago with that Highways Act saying we couldn't play football on the streets in the town and that hasn't stopped us. So, let's not let them win now."

"Have you seen this?"

A thickset long-haired fellow, with an untidy beard and curling moustache, took off his cap and tried to read out the scrunched piece of paper that had been shoved in front of him. Apparently, a new Police Act had been passed in Parliament on the previous Saturday.

'It having been represented to the Commissioners of the Police of the metropolis that great annoyance to the passengers and detriment to the inhabitants, has been occasioned by the practice of kicking a foot-ball in the public streets and thoroughfares of the parish of Richmond on Shrove-Tuesday. All persons are hereby cautioned that such a practice is illegal and any one committing the offence is liable to a penalty of 40s (shillings). The police have accordingly been ordered to prevent this offence and to take into custody any person committing the same after this notice.'

(Signed) Richard Mayne, Commissioner of the Police of the Metropolis – Whitehall Place, Feb. 29 1840.

It was fast approaching noon and there were rumours abounding that a large number of policemen had arrived earlier that morning and were ensconced in the local police station. The crowd was by now nearly two hundred strong and the signal was given to head across The Green and over to the houses on George Street. John followed and he could see that the locals had closed up their houses and boarded up their windows in readiness for the upcoming match. Everything passed on very quietly until about half-past two when the balls were suddenly thrown down at the top of George Street and amidst loud cheers the sport commenced.

The rules were simple. The balls would be carried through the town's streets and down by the river. The team that got the balls back to the meeting place by five o'clock would be announced as the winner.

The balls were thrown high into the air and great excitement followed as the crowd swarmed forward and tried to get a touch or kick on the ball. Then suddenly, just as they started to move, a body of about 50 police constables, headed by the Superintendent and Inspector, were observed marching up the street. As the balls rebounded, the police immediately seized two men who were kicking them and they conveyed both the culprits and the balls towards the Station-house.

They had not proceeded far before a cry of "Rescue, Rescue" was raised and John and a group around him, adrenalin still pumping, picked up some stones and missiles to try and prevent their fellow footballers from being arrested. The police counterattacked and stormed into the crowd. John could feel his jacket being pulled. Suddenly, his neckerchief was ripped off and two policemen threw him to the ground.

"You're nicked."

The rest of the police advanced towards the angry crowd who, upon seeing their friends arrested, fled in all directions. During the remainder of the afternoon, although people were gathering in large groups, there was no further disturbance.

On what was supposed the greatest day of his life, poor old John Newman was now facing his biggest nightmare. He wouldn't be returning home to his family that night. In fact, he wouldn't be seeing them for another month. The following day, he and the five other prisoners were taken from the cells in Richmond prison to appear in front of the local magistrates, Messrs. Paynton and Price, who were sitting in petty sessions in the vestry room near the local church.

After a lengthy examination two prisoners, Joseph Aston and Samuel White were fined 10 shillings each plus 6 shillings costs for having created a disturbance by kicking a football around the public streets of Richmond contrary to the Act of Parliament. Alternatively, in default of this payment, they could endure 14 days of imprisonment. A Charles Norman was fined 30 shillings plus 7 shillings costs or he could serve 21 days imprisonment for being disorderly and assaulting the police. Robert Atkins was fined a similar sum for rescuing a person from the custody of the police. A John Merchant was fined 40 shillings plus 7 shillings costs for resisting the police whilst arresting the above prisoner.

Poor old John Newman received no option of paying a fine but rather was sentenced directly to one month's imprisonment for being disorderly and for throwing stones at the police. All of the defendants paid their fines and John was removed to Kingston Gaol to undergo his imprisonment.

All this in the name of football.

Mob football – Kingston-upon-Thames
(Illustrated London News – 28th February 1846)

The myth surrounding the advent of football on our native shores apparently arises from Anglo Saxons resisting the Danish invasion in 1015. On one occasion, a Shrove Tuesday, the Danish general leading the charge was captured, slain and his head cut from his body. In celebration the townsfolk proceeded to kick the head around the town as a symbol of victory.

In the eyes of authority and the well-bred, the ensuing annual 'mob football' match was a vulgar, rowdy pastime and from the fourteenth century onwards the respectable and the Godly observed it with distaste and made constant efforts to suppress it. It kept men from the exercise of their Christian duties and distracted them from focusing on their work with their employers. Also, it wasted time that might profitably and decently be used in the practice of archery and other military skills. But although the law-abiding mayors, sheriffs and clerics tried to stamp it out, their efforts had little or no effect. One of the earliest written references, showing the authorities opposition to football, was to be found in the provincial newspaper the 'Stamford Mercury' on 18th April 1717.

On Monday last the Commons gave leave to bring a bill to prevent the mischiefs which frequently happen by throwing at Cocks, and kicking footballs within the City of London and Westminster.

The game of football was, of course, not restricted to London and its environs but rather was a national game being played the length and breadth of England on its green and pleasant pastures. It was even to be found played in churches!

'Letters from Chester advise, that at six o'clock prayers at the Cathedral on Christmas morning, the Mob kicked a Foot-Ball in the Broad aisle at the beginning of the Divine Service, and about the middle of it, went into the choir, put out the candles, abused and pulled the reader out of the desk, and the congregation went out in the dark, as well as they could.' (St. James' Evening Post – 4th January 1732)

You could understand why the game of football wasn't endearing itself to the upper echelons of society. However, over the years the game continued to develop and some indication of the nature of this development and the importance of the game to the British people could be found in two matches played near Bedford and Bath in October 1726.

Bedford: 'On Wednesday the 23d Instant; a most obstinate and hard match at Foot-ball was played near Great Harwood in this County, between 7 men of the village of Ranse and the like number of Great Harwood; which last had challenged the whole Kingdom to match them. The Contest was so great between them, that one of the Harwood's Champions dropped down dead on the spot. His brother being engaged on the same side, would not leave off till the Decision of the Game, which ended in favour of their Antagonists, the Ranse Men.' (Ipswich Journal 6th December 1726)

Bath, Oct. 4. 'Yesterday a new and extraordinary entertainment was set on Foot for the Diversion of our polite Gentry, and what should it be but a Match at Foot-Ball, played by six young Women of a Side, at the Bowling Green.' (Ipswich Journal 8th October 1726)

So, football was starting to evolve and gain some kind of structure. Small sided games, with set time periods, were starting to take place (between men and women) and another more illicit type of sport was also starting to appear, that of gambling.

'This is to acquaint all Lovers of that manly Exercise of Foot-Ball Playing, THAT there will be Ten Hats played for on Bury Race-Ground, by Ten Men a Side, on Saturday the 24th of May instant ; to meet at John Place's Booth, at the sign of the Three Pidgeons, at Three o'clock in the Afternoon ; to pay the best of three-quarters of an Hour: The Ball to be thrown off at Six o'clock; where all Gentlemen and others shall meet with a hearty welcome from their humble Servant, JOHN PLACE. N. B. There will be a Foot-Match the same Day for Ten Guineas; to run four Miles.' (Ipswich Journal 10th May 1755)

'Mob football' was still being practised up and down the land including in Scotland and across the water in Ireland. However, this type of football in particular was still frowned upon and matches like the following two 'mob' games in Premnay in Aberdeenshire, Scotland and in Wakefield, Yorkshire, did nothing to help its reputation.

'ON Tuesday last, the following melancholy accident happened in the parish of Premnay, about sixteen miles from this place. Several young lads had met to play at foot-ball (being the day kept in the country for Fastens-eve – Shrove Tuesday) and after their diversion, adjourned to a public house where a quarrel ensued betwixt two of them, viz. William Milne and James Wilson. They started to fight and struggle and when the former, having thrown down Wilson, the said Wilson then gave the other a mortal stab with a knife, of which he died in a few minutes. (Aberdeen Press and Journal – 21st March 1763)

'Last Monday a foot-ball match was played upon Heath Common betwixt the gentlemen of Sharlston, and the gentlemen of Crofton, two neighbouring villages, near Wakefield in Yorkshire, for forty guineas a side. After they had played a full two hours, in which time there was a great many smart falls and ill bruises given on both sides, the gentlemen of Sharlston got the first goal. On beginning a second time, the gentlemen of opposite parties met together at the ball with such violence, that one of them had his leg broke, and the other his shoulder dislocated. The mob immediately rushed in, in such a manner, that they were obliged to give out, and it cannot be decided until the two gentlemen get found again, as neither of the parties were willing to yield. There was some

12

damage sustained by the rudeness of the mob. A fine boy, about eight years of age, was thrown down among them, and unfortunately trod to death. It is very surprising that persons who call themselves gentlemen, should be fond of encouraging such dangerous exercises. (Kentish Gazette – 26th October 1771)

However, football had now worked its way into the British psyche and was firmly established in its culture. It even got the Royal seal of approval at the birthday celebrations of the Prince of Wales and the Duke of York at Brighthelmstone in Sussex where, after a game of cricket, the other amusements of the day consisted of;

I. A game of football, eleven on each side, by the inhabitants of Brighton, for a sum of five guineas.

II. A game of foot-ball, by young women, eleven on a side, for the like sum.

III. A jingle-match, won by one John Baker, who, dressed up with bells, escaped the pursuit of ten persons blind-folded, for half an hour, and obtained the prize of a jacket, waistcoat, and gold-laced hat. (Chester Chronicle – 3rd September 1790)

So, there now seemed to be two strands to football in Britain at the end of 18th Century. The aristocracy, who were starting to adopt the game for exercise, relaxation, pleasure and the odd bet or two. Then there was the game of people, like young John Newman, who saw their 'mob football' as an escape from the hardships of a working-class life and who felt they had a primeval right to play the game.

***

Author's Note:

The story of the mob football match in Richmond-upon-Thames is based on a true event and the details are taken from the newspaper report which can be found in the London Evening Standard - Thursday 5th March 1840. John Newman was arrested and gaoled as described although whether the gentleman involved was the John Newman from Isleworth is conjecture on my part and based on the nearest John Newman I could find to Richmond in the census of 1841.

Chapter 3: 'Made of Steel'
The Creation of the Sheffield Football Club
(24th October 1857)

HALLAM CLUB versus SHEFFIELD FC

Saturday 26th December 1860
Sandygate, Hallam
(Kick-Off : 1.00 - 1.30 p.m.)

"Bloody hell, it's cold lad! We must be mad playing football on't day like today. It's blooming snowing!"

"Aye, but we've had enough matches cancelled this winter and we need t'work off all that roast beef, Yorkshire and plum pudding. That were one hell of a meal that we ate yesterday for Christmas Dinner and anyway, what were you going t'do today? It's Boxing Day. Time to get out of t'house and get some fresh air and exercise."

"Ye're right. I'm looking forward to getting reet stuck in. This is a matter of local pride. We can't afford to lose against our local rivals."

Nathaniel Creswick and William Prest sat in the wooden changing rooms of the Hallam cricket pavilion. The surroundings may have been fine for a cricket match on a warm mid-summer's day but today it was absolutely freezing and you could hear the wind blowing through the slats of the wooden walls. The match was supposed to have taken place on the 10th November 1860 but due to the awful weather conditions the match had been postponed until today and nothing was going to stop it going ahead this time.

It was 26th December 1860 and the Sheffield FC team caught the horse-drawn omnibus, leaving at 12 o'clock from the Angel Hotel in Sheffield to complete the short three-mile journey to Hallam. There had been a fight for the downstairs seats as, given the freezing conditions, none of the players wanted to sit on the top deck which was open to the elements. The unlucky few sat huddled together on the exposed top seats in their thick Ulster overcoats and caps. At least the views were magnificent.

Joseph Tomlinson & Sons, a Sheffield Funeral Director and local provider of horse drawn 'omnibuses'

The omnibus finally pulled up at the Plough Inn just outside the cricket ground on the Sandygate Road. Apart from a few houses, a Victorian mansion and the pub there was nothing but open Yorkshire countryside all around them and the glistening snow sparkled on the surrounding hills. Despite the cold it was a beautiful winter's day and there was no way they were going to let the large number of spectators gathered around the Hallam cricket pitch down this time. The match was due to kick-off at 1.00 p.m. and they would keep playing until it was dark. The communications on the time and location of the match had been posted in the local press by the Clubs' secretaries. Confusingly, the Clubs' Secretaries, Nathaniel Creswick of Sheffield FC, who stated in the Sheffield Telegraph that the match would kick-off at 1.00 p.m. and, John Shaw of Hallam, who quoted 1.30 p.m. in the Sheffield

Independent. With telephones still to be invented I'm sure this kind of confusion regularly took place.

As the Hallam Club was new to football, the original idea had been that 15 players of the Sheffield Football Club would take on 20 of the Hallam and Stumperlowe Football Club. However, this match didn't take place because of the atrocious weather. The rearranged game was less charitable in that it was to be 16 a-side. The combination of the continuing inclement weather and the retributions from the players' wives, who had chastised their husbands for wanting to go and kick a piece of leather around a field on Boxing Day, meant the numbers on the Hallam side were reduced.

The match duly kicked off and the crowd laughed as the men went slipping and sliding on the icy ground. One Hallam player went to charge a Sheffield forward but due to a successful 'dodge' on the part of the latter, the Hallam player went skidding across the snow and headlong into a dry-stone wall which ran the length of the pitch.

"Hey lad, thou'st dislodged a few of t'top stones there and wall's collapsing at the back. You'd better fix that after t' match or we'll have the farmer on t'us."

The players looked magnificent, with the scarlet jerseys and white shorts of the Sheffield side and the blue garments of the Countrymen (the Club's nickname) of Hallam, contrasting beautifully against the brilliant white snow. It soon became evident that the more experienced Sheffield side were more scientific in their play and more alive to the opportunities to take advantage of the game and upset their opponents. Luckily, and despite the conditions, there were no serious accidents and the game was played with 'good temper and in a friendly spirit'.

As darkness rolled in across the hills, the Sheffield Football Club had managed to score two goals to Hallam's nil. They had won the first-ever Sheffield 'derby'.

***

In the 19th century, the city of Sheffield was at the heart of Britain's Industrial Revolution. The natural resources of coal and iron ore to be found in the surrounding hills, plus the fast-flowing rivers of the Loxley, Sheaf and Don, meant Sheffield was the ideal location for the production of steel. It wasn't long before spin off industries, manufacturing items such as cutlery-ware, sharp knives, razors and axes, were springing up around the city. The high demand for Sheffield steel meant the iron ore forges were working around the clock to put silver-plated knives, forks and spoons on the dining tables of Victorian society. The downside of a rapidly developing industrial city was the inevitable pollution from the constant smoke and acrid fumes, billowing across the city, which blackened the stone walls of the surrounding buildings.

Sheffield's industrial skyline as viewed from the Dales (E. Blore 1819)

By the mid-point of the 19th Century, the sons of these pioneering and successful industrialists were looking for an outlet for their new found wealth and seeking activities that were good for their general health and well-being. It was on a summer's evening walk at the end of the cricket season that a young Nathaniel Creswick (26), the son of a silver plate manufacturer, and William Prest (25), the son of a wine merchant, discussed their plans to form a football club for the young gentlemen of Sheffield. A game was arranged for 24th October 1857, the day the club were formed, at Frederick Ward's (soon to be the first President of the club) Park House in the East Bank area of the city. A greenhouse served as the changing room and from this initial match, between a number of local enthusiasts, emerged the Sheffield Football Club. The all-encompassing name of the club revealing the ambition of its founders.

In its early days the club would mainly be renowned for its athletics events which drew large crowds in their thousands to watch the races, wrestling, throwing the hammer, cricket ball etc.

Nathaniel Creswick and William Prest.
Co-founders of Sheffield Football Club – 24th October 1857

As there were no established football clubs in the area, the early days of football were confined to matches between the members of Sheffield FC and would typically feature arbitrary games between players whose surname was in the first part of the alphabet against a team from the rest. However, this always pitched Creswick against Prest and it also seemed that the 'A to M' team had the more naturally gifted players and so other permutations for sides were sought. A favourite of these was the professional men against the steel merchants and manufacturers. From these resulting line-ups, you could clearly see that the Sheffield Football Club was not made up of players from the working-classes. The list of members in 1858 showed that eleven were manufacturers and the rest included doctors, surgeons, dentists, solicitors and architects. In its early days, the Club would be called 'The Gentlemen'.

Inter-club matches continued to be played at Park House but, as no football jerseys existed, the players were expected to provide themselves with one blue and one red flannel cap for the purposes of identifying the side they were playing on. Amusingly, the Club's first meetings were held in that same greenhouse in the garden and ballots would be decided by using potatoes or matchsticks as counters.

The Sheffield Football Club quite quickly realised that they needed to draw up some rules and regulations to give a structure to the Club and to the playing of football matches. Consequently, the committee drew up a list of 17 rules. (See Appendix 3) It is interesting to note that in Rule 5 of the Rules, the annual membership subscription of half a crown (two shillings and sixpence or twelve and a half pence) also included their beer and tobacco ration for the year.

Both Nathaniel and William, as well as being good cricketers and exceptional athletes, had an extremely admirable moral compass. In the 1850s there was the serious threat of the invasion of the British Isles by Napoleon and it was decided to set up regiments similar to what we know as the Home Guard. The two Sheffield FC men were instrumental in the creation of the Hallamshire Volunteer Rifle Corps. It was actually this latter connection that had provided the Sheffield Football Club with its first competitive opposition with a match against the appropriately named 58th (Rutlandshire) Regiment of the 'Foot' in December 1858. The club played numerous games against the soldiers of the garrison, sometimes playing at the Regiment's barracks near Owlerton, Hillsborough, Sheffield.

In the October of 1858, the club produced a set of twelve laws to enable the game to be played against any new clubs being formed in the Sheffield area (See Appendix 4). Rule 5 of the Laws stated that *'No pushing with the hands or hacking, or tripping up is fair under any circumstances whatsoever.'* Unfortunately, this didn't prevent two soldiers playing for the 58th Rutlandshire Regiment ending up with fractured ribs.

So, how did the first Football Club come to be created in the north of England, well before the emergence of other Clubs in the country and how did Sheffield FC become England's oldest Club? I say England's and not the World's as there is some evidence of a John Hope Football Club being formed in Edinburgh in Scotland as early as 1824-25. In 1833, the John Hope Football Club produced its own set of rules, thus establishing the first written rules of football to be found anywhere in the world. These were followed by the rules of the Surrey Football Club in 1849 and then Sheffield FC's rules nine years later.

The first place to look for an answer to this question was in the development of 'mob' football or 'folk' football as it was to become. The annual 'mob' football still took place across the country as can be evidenced in Sheffield by an account of a game at Bents Green in 1793:

'There were selected six young men of Norton, dressed in green; and six young men of Sheffield, dressed in red. The play continued for three consecutive days. At the arch which was erected at each end of the place selected, there was a hole in the goal, and those of the Sheffield side would prevent the ball from passing through the hole. Then those on the Norton side (not being so numerous as those of Sheffield) sent messengers to the Peak and other places in the county of Derby; in consequence thereof, a great number of men appeared on the ground from Derbyshire.

Then those from Sheffield sent fife and drum through the streets of the town, to collect recruits and sufficient force against the Derbyshire men. The fashion then was for all responsible gentlemen, tradesmen and artisans of Sheffield to wear long tails. Hence, at the conclusion of the third day, a general row or struggle took place between the contending parties, insomuch that the men of Derbyshire cut and pulled nearly all the tails from the heads of the gentlemen of Sheffield. I understand there were many slightly wounded, but none were killed; thus ended the celebrated football match which aroused the bad passions of humanity for many years afterwards, insomuch so that the inhabitants of Norton felt a dread in coming to Sheffield, even about their necessary business.'

Despite the violence of mob football, a more regular type of football was transferring to the green fields of England. In the 1840s this so called 'folk' football was to be found in a concentrated area to the north-west of Sheffield, in a corridor containing the villages of Thurlstone, Thurlstoneland, Denby, Penistone, Thurston Upper End, Holmfirth and Hepworth.

Two key men in the story of the development of Sheffield football came from these villages. John Shaw, who we have already come across as the Secretary of Hallam and Stumperlowe FC, came from Penistone and went to the local grammar school. Here he would get to know John Ness Dransfield, who was also born in the village, became a solicitor and then also became a member of Sheffield FC in 1860-61. Other members came from the Sheffield schools and Nathaniel Creswick and sixteen other pupils from the

Sheffield Collegiate School formed a large part of the original membership.

So, whilst these two sources provide a clue as to the origins of the membership of the Sheffield Football Club, the greater question arises as to what drove them to create their own unique set of rules. One answer could be that William Prest had a brother Edward who went to Eton School and Cambridge University. At Cambridge, Edward was a contemporary of John Charles Thring who in 1846 had been instrumental in trying to create a common set of rules for football. These would then be used to play matches between the various students arriving at Cambridge from different public schools who wanted to continue playing the game. Was it any coincidence that the Sheffield rules bore some resemblance to those of Cambridge?

A second factor could be the strong connection with the local volunteer movement where both Creswick and Prest soon achieved the rank of Major. They most certainly would have rubbed shoulders with officers with strong public school and university backgrounds. The stories they would have heard about the various forms of football encouraged the Sheffield men to write to several public schools to ask them to send them a copy of their printed rules where available. These would have been studied and laws adopted where they suited the Sheffield Club. One such rule was the rule about catching which, whilst not central to the style of football they wished to play, was practical on the hilly pitches of the Dales. Here, catching the ball could prevent the halting of the game due to the players chasing down the hill to recover it.

The advantage the Sheffield Club had over other clubs was that it was not bound by the prejudices of the public-schools, who were against adopting a common set of rules and who, as we shall see later, struggled to expand the game. Sheffield was a club that could fashion the rules for its own purpose and create a game that could be played against any other team. It was therefore no surprise that within five years there were fourteen football teams in the Sheffield area all playing to the Sheffield rules.

And it wouldn't end there. This was just the start of the City of Sheffield's impact on the national game. It's influence on the future development of the sport we know and love today would be substantial in the years to come.

HALLAM CLUB V. SHEFFIELD FC

Saturday 26th December 1860
Sandygate, Hallam
(Kick-Off : 1.00 - 1.30 p.m.)

HALLAM FC (0)	SHEFFIELD FC (2)
(Blue)	(Red and white)
John C. SHAW (c)	Nathaniel CRESWICK (c)
F. VICKERS	William PREST
J. SNAPE	W. BAKER
G.H. WATERFALL	J. APPLETON
Wm. WATERFALL	Harry W. CHAMBERS
F. WARBURTON	J. DIXON
B. ELLIOTT	Robert FLAVELL
Alfred WATERFALL	W. TURTON
George ELLIOTT	J. WILD
A. HOBSON	A. WIGHTMAN
A.W. PEARSON	T. GOULD
J.W. PYE SMITH	T. MOORE
H. MOORE	M. HALL
Capt. T. VICKERS	David SELLERS

*Note: List of 14 reported players taken from a return match
at Hyde Park, Sheffield in 1861.*

Chapter 4: 'Cock of the North!'

Cock House Cup Final – Harrow School
(Tuesday 30th November 1858)

Charles Alcock sat on the hard, wooden bench of the small, cellular brick room that served as a changing room for the sportsmen of Harrow School. Today was the day. It had finally arrived. It was the final of the 'Cock House' Cup.

Charles was happy this morning's lessons were finally over. He hadn't been able to concentrate on the Greek quotations and algebraic equations which had been scrawled in dusty chalk on the blackboard in front of him. It was time to escape the dark oak-walled classroom with its high stained-glass windows and the pervading acrid smell of ink. His mind was focused on more important matters. 'Footer.'

Charles wasn't particularly academic. In his four years at Harrow, he hadn't excelled at the classic subjects of Mathematics, English, Ancient Greek and Latin and, given the superior knowledge of some of his classmates, he'd accepted his place in Harrow's pecking order. He wasn't thick, however. Perhaps his accent was. He'd moved down from Sunderland, in the north-east of England, four years ago with his brother John Forster Alcock. They got a bit of a ribbing from some of the posher lads but being canny and brought up near the shipyards of Wearside in Sunderland (The Alcocks' early residences were in Bishopswearmouth, just a stone's throw away from the Stadium of Light – current home to Sunderland A.FC) and they had been accepted into school life particularly as they were pretty good at the new sport of football.

Charles was two days away from his sixteenth birthday and next year would be his last year at Harrow and whilst, in his earlier years, he'd been described as being of 'delicate health', he was now turning the corner into adulthood and delicate he was not. In fact, quite the contrary, he had discovered only quite recently that on the fields of Harrow he had a talent for out-muscling opponents and dribbling & shooting a heavy Harrow football accurately between two upright posts.

Charles stood up and pulled on his red and black football shirt, the colours of his house team 'Drury's'. Next, it was a pair of knickerbockers and a pair of thick woollen socks. Tying up his boots he reached forward and took the red and black house cap, shaped like a fez, off his coat peg. It was time to go.

It was quite a long walk down from the school buildings, perched on the top of Harrow Hill, to the football pitches in the valley below. Charles didn't mind. It gave him time to shake off some of his pre-match nerves and collect his thoughts for the game ahead. As he followed his team-mates down the pathway, he could see a large crowd was collecting at the pitch side. The whole school would be out today along with all the parents of both teams, who were here to witness the winners of the 'Cock House' Cup, the most prestigious tournament of the Harrow school year. Over the last few weeks there had been a knockout tournament taking place between the existing school houses at Harrow (Reverend B.H. Drury's, Reverend T.H. Steel's, Reverend Dr. Vaughan's (Headmaster's), Reverend R. Middlemist's, Reverend W. Oxenham's, Mr. G.F. Harris', Reverend R. Rendall's and Mr. E.H. Vaughan's.) all of whom had the same aim to become the 'Cock House'. In the early rounds (First Ties) the whole house had featured in their house team resulting in boys from the ages of six to eighteen playing together. This was seen as character building. A few hard knocks would do the youngsters good as they took to the field with their elder, sporting heroes. Surely this sporting occasion would inspire them to want to lead their house to future 'Cock House' Cup victories? The consequence of this was that there were often games of twenty players playing twelve depending on the size of the houses. However, in the latter stages of the Cup the sides were reduced to the eleven best players.

The draw had been made and from the original eight houses, the four winners of the First Ties had proceeded to the Second Ties.

This had resulted in the following house draw.

SECOND TIES

Rev. B.H. Drury's versus Mr. G.F. Harris'
(Tuesday 16th November 1858)

Charles' house, Rev. B.H. Drury's, had a comfortable win against Mr. G.F. Harris' running out victors by four bases (goals) to one with two bases scored by Rob Burton, one from Charles Weekes and one from Will Smyly. However, this victory had come at a cost as Drury's lost the services of Sam Ashton, a member of the school football XI, who was seriously injured at the start of the game and was now a serious doubt for the final in two weeks' time. Sam was absolutely gutted. This would be his last chance to play in a Cock House final as he was due to leave Harrow in December.

Rev. Dr. Vaughan's versus Rev. T.H. Steel's
(Saturday 20th November 1858)

The other second tie was a much closer contest with the Headmaster's House, Rev. Dr. Vaughan's, coming out narrowly on top with two bases scored by Walter Medlicott, versus a single base from a Cecil Frederick Reid (later to play for Hitchin FC) of Rev. T.H. Steel's. Apparently, Walter Medlicott's play was absolutely 'first rate' and also George Webster 'distinguished himself as usual.' Here were two players that Charles' house would be watching out for in the Final.

So, now there were just two houses left to contest for the title of Champion House and become the 'Cock House' of the school.

At last, it was the final.

HARROW COCK HOUSE CUP
THIRD TIE (FINAL)
Rev. Dr. Vaughan's versus Rev. B.H. Drury's
(Tuesday 30th November 1858)
Kick-Off: 2.30 p.m.

Charles jogged onto the pitch. He needed to keep moving as there was a chilly easterly wind blowing driving rain across the pitch. Charles didn't mind as he was used it. The 'Cock House' Cup was always played in the winter months of October and November when the football pitches were particularly susceptible to flooding. The rainwater would collect on Harrow-on-the-Hill and seep down the slope forming pools on the clayey, clinging soil in the valley below. Today the pitch looked awful. The previous rounds of knockout matches had torn the field to shreds. The centre of the pitch was pitted with footprints and was like a quagmire. In some places you could easily lose your footing and your boot could sink into the ground. For this very reason the Harrow football was not entirely round but slightly flat-sided to stop it sinking in the mud. It was really only at the edges of the pitch where swathes of decent grass could be found. Charles looked all around him making a mental note of the best areas to dribble the ball and marking the location of any deep potholes that could compromise the accuracy of his shooting.

The Harrow match ball resembles a giant pork pie and is about 18 inches in diameter and 12 inches deep.

The pitch itself is rectangular in shape, around 150 yards in length and 100 yards wide. On the goal line at each end of the field is a 'base' which looks like rugby posts with their crossbar removed and a base (goal) may be scored at any point through them. The inner edges of the base posts are twelve feet apart. The field itself has no markings except for some flag posts marking the four corners of the pitch and two additional flag posts that indicate the half-way line, itself equidistant from each goal line. Coloured flags had been tied to the tops of the posts to stop any day-dreaming spectators inadvertently walking into them and injuring themselves.

The toss had been made and each team of eleven players took up their chosen positions on opposite sides of the half-way line and proceeded to have a preliminary kickabout between themselves.

It was going to be a tough match today. The opposition was none other than the Headmaster's House itself. The Reverend Charles John Vaughan was the current man in charge of Harrow School and he'd been Headmaster since 1845. The colours of the Headmaster's team were an unusual choice of pink and white which perhaps wouldn't be the most practical colours for an afternoon of playing football in the mud.

The formation of each team tended to be three players at the back in defence, 'The Threes', with two wingers on each side of the pitch and four strong forwards whose aim it was to propel the ball towards the base. One of the three backs would tend towards being the base keeper whose obvious mission was to protect the space between the posts and stop the ball passing at all costs. Base keeping was a skill that required strength in the upper & lower body and excellent judgement in the flight of the ball.

Most of the game was to be played with the feet although a player could catch the ball from an opposition kick in the air and shout 'Three Yards'. He would then be awarded with a free kick from the point (mark) where he had caught the ball and he could then run three yards further forward from this mark before kicking the ball again. Each of the houses have provided an umpire with a stick to mark the spot where 'Three Yards' had been called.

The school clock on the top of the hill struck two-thirty and it was time for the kick-off. The leader of the forwards shouted out:

"ARE YOU READY?"

"YES!", came the enthusiastic reply.

There was a loud cheer from the crowd and the match was started with a kick of the ball out of the hands. The opposition wingers and backs were strategically placed to make the first mark if required.

Football match being played on the Harrow School footer field, painted by Thomas M. M. Hemy 1888.

Charles stared deep into the eyes of his fellow team mate, 'Art' Daniel to check if he was fired up and ready to go. Arthur was a forward and winger like himself. He was also a key player in both Harrow's cricket and football school XIs. 'Art' could be relied on for a turn of speed as he was an all-round sportsman, a good rackets player and you just try and catch him in a race over the hurdles.

The match started and the players of both teams rushed forward to try and gain possession of the ball and propel it into the opponent's territory. Charles was immediately shoulder barged (boshed) out of the way which was legal even though he didn't have the ball. Picking himself up from the mud he could see that the culprit was the burly George Webster who had played well in the Second Ties. George was what was known as a Home Boarder, a day boy who lived at home with his parents in Harrow. George had been born in Argyllshire in Scotland and was fiercely proud of his roots and his Scottish heritage. Charles wasn't quite sure why he was playing today. Normally, the Home Boarders had their own team.

Still, no damage had been done but from now on Charles would keep an eye on the Scot as maybe he'd been given the task to take him out of the game. Suddenly the ball came loose and Charles managed to get a foot to the ball. He dribbled for a few yards and then passed the ball to Billy Sparks a tough lad from Crewkerne in Somerset. Billy was immediately surrounded by the opposition's defence and Henry Swinny from the Headmaster's House managed to tackle him and boot the ball out of bounds.

One of Charles' mates Will Smyly, a Dubliner from the year above and another member of the school football XI, recovered the ball and proceeded to kick it back into play and towards Charles. Charles made sure that the ball didn't touch his hand and that he'd controlled it without it touching his arms anywhere below the elbow. Having got control of the ball, he headed straight towards the opposition's baseline, swung his leg back and took a fierce shot. It looked like a certain 'base' but the ball flew 'out of bounds' just inches away from the post. Sam Hoare, an adversary of Charles at football as well at cricket, ran and recovered the ball and then launched it back into play. As it soared over the player's heads, the Drury's team knew that nobody else could touch it until they themselves had a touch.

The ball fell to Billy Benyon, a Yorkshire lad from Leeds, and he tried to kick the ball forward. However, it took a unlucky deflection off one of the opposition's players and suddenly Vaughan's were on the attack. An optimistic punt was hit high into the afternoon sky and as it fell back towards earth, Rob Burton the scorer of two bases in the Second Tie, caught the ball and cried 'Three Yards'. Nobody had managed to arrest the ball from him before he made the call and so he was entitled to a 'Three Yard' kick. One of the two umpires rushed onto the field and proceeded to push his stick into the exact same spot where Rob had caught the ball. Rob took his time. He looked up to make sure that none of his teammates were 'Behind' (offside) then proceeded to run up to the stick. He knew he could go another three yards further forward before he needed to launch the ball again.

Time was marching on and despite a few thwarted attempts on each other's bases, 40 minutes had expired and half time was called. The Drury's players got together and during the fifteen-minute break they discussed the plans for the second half.

"We've got to be cute this half, lads," said John Griffith Lock in his clipped Welsh accent. "Those forwards have been doing a bit of shinning and both of the umpires have missed it. If there's any shinning going on in the second half, we need to make sure the umpires are aware of it and we get a free kick."

"Yeah, I've been tripped twice and nobody's noticed. And I've had my shirt pulled," replied Charles. "Come on lads, we're by far the better side."

As no bases (goals) had been scored before half time the sides changed ends. Had a few bases been scored then ends would have automatically changed after each score.

It was 'Boston' Billy Garfit from Lincolnshire's turn to kick-off the second half for the Drury's. The ball was really heavy now. It was caked in mud and the worn leather had soaked up a lot of the rainwater giving it the feel of a heavy medicine ball that could be found in the school's gymnasium. Still, Billy was a strong lad and getting a good connection on the ball he managed to launch it over the heads of the Headmaster's players. The Drury's supporters knew something had to give soon and if justice were to be done that day, a base would soon be scored on behalf of their team.

The second half was much like the first and the red & black (and now brown) shirts of the Drury's team swarmed forward and peppered the Headmaster's goal with some scintillating shots. The Headmaster's players were also covered in slimy thick brown mud and their pristine pink & white shirts now resembled the colours of a rapidly melting Neapolitan ice cream.

Charles was seeing more & more of the ball and, working in tandem with the other forwards, they were succeeding in wearing down the opposition. Luckily there had been no 'Three Yard' shouts in front of either goal. Charles thought this was a stupid rule as, if you caught the ball in front of the opposition goal, you could then run the three yards unopposed past the umpire's stick, cross the baseline and score. That just wasn't 'footer' at all.

Deep into the second half one of the opposition players, who was obviously tiring, allowed the ball to hit his hand. From the resulting free kick, Will Smyly managed to get the ball through to Charles. Charles then went on an amazing dribble and took the ball past the opposition's 'Three Backs'. Suddenly, the posts were wide open in front of him. Charles lifted his head, measured his shot and the ball flew in between the posts. The crowd went wild and the chant of 'Drury's, Drury's' could be heard floating across the crowded playing fields of Harrow School.

The two sides changed ends again and despite some desperate defending in the last few seconds Drury's managed to protect their base. After what seemed an age, the old school clock struck half past and the two umpires called full time. The 'Cock House' Cup had been won and young Charles Alcock had scored the vital winning base (goal)!

The crowd cheered the players all the way back up to the school. Some threw their boaters into the air shouting 'Hoorah for Drury's. We are the 'Cock House' tonight.'

Both the players and spectators climbed the stile at the end of the field and worked their way back up the hill. The players would get showered & changed and prepare themselves for the house supper that evening. Over a hearty meal the match would be discussed from beginning to end with a few of the parents discussing inter-house games played in days gone by. Charles sat on a long bench at the end of the table and a warm glow spread across his face. This was his game and he knew he wanted to play football more than anything. His thoughts started to turn to life after Harrow.

What though the Hill be muddy and begriming,
Victory yet can make it easy climbing.
Bless the bell, for the triumph it is chiming.

(Harrow School)

***

HARROW COCK HOUSE CUP
THIRD TIE (FINAL)

Tuesday 30ᵗʰ November 1858
Kick-Off 2.30 p.m.

REV. DR. VAUGHAN'S	REV. B.H. DRURY'S
(Pink and White)	(Red and Black)
Samuel HOARE	William SMYLY
Henry SWINNY	Arthur DANIEL
George WEBSTER	John LOCK
Charles HAMILTON	William GARFIT
Cecil WATSON	James LE MESSURIER
Thomas MADDY	William SPARKS
Thomas USBORNE	Evelyn SKINNER
Herbert PRAED	William BENYON
John TOMPSON	Robert BURTON
Walter MEDLICOTT	Charles ALCOCK
Edward BARTON	Benjamin MORLAND

SCORER: Charles William Alcock – 1 base
Rev. B.H. Drury's become the Champion House 1858

Author's Notes:

The match details of the 'Cock House' Cup Final of 1858 are taken from the book 'House Matches at Rev. Dr. Vaughan's and Rev. Dr. Butler's (1845 – 1864);

The details of the pupils who played in the final are taken from the members of Drury's House and the Rev. Dr. Vaughan's (Headmaster's) House as listed in the Harrow School Register 1800 – 1911.

In an interview with A.W. Bettesworth entitled 'Chats on a Cricket Field' in 1910, Charles Alcock states that he 'was fortunate enough to score the goal which made us the Cock House.'

Alcock himself was a great friend of the legendary cricketer W.G. Grace who was later to state in his 'Personal Recollections and Reminisces (1899)' that Charles Alcock played no games until his final year when he took to football.'

The two good friends W.G. Grace and Charles W. Alcock photographed in later life outside The Oval pavilion.

Charles left Harrow in July 1859 and I have based the imaginary 1858 'Cock House' Cup Final on the above notes along with the Rules of Harrow Football 1858 (see Appendix 1) and a newspaper report that appeared in The Sportsman newspaper on the 22nd January 1867 entitled 'A Match at Harrow'.

And so, the game of football had survived and despite the negativity surrounding the game and the attempts to suppress it by the authorities, it had found its way into the public schools of England where differing codes and rules were being applied, bringing a structure to the sport.

Winchester School rules	(1825)
Rugby School rules	(1845)
Eton School rules	(1847)
Cambridge University rules	(1856)
Harrow School rules	(1858)
Sheffield rules	(1858)
Uppingham School rules	(1861)
Charterhouse School rules	(1863)

However, that in itself was a problem as each school codified the game and played to their own set of rules, it soon became impossible to play inter-school matches. The only way to play was to have a composite set of rules agreed before the match. This often led to confusion and arguments during the play. A major row on this subject took place in the national press in January 1859. The editor of the 'Bell's Life in London and Sporting Chronicle' was so disgruntled at this mudslinging between the public schools defending their own rules and slagging off the others, he felt he had to take to writing the following:

'We have received many other letters on this subject (uniformity of rules) from public schoolmen, but they are so mixed up with abuse of each other that we consider them best unpublished, and the correspondence closed. The inference seems to be that it will undoubtedly be unadvisable for different schools to meet at this game. We should have seen with pleasure some proposition for a generalisation of the rules, but there seems no disposition on any side'

It is interesting to note that two weeks before the following letter appeared in The Portico, the in-house magazine of Harrow School:

Editor, you would favour me much if you would insert in your next number of the Portico this short letter.

'Would it not be much better if there were settled rules and laws for the game of football, and as have been, for many years past, founded for the game of cricket? Rules which public schools, universities and the few clubs that there are at present, might follow; which might be kept with the greatest strictness, and adhered to by all players. At the present time the rules of no two public schools, in this game, at all agree; in fact, I do not hesitate in saying that, at different schools, the game is often entirely different, and would scarcely be recognised by a boy going from one to another.'

A LOVER OF FOOTBALL, THE PORTICO, VOL II, No. XIII – 1st January 1859.

Could this have been the young Charles Alcock expressing his views on the subject in this his last year at school?

***

'Mob football', on the other hand, was still being practised throughout the country despite the best efforts of the authorities and police to stop it. The Shrove Tuesday match was still very much an annual event in places like Kingston-upon-Thames and Dorking in Surrey, Laxton in Nottinghamshire, Stoneyhurst and Kirkham in Lancashire, Scarborough and Whitby in Yorkshire, Chester-Le-Street in County Durham and Ilderton in Northumberland.

One of the most notorious of the Shrove Tuesday games was held at Ashbourne in Derbyshire. The authorities had managed to stop the game in 1846 by bursting the ball on two occasions and in 1860 there was a riot in the town with the newly recruited police trying to disperse the 500 or so participants. Despite this the game survived and in 1891 it even attracted its own song:

There's a town still plays this glorious game
Tho' tis but a little spot.
And year by year the contest's fought
From the field that's called Shaw Croft.
Then friend meets friend in friendly strife
The leather for to gain,
And they play the game right manfully,
In snow, sunshine or rain.

'Tis a glorious game, deny it who can
That tries the pluck of an Englishman.
For loyal the Game shall ever be
No matter when or where,
And treat that Game as ought but the free,
Is more than the boldest dare.
Though the ups and downs of its chequered life
May the ball still ever roll,
Until by fair and gallant strife
We've reached the treasur'd goal.

A Shrovetide ball goaled by H. Hind on Ash Wednesday 1887 .

However, even though the Shrove Tuesday match continues to this day, it can't be said that the rules have mellowed.

Rules:

1. Committing murder or manslaughter is prohibited. Unnecessary violence is frowned upon.
2. The ball may not be carried in a motorised vehicle.
3. The ball may not be hidden in a bag, coat or rucksack etc.
4. Cemeteries, churchyards and the town memorial gardens are strictly out of bounds.
5. Playing after 10 pm is forbidden.
6. To score a goal the ball must be tapped three times in the area of the goal.

I suppose with rules like that football fans shouldn't really moan about the introduction of goal-line technology or VAR !!

Chapter 5: 'On the Origin of Species'
The formation of the Forest Football Club
(1859)

" If I may be allowed to inquire," said the Bishop of Oxford, "would you rather have an ape for your grandfather or grandmother ?"

"I would rather have had apes on both sides for my ancestors," replied the naturalist, unabashed, "than human beings so warped by prejudice that they were afraid to behold the truth." *(The Era - Sunday 26th August 1860)*

The autumn of 1859 was a significant period for Victorian society. Not only did the chimes of Big Ben ring out across London for the first time but in late November an extremely controversial piece of writing appeared in the book shops of England. It had the catchy title of 'On the Origin of Species by means of Natural Selection, or the Preservation of Favoured Races in the Struggle for Life.'

Hardly a title to capture the imagination. However, its content was to send shockwaves throughout the theological and scientific world. In the book the naturalist, Mr. Charles Darwin, explained his theories that all animals and plants may have evolved from one original species and the process of natural selection (survival of the fittest) had dictated the current species in the world today.

The young Charles Alcock was probably oblivious to all this as he left Harrow School at the end of the July in the same year and returned to his parents' (Charles and Elizabeth) house in Chingford, Essex. Here he was reunited with his elder brother John Forster Alcock, another keen footballer, who had left Harrow two years earlier. He was also delighted to see his younger brother Arthur and his tiny sisters, Anna and Ada, whom he hardly knew since leaving home for Harrow. It was around this time that Charles became Charles William Alcock. The addition of William probably being in memory of his eleven-year-old brother William, who had died suddenly of heart failure in 1858.

Why the Alcocks chose Chingford in Essex as their London home, when relocating from the north east of England is unclear.

Chingford was 'a small rural community with fishermen's' cottages built along the River Lea and agricultural labourers' cottages around the village green.' There were also no direct train connections into central London where they had based the family business. The train route into Liverpool Street station would not arrive until late in 1873. Maybe it was the fact that Chingford is to the north-east of London and land was cheaper in the area. One thing is for certain was that the Alcocks family residence was called Sunnyside, surely named after the similar sounding 'Sunniside' district of Sunderland, from which they had all just recently moved.

The original gatehouse to Sunnyside Lodge, home to the Alcock family, Chingford, Essex.

Having left Harrow Charles didn't go on to university like many of his schoolmates as he was bound to join his elder brother John at the Central London branch of their father's marine insurance business based in Fenchurch Street.

It was now the autumn of 1859 and after Charles' successes on the sports field at Harrow he wanted to continue to play the sport he so loved. His brother John had also played football whilst at Harrow School and was also desperate to play the game. Over dinner one night the two brothers started to hatch a plan to form a football team. John had lived at home for a couple of years now and knew the area quite well.

"I've been thinking for some time now how best to get a football side together. There's not much interest or even knowledge of the game around here and most of the locals are too busy working or labouring to be able to get the time off for sport. What we need is a group of ex public-schoolboys who have played the sport before and are looking to keep fit in the winter. Do you remember John

Pardoe? He was at Harrow at the same time as us, two years above, in Mr. Rendall's house. He was a good football player and he'd be keen to set up a team with us. He is studying at Trinity College in Cambridge at the moment where he continues to play football but with slightly different rules. John's father is the Reverend John Pardoe, the Vicar at Leyton and they live in the vicarage around five miles from here.

Also, as if by coincidence, the Tebbut family have just moved into a house called 'The Cedars' down the road from John. You know the Tebbut brothers of 'Tebbut, Stoneman and Spence', the shipbuilders we have dealt with in the past. Well apparently, both brothers, Charles and Arthur, would be keen on playing for us. Not only that but Sam Bigland, who is also a marine insurance broker, lives on the same road. He's the same age as me and has played football before. He's convinced his younger brother Compton will also turn up and play."

"Crikey, that's seven of us already. More than half a team. Good work John," replied Charles, he could feel the adrenalin pumping already, "but where could we play?"

Leyton Flats today – Original home of the Forest Football Club

John was quick in his response, "Across the road from the Tebbuts' and the Biglands' house on Whipps Cross Road in Leytonstone is a vast expanse of land on the edge of Epping Forest called Leyton Flats. We could play there. We may need to watch out for a few boggy areas near the open ponds but other than that it's ideal and as the name indicates it's flat."

"Well, it can't be any worse than the Harrow School playing fields, can it? Wow, it's all coming together. Leytonstone is about four miles from here and Leyton Flats can't be far away from the Forest School where our brother Arthur goes. Maybe we could get a couple of players from there?"

And so, the dream of getting a football club together began. During the winter of 1859 and the spring of 1860, they started to attract a number of players from the Leytonstone and Woodford areas of East London. A new member arrived from the nearby Forest School. David John Morgan was sixteen and lived in the White House next to the Tebbuts' house 'The Cedars' in Leytonstone. Then a couple of local lads saw the team training and came down to join in. The unusually named Cowper Donne Jackson came from nearby Woodford. A native of Blackheath, he had come across the football/rugby game in his youth but found it to be too violent. Cowper was studying to be a mechanical engineer and he couldn't afford to get injured and have time off work. However, the game this team were playing seemed more sedate and involved more kicking of the ball with the feet than the games he had seen played in Blackheath which involved kicking the opposition on the shins.

And so, the nucleus of the side was coming together. The area of the ground they had chosen to play on was known locally as Forest Place and in the distance, they could see the imposing structure of the Infant Orphan Asylum in the adjoining town of Snaresbrook. Built in 1843, in the Jacobean Gothic style, the philanthropist Andrew Reed commissioned the building to house children under seven years of age who were either fatherless or entirely orphaned. It was a lovely backdrop to the Leyton Flats and the nearby Eagle Pond made it a gorgeous setting and the perfect place to play football.

"So, what are we going to call this new team of ours? We need a name that reflects the ambitions of the club," said Charles.

"And what are they?," replied John. "We need some local teams to play against first."

An aerial view of the Infant Orphan Asylum at Snaresbrook.

"Yes, I know," Charles continued, looking out across their beautiful new pitch. "Football is becoming more popular day by day. Not just in the schools, but elsewhere in London and across the country as a whole. It is rumoured that there are a couple of clubs that have been formed up in Yorkshire around Sheffield. I've also heard there may be a few more clubs being formed in the London area by ex-public-schoolboys, but what rules they are playing to, I don't know. Also, there are some cricket clubs who are looking to take up football to keep fit during winter and factory workers who are looking to have some fun and entertainment now that their working hours are being reduced and they have more time for leisure. Our ambition should be to help spread the development of the game and, as you know, I fully believe we should have a uniform set of rules so that one side can play the other without argument. You remember what happened when the Harrow School XI used to try and play a game against Eton or another public school. Nobody would concede to change their rules and the game became a farce with both sides' umpires arguing they were correct."

"True," said John, looking out towards Epping Forest. "Well, it's obvious, isn't it? We're on the edge of a Forest. We're playing at Forest Place, a few hundred yards from Forest School and my middle name is Forster. The Forest Club it has to be."

Charles readily agreed.

Forest Foot-Ball Club, circa 1863

Left to right: John Pardoe, Francis C. Adams, R Edmunds, Compton Bigland, John Forster Alcock, Charles William Alcock, Cowper Donne Jackson, Charles M Tebbut, William B. Standidge, Arthur M. Tebbut & Arthur L Cutbill.

"So, now we have a name, next we need a structure to run the club. You can be the captain John but we need some other members to be on the Committee. I don't really know all these local lads that well. They seem good fellows but some of them are quite young and we need someone we can rely on."

"Don't worry Charles. I've already thought this through. John Pardoe will be back from Cambridge this summer. He's 21 and as the son of a vicar I'm sure he can be totally relied on to come on board."

Another key recruit to the Forest Club during this time was Alfred Westwood Mackenzie. Alfred had been born in Leytonstone and had been a pupil at Walthamstow House School. Alfred had a difficult start to life. When he was only 11 years old his father, Stephen Mackenzie, had been killed when he was thrown forcefully from his cob carriage into the trunk of a chestnut tree. As a consequence, Alfred had to leave school and start work straight away to save the family from becoming destitute. He set up a successful wharfinger business in Lower Thames Street in Central London, taking custody of the goods being delivered by vessels arriving on the docks of the River Thames. Alfred's wharf was within walking distance of the Alcocks insurance offices in Fenchurch Street. Unfortunately for Alfred, his wharf was seriously damaged by a fire just as his business was starting to become successful. Let's hope he had taken out some insurance with 'Alcock and Sons'.

Despite this devastating setback Alfred was soon to resurrect his career and ventured into the insurance business himself ending up as one of the leading officials of the Guardian Assurance Company. Alfred possessed good administration skills and he was soon to become the first Secretary of the newly formed Forest Club, along with the two Alcock brothers and John Pardoe who had returned from university. The first item they had to agree on was what rules the club should play to.

"That's easy," said John Pardoe, "the rules I played to at Cambridge weren't that dissimilar to the Harrow School rules. In fact, at Cambridge we've been playing an annual match against Harrow without any problems. What you will like Charles is that these new rules remove the 'Three Yards Rule' that you so dislike. They call a 'base' a goal. Also, there is a tape tied across the top of the base posts, eliminating any arguments about whether the goal is valid, as the ball has to be seen to pass under the tape. The offside law is a bit lax but it keeps the game going."

"That's a spiffing idea." the brothers replied in unison. "let's add some of our own club rules as well and then we can start seeking more teams to play against."

To show their intent and to add gravitas to their new rules a system of fines was introduced. It read 'for any wilful infringement of the rules of the game, a fine of Two Shillings and Sixpence be inflicted.' *(See Appendix Two: The Forest Club rules 1858)*

To put this in perspective the average weekly wage for an agricultural labourer in Victorian times was around ten shillings. As to who to play, this was to prove a more difficult task. Reports had been published in the national press, in such respected journals such as the 'Bell's Life in London & Sporting Chronicle', showing that Dingley Dell FC (The club's name had been taken from a fictitious cricket match in Charles Dickens 'Pickwick Papers') formed in 1858 and The Crusaders FC formed in 1859 were playing football matches against public schools such as Charterhouse and Westminster. The clubs were scratch teams made up of ex-public schoolboys looking to continue playing the game like Charles and John Alcock. However, they were from a different clique of schools and weren't playing the type of football the newly formed Forest Club wished to play.

So, for early games John and Charles turned to a newly-formed club to be the first of the Forest Club's opponents. As coincidence would have it, at the bottom of Fenchurch Street, where the Alcocks offices were to be found, was a short street called Mincing Lane. Here, a number of merchants had formed an athletics/football club called Mincing Lane FC (1859). Most of the members were merchants of imported goods such as tea and coffee or cotton and rice. As they were new to football, they were happy to play to the Forest Club rules.

By the start of the 1861-62 season, the Forest Club were desperate to find another club to play against. As it happened there were a number of brothers who attended the Forest School with the surname of Cutbill. They lived in Beckenham and were playing cricket for the nearby Crystal Palace - the majestic home of the Great Exhibition of 1851. The cricket club had been formed by some of the officials and members of the Crystal Palace Company and they were looking for some winter exercise. To this end they gravitated to the new sport of football and the Crystal Palace Club was formed in 1861. Their first competitive match was to be against the Forest Club. It was organised with the assistance of the Cutbill family and a date agreed for the 15th March 1862. The match was to be a 15 a side game and would be hosted by the Forest Club at their ground at Forest Place, Leytonstone.

The match kicked off at 2.30 p.m. and on a bright spring day the Forest Club walked out onto the pitch in their dark red and black jerseys, (the same colours as Drury's house at Harrow) contrasting against the lighter sky blue and white halved shirts of the Crystal Palace Club. The match was keenly contested and the Forest Club were taken by surprise by their newly formed opponents. The Crystal Palace team, despite not being familiar to the rules, played admirably showing a good eye for the ball that had been developed on the cricket pitch. After two hours they had conceded only one goal and left the pitch with their heads held high. The game was such a success that a return match took place on the Crystal Palace cricket field just three weeks later.

Again, the Forest Club were victorious, running out easy winners by four goals to none. However, the conditions were wet and the ground was not 'first rate'. This probably suited the Forest Club and the Old Harrovians who had learned their dribbling skills on the muddy playing fields of Harrow. John Pardoe in particular excelled, scoring three goals, the other coming from Compton Bigland.

For Charles Alcock this was a culmination of a vision he'd had since scoring that goal in the Cock House Cup Final. The Forest Club was up and running. The Cambridge rules had worked well and now it was time for the Club to seek out more opponents and spread the word about this wonderful game. Years later Charles elegantly but rather grandly stated:

'..the Forest Club, having fulfilled its mission of pioneering work, after two winters had already begun to feel the necessity of a more extensive field of operations. It was gradually overstepping the circumscribed limits of a local habitation.'

Whether a couple of matches against two sides constitutes an expansion of the beautiful game is up for debate but the intention was there and the following autumn this advert appeared in the national press.

> The Hon. Secretary of the **FOREST FOOTBALL CLUB** will be happy to make arrangements with secretaries of similar clubs for **MATCHES**, to be played during the coming season, on the rules of the University of Cambridge. Address, Alfred W. Mackenzie, Hon. Sec

FOREST CLUB V CRYSTAL PALACE

Saturday 15th March 1862
Forest Place, Leytonstone
(Kick-Off : 2.30 p.m.)

THE FOREST CLUB (1)	CRYSTAL PALACE (0)
(Red and Black)	(Sky Blue and white)
John F. ALCOCK (C.)	William ALLPORT
Charles W. ALCOCK	Walter CUTBILL
Henry BIGLAND	Edward CUTBILL
Compton BIGLAND	Francis DAY
Cowper JACKSON	Henry HEAD
Alfred MACKENZIE	Alfred LLOYD
George MACKENZIE	Henry (Harry) LLOYD
Fred WOODWARD	Theodore LLOYD Jun.
Charles TEBBUT	John SHARLAND
Arthur TEBBUT	James TURNER
John PARDOE	Frederick URWICK
John MORGAN	T. JACKSON
J. ROBERTSON	BELL
M. SAVILL	MEDWIN
J. E. WHITE	PHELPS

Author's Notes:

The above description of the origins of the Forest Football Club is based on the following information:

There are no press reports of Mincing Lane Football Club in 1859-60 but Charles W. Alcock states he was playing against them in that period:

'Their (Forest FC) opponents at the outset were few in number, and as far as I can remember Mincing Lane furnished the bulk of the opposition.'

In his obituary in the Acton Gazette on 11th April 1924, Alfred Westwood Mackenzie is quoted as having said:

'When I first began to play in 1859, the few clubs represented were a law unto themselves.'

In an article in the 'Leytonstone Express and Independence' in 1909 Alfred Westwood Mackenzie also states:

'One of them was playing football in front of Forest Place where I was the first secretary of the 'Forest Football Club' founded in 1861.'

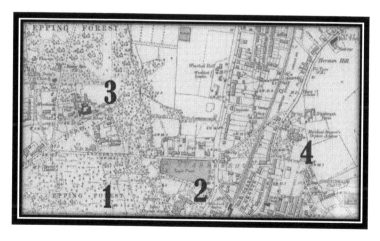

Map showing the location of the Forest Club pitch at Forest Place (1), in the shadow of the Infant Orphan Asylum (2), the Forest School (3) and the Merchant Seaman's Orphan Asylum (4).

Charles W. Alcock made the following statement about the Forest Club:

'... was a club known as the Forest Club. Founded in 1859, by a group of old Harrovians under the captaincy of J. F. Alcock, the Forest Club used a pitch in Epping Forest – near the Merchant Seamen's Orphan Asylum at Snaresbrook.'

The location of the Forest Club pitch is quite clearly defined in 'The Sportsman newspaper' dated Thursday 29th October 1868 (below) which states that the ground was in Forest Place next to the Infant Orphan Asylum in Snaresbrook, rather than the Merchant Seaman's Orphan Asylum. Also, the group of Old Harrovians appear to be just three, the two Alcock brothers and John Pardoe. Charles William Alcock was not always accurate in his statements or in his recollections of games gone by.

After the Forest Club evolved into Charles Alcock's Wanderers team in 1864 the Club was disbanded for a number of years. However, on the 29th October 1868 a few ex-players reformed the Club and of course their first match had to be against the Wanderers on the 23rd January 1869. Amazingly, John Forster Alcock captained the Wanderers side in place of Charles and led the Wanderers to a 3-1 victory. The Forest Club continued playing matches for a few years until the 1871-72 season after which they disappeared.

FOREST CLUB

This club, a few years ago one of the prominent of the 'dribbling clubs' has been revived under the management of the following players – P.G. Rouquette (captain), J. Conquest, A. Frost, A. Lloyd, W. Man, jun., C.M. Tebbut, J. Townsend, R. Piper (hon. sec. and treasurer). Practice will take place on the old ground in front of Forest-Place, Leytonstone, on Saturdays, commencing at three o'clock.

Chapter 6: All the President's Men
The Formation of the Football Association
(1863)

'The sturdy plowman, lustie, strong and bold.
Overcometh the winter with driving the foote-ball,
Forgetting labour and many a grievous fall.'
(Alexander Barclay – 1530)

"This'll be fun," John Forster Alcock laughed out loud, teasing his younger brother, Charles. "This'll be the first time we've played against each other in a competitive match. We'll see who's the best at football now. What do you reckon your chances are?"

"Pretty good," replied Charles, who had not long celebrated his 21st birthday. "I reckon I've chosen wisely and I've got the lad from the Sheffield Football Club, Harry Chambers, on my side. They're made of tough stuff up in Yorkshire. They'll play in a foot of snow; never mind a thick frost and he should have no problem playing to our new Association rules. They might even adopt them 'up north' if today's match goes well. Their rules aren't that much different to ours."

The two brothers stood outside the imposing Albert Gates at the entrance to Battersea Park waiting for the other members of the two teams to arrive. It was a bitterly cold day with an easterly wind blowing down the River Thames and across the park. There had been a severe frost and it was rumoured that the locals had taken to ice skating on the Battersea Park boating lake. The deer that could be occasionally seen roaming the park were well hidden, seeking warmth huddled together in the undergrowth of the surrounding bushes.

"At least the match hasn't been called off. We should be able to play today even if the surface is going to be rock hard. Mind you, there might be a few injuries out there today."

Suddenly, they could see a few of their fellow Forest Club team-mates walking down Park Road towards them. The Tebbut brothers were also going to be on opposite sides for the first time and they were looking forward to it. Charles, the elder of the two Tebbut brothers spoke first, "How come you didn't pick me on your side, Charles boy? You're going to regret it!"

"Well, I couldn't have two Charles in my team, could I? One is enough and anyway Arthur is younger and faster than you. I've also got the Crystal Palace back, James Turner, in my side. You just try and get the ball past him; you've got no chance!"

"Did you have a good New Year's Eve? We celebrated with a few egg nogs and some homemade black bun and it was delicious. Mind you we didn't have too many snifters as we wanted to be ready for today. They say that what you do at the beginning of the year, you will carry on all the year through and I want that to be playing football!"

There was a nodding of heads all round. Mind you they weren't in the mood for stopping and chatting. The players were all wearing their thick long overcoats made from the best tweed. The coats were buttoned up to their necks to keep the cold wind out. Cowper Donne Jackson, also of the Forest Club, suddenly shivered; "C'mon, let's keep moving. Where are the changing rooms? I need to get out of this biting wind."

John Alcock started walking and said, "Follow me, the landlord of the Albert Tavern is letting us use the backroom of his pub to get changed in. It's very kind of him but I think he's hoping we'll purchase a few 'winter-warmer' drinks after the match to thaw us out. He's not daft, is our George."

John Forster Alcock – FA Committee Member 1863-66 and one of the founding fathers of football.

It was the start of a new year and the start of a new era for English football. Today's game would be the inaugural match to be played under the new rules of the newly formed Football Association. After six meetings over the last two months, the committee had finally managed to agree a set of rules that could be played by all the clubs belonging to the Football Association. This would eliminate the constant arguing during matches and the wasted time trying to agree the rules before the matches kicked off. It had meant a falling out with some of the clubs that preferred the 'rugby' style of play but that was a small price to play to secure a style of football being played increasingly with the feet rather than with the hands. Unfortunately, Arthur Pember (the first FA President) and Ebenezer Cobb Morley (the first Secretary) hadn't been successful in eliminating handling entirely. You could still catch the ball before it bounced and claim a free kick (as in rugby). Also, the offside rule meant that everyone had to be behind the ball before it was passed, which was quite restrictive to the game as a whole. However, the football game was advancing and it would now be a less violent game with shinning (kicking the shins) and hacking (tripping an opponent by kicking in the knees) abolished. This suited the up-and-coming young businessmen that were now playing the game for leisure.

As it happened, none of the public schools accepted the invitation to attend the meeting, apart from a representative from the Charterhouse School who, on his 19th birthday, attended the first meeting as an observer.

Watercolour of Freemasons' Tavern by John Nixon circa 1800

And so, on the 26th October 1863, 16 representatives (the captains plus others) of football clubs in the locality, met at the Freemasons' Tavern in the Covent Garden area of London to form an Association which could manage the developing game of football. The sixteen individuals representing thirteen different clubs at the first meeting of the Football Association were:

Representative	Club	Age
Ebenezer C. Morley	Barnes FC	(32)
Thomas D. Gregory	Barnes FC	(28)
Arthur Pember	No Names Kilburn	(28)
Alfred W. Mackenzie	Forest Club	(23)
John Forster Alcock	Forest Club	(22)
Francis M. Campbell	Blackheath	(20)
Frederick H. Moore	Blackheath	(24)
William H. Gordon	Blackheath School	(18)
Herbert T. Steward	Crusaders	(24)
Francis (Frank) Day	Crystal Palace	(25)
James Turner	Crystal Palace	(24)
William J. Mackintosh	Kensington School	(18)
George W. Shillingford	Pereceval House School	(19)
Theodore Bell	Surbiton & Dingley Dell	(23)
George T. Wawn	War Office	(23)
Bertram F. Hartshorne	Charterhouse (observer)	(19)

It took until the sixth meeting of the Football Association on the 8th December 1863 for the final rules to be agreed. This had been done with a great degree of skulduggery as the successful vote on removing 'hacking' and 'carrying the ball' had been taken when the unsympathetic (rugby) members of the association had either been unwilling to attend or unable to because of school holidays.

A new committee was formed with

Arthur Pember (N.N. Kilburn) – President
Ebenezer Cobb Morley (Barnes Club) – Hon. Secretary
Francis Maule Campbell (Blackheath) – Treasurer

The Freemasons' Tavern as it is today at 61-65 ,Great Queen Street. The plaque commemorating the formation of the FA is to the right of the entrance. The building is now an event venue called the 'Grand Connaught Rooms'

That night Ebenezer Cobb Morley, the new secretary, returned to his substantial residence at No. 26, The Terrace in Barnes in south-west London and drafted the first set of rules of the Football Association. As he sat at his candle-lit drawing room desk and neatly transcribed the thirteen rules in his own copper plate writing, little did he realise the impact this small document would have on the future of world football. (See Appendix 5)

It had also been agreed at the meeting that a football match would take place, as soon as possible, to put the new rules to the test. This match would be a 14-a-side game between a President's

XIV and the Secretary's XIV. It would be played on the 2nd January 1864 with a 2.00 p.m. kick-off in Battersea Park. The players selected for the match were to be chosen by the Alcock brothers, highlighting their importance and influence in this new Football Association.

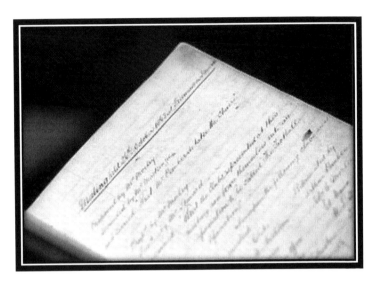

The first set of Association football rules hand written by Ebenezer Cobb Morley is now on display at the National Football Museum, Manchester.

***

The pitch where this historical game was to be played on was at the Battersea end of the park, in the north-west corner near the Albert Tavern. The players could see that quite a large crowd had gathered to witness this inaugural match. Most of them were moving and stamping their feet and blowing on their hands to keep warm.

The pitch had been marked out with flags and was laid from east to west across the park on the western practice ground which was normally reserved for cricket. It was 100 yards in length and 80 yards in breadth, so well within the new rule of 200 by 100 yards and it seemed an adequate size for 14 players a side.

The players entered through the front porch of the Albert Tavern which was still full of midday regular drinkers. Some of the crowd were partaking in a pre-match imbibement as well as keeping warm by the large wood fire in the centre of the bar. Two of the back-rooms of the pub had been put aside as changing rooms for the teams and Charles could hear the loud deep voices of the opposition as they partook in some friendly banter before the game.

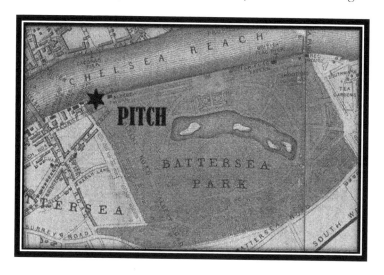

Plan of Battersea Park (c. 1852) showing the Albert Tavern in the top left corner of the park (*) not far from the Albert Bridge. The Surrey rowing club would often race from here to Westminster Bridge.

The Baker brothers, from the No Names Kilburn side, had been selected to play for the Secretary's XIV and were complaining about there being no caps to wear given the freezing conditions outside. "With no caps or head garments to wear we shall be 'roofless' and the heads of our 'full-backs' will turn blue with cold whilst waiting for an attack from the opposition."

John Alcock heard this as he entered the room, "Don't worry lads. They're going to get nowhere near our full-backs today. In fact, the backs can join us up front and help us score more goals. That'll keep them warm. You just make sure that your boots conform with the new rules and that none of us have any dangerous nails or rubber protruding from the soles. We don't want to lose a player before the match has even kicked off."

A check had been made on each player's boots as they exited the Albert Tavern in their brightly coloured woollen jerseys which at least gave some protection against the bitterly cold north-easterly wind, which although light, cut through you like a knife.

There was an inevitable delay to the 2 p.m. kick-off as the 28 players plus officials, who were travelling from all sides of the capital, got waylaid for one reason and another. Eventually, everybody was ready and the match kicked off at just past 2.30 p.m. Given the time of year the team playing at the east end of the pitch were already getting the sun in their eyes. There was however still time for a decent match before dusk fell at around 4.40 p.m.

The toss was made and won. The ball in play was a leather football made by Mr. John Lillywhite's sports company in Euston Square, North West London. Lillywhite's had also produced printed copies of the new rules which could be purchased for 6d. (two and a half pence) A few of the spectators were keenly reading them through on the touchlines.

The wind, despite not being that strong, was disturbing the players rhythm and consequently many of the shots on goal were missing the target by miles. The game was played hard but fair and although shinning was banned from the play, the players sometimes 'shinned' an opponent by accident when going for a 50/50 ball. Suddenly, a goal was scored for the President's XIV and it was none other than that man Charles Alcock. The crowd roared their appreciation and memories of the Cock House Cup Final, only four years ago, came flooding back.

The teams changed ends as the rules dictated and play continued. The ball was mainly being kept on the pitch and on the odd occasion that it did go out of touch it was promptly thrown in again. (at right angles to the pitch, as in today's rugby) Some of the players struggled with the offside rule but to be fair most of them tried to hold their positions.

As the game wore on it soon became evident as to which was the stronger team. Harry Chambers of the Sheffield Football Club 'gave a capital taste of his quality' for the President's XIV and his captain, the FA President, Arthur Pember also put on an impressive display. Harry had been invited to play in the match as the Sheffield player was studying for his law exams in London. He was the perfect person to make a comparison between the two sets of rules. The rule he was really struggling with was the Football Association's offside rule.

"I'll tell thee what," he said in a broad Sheffield accent, "this 'offside' rule of yours is crackers. It's amazing you ever score any goals at all. As soon as we get the ball for'ard the whole team has to stop and wait for their backs to catch the ball up before we can charge their goal. We have none of this nonsense 'oop north' and the game flows much better. End to end with no stopping. Mind you, your goals are twice the width of ours so you can't miss when you hit the ball can you?"

Arthur Pember had some sympathy with the Yorkshireman.

"I understand your frustration Harry but it's taken a lot of long meetings and a lot of arguing just to get these rules agreed and we've now succeeded in eliminating shinning and hacking. Most of our players are used to the offside rule having played it at their schools. Maybe one day we'll take a look at other rules and consider a possible amendment."

It wasn't long before a second goal was scored for the President's XIV and again it was none other than Charles Alcock. Charles had been on one of his renowned long dribbles and his subsequent shot, whilst flying high over the goal, was definitely between the goalposts. (There was no tape across the top of the goal posts at this stage and it was up to the umpires to agree that the ball had passed between the two posts at whatever height it was struck. This tended to negate the need for a full-time goalkeeper in a match as many shots were out of reach.)

The two umpires conferred and agreed that a goal had been scored and the crowd roared their approval again. This proved to be the decisive goal and so the match was won by two goals to nil. No 'touch downs' had been scored by either side. (Touch downs were similar to a try in rugby and could be scored on either side of the opposition's goalmouth. They were used to determine the final result in case of a drawn match.)

John Alcock looked at his younger sibling and admired the way he had grown as a player in this game. Mind you he wasn't looking forward to the inevitable ribbing he would receive as the players dined that night in the restaurant of the Grosvenor Hotel, built in 1862, next to the recently opened Victoria railway station in Pimlico. After dining on some fine food and tasting some fine wines, Arthur Pember raised his glass to the gathered members of the Football Association, and uttered the following words;

"Success to football, irrespective of class or creed."

The Grosvenor Hotel, next to the Victoria rail station, built in 1862.

The Grosvenor Hotel today, 101, Buckingham Palace Road, London, SW1

THE FIRST FA COMMITTEE – 1863

Arthur Pember
(FA President)

Ebenezer Cobb Morley
(FA Hon. Secretary)

Francis Maule Campbell
(FA Treasurer)

PRESIDENT'S SIDE V. SECRETARY'S SIDE
Saturday 2nd January 1864
Battersea Park, London
(Kick-Off : 2.00 - 2.30 p.m.)

PRESIDENT'S XIV (2 GOALS, 0 T.D.)

Arthur. PEMBER (Pres.)	No Names Kilburn FC
Charles W. ALCOCK	Forest Club **(2 GOALS)**
Harry W. CHAMBERS	Sheffield FC
Arthur M. TEBBUT	Forest Club
Horace W. GRAY	War Office
DREW	Unknown
Robert G. GRAHAM	Barnes FC
Walter .J. CUTBILL	Forest Club
Alexander MORTEN	No Names Kilburn FC
James TURNER	Crystal Palace
MORRIS	Crystal Palace
A. RENSHAW	No Names Kilburn FC
LEUCHARS	Barnes FC
A. SCOTT	Unknown

SECRETARY'S XIV (0 GOALS, 0 T.D.)

Ebenezer C. MORLEY (Sec.)	Barnes FC
John F. ALCOCK	Forest Club
Charles M. TEBBUT	Forest Club
A. LLOYD	Crystal Palace
C. HEWETT	Unknown
George .T. WAWN	War Office.
J.P. PHILLIPS	War Office
INNES	Barnes FC
McCALMONT	Barnes FC
NEEDHAM	Unknown
H. BAKER	No Names Kilburn FC
Alfred J. BAKER	No Names Kilburn FC
HUGHES	Unknown
Cowper D. JACKSON	Forest Club

T.D. = Touch Downs.

Author's note:

I have given a very brief description of the evolution of the rules of the Football Association from the six meetings that were held at the Freemasons Tavern in November and December 1863. The full details can be found in many of the books that are quoted in the bibliography in the rear of this book.

The details of the match that took place on the fields of Battersea Park are taken from an in-depth description of the inaugural match that can be found in the 'The Field, the Country Gentleman's newspaper – 9th January 1864.' I reproduce this article in its entirety as readers may find it of both historic interest and some amusement. (See appendix 6)

The match is commonly believed to have taken place on the 9th January 1864 and the plaque erected in Battersea Park by Wandsworth Council quotes this as being the date.

However, this date is in fact incorrect and is based on an error to be found in a match report in the Bell's Life newspaper dated 16th January 1864, which quotes the incorrect date of the 9th. The correct date of the 2nd January 1864 can be found in the following newspapers;

Sporting Life - Wednesday 6th January 1864
Bell's Weekly Messenger - Monday 11th January 1864

The detail of the weather conditions on the day is taken from the Meteorological report for London on Saturday 2nd January as found in the London Daily News – Monday 4th January. The temperature was 29 degrees Fahrenheit (minus 2 degrees Celsius) and the wind was east-north-easterly.

This was not to be the first-ever match to be played to the Football Association's new rules. In fact, Ebenezer Cobb Morley was so keen to try out the new rules he arranged a 15-a-side match between his Barnes Club and another local side, Richmond, on Saturday 19th December 1863. It was said that the two teams had very little difficulty in understanding the new rules and the game was played in good temper with no disputes. However, despite Barnes having six 'tries' at the goal they didn't succeed in scoring and the match ended up goalless. The reporter of 'The Field' newspaper was not very complimentary about their play stating that if the match had been played after Christmas it might have accounted for their 'slowness and want of condition'.

At this point, there were 19 members of the Football Association who were due to pay their one guinea (£1, 1s.) subscription.

Barnes FC
Blackheath
HM War Office (Civil Service)
Crusaders
Crystal Palace
Forest Club, Leytonstone
No Names Kilburn
Surbiton
Perceval House (Blackheath)
Blackheath Proprietary School
Royal Naval School (New Cross)
Wimbledon School
Forest School, Walthamstow
Kensington School
Sheffield FC
Royal Engineers
Lincoln Football Club
Aldershot
Uppingham School

Chapter 7: North versus South
London v. Sheffield
Saturday 31st March 1866
Battersea Park, London

After the euphoria of agreeing the new rules of Association football, the forefathers of the new game suddenly found themselves rather isolated. The series of meetings that had been contrived to drive hacking out of the game had also been held at a time when most of the public schools could not be present. Consequently, those clubs and schools with a preference for the 'Rugby' style game pulled out. Those clubs that remained in the FA, numbering only nine (i), gave only a passing nod to the new rules. Sometimes in matches they would agree a variation to the rules between themselves; or sometimes adopt local rules in preference to the FA's.

By the time of the Football Association's A.G.M. on the 28th October 1864 the game and the Committee were in disarray and as a consequence no business was conducted. They would not meet again for another 16 months (22nd February 1866) and it might be considered that the new experiment had failed.

Meanwhile, Charles Alcock had plenty to be positive about in his personal life. In December of 1864 the twenty-two-year-old had married his new found love, Eliza Caroline Ovenden, at the church of St. Philip the Evangelist in Islington. They immediately moved into the area and took up residence at No. 33, Sherborne Street. Charles was not a man to hang around and by the turn of the New Year, Eliza had fallen pregnant and the Alcocks were expecting their first child.

Mind you, the prospect of married life and parenthood had not curtailed Charles' football career and during 1864 the Wanderers club was formed out of the 'chrysalis' (ii) of the Forest Club. The newly fledged 'butterfly' of a team would have no fixed ground and, as their name suggested, they would wander from ground to ground, taking on opponents on their home territory. Being a butterfly and flitting around the metropolis, they also took on the appearance of the red admiral of the species, and their new team shirt was a magnificent set of hoops, coloured orange, violet and black. The Wanderers first match had been played against the No Names Kilburn Club on the 2nd April 1864 and had resulted in a one-nil victory. The match report is worth recording for its fascinating insight into the methods of travel available to the Victorian footballer and the lengths they had to go to get to a match.

WANDERERS versus NO NAMES KILBURN

Responding as they always do with alacrity and cheerfulness to an invitation received at the eleventh hour, the Wanderers prepared their 'costumes de foot' on Saturday, April 2, and according to their usually 'one'-dering individual style of travelling started off by different routes to arrive at their destination, the Victoria Tavern, Kilburn, as may be expected, widely different hours. Some, evidently relying on the old proverb that 'hansom is that hansom does,' chartered the fashionable two-wheeler, and were quickly landed at the house of call. While others, eager to take advantage of the opportunities for speedy (?) transit afforded them by the North London Railway, safely accomplished the distance (six miles) in the incredibly short space of 1 hour 10 minutes. The roving band was at last, however, satisfactorily collected together, and soon made its appearance on the field of battle, where it was very graciously received by a sharp, cutting wind, which was blowing straight down from the upper to the lower goal. By acquaintance with the chief points of the art of tossing, as exemplified through the medium of a shilling piece, the choice of goal was won by the rovers, who, unwilling as they always are to turn their backs on friend or foe, selected the upper goal, with the wind and sun (two valuable auxiliaries as it proved) behind them. For an hour, in spite of the heaviness of the ground, the game raged furiously, only one goal (kicked for the Wanderers by A. M Tebbut) being obtained by either side. The sides were:

Wanderers: C. W. Alcock (capt). C. Absolom, C. Bigland, F. Desborough, G. H. Edmunds. T. Greaves. J. Hillhouse. A. M. Tebbut. C M. Tebbut, and A. Thompson.

N.N.'s: A. Pember (capt). G. Baker. H Baker. W. Baker, F. Giles, W. H. Lendrum, G. Michel, C. Morton, A. Pothonier, and A. G. Renshaw.

The question arises as to why the new club was formed? It is commonly reported that the Forest Club ground at Snaresbrook was becoming too expensive to maintain which is surprising given the team consisted of a group of up-and-coming businessmen. After all the land was common ground and any ground rent can't have been beyond their means. Perhaps it was just a natural evolution of the club. As we know, Charles would soon be leaving his home in Chingford and maybe it was time for pastures new. Charles himself, later stated: *'a variety of causes led to the decision of the old Forest Club , after four years of unbroken triumph, to seek a wider scope of football utility. The chief of which was the fact that the local element had become fine by degrees.'*

What we do know is that a handful of the Forest Club players followed Charles on his travels and these included the Tebbut brothers, Compton Bigland, and Charles Absolom. Conspicuous by their absence were three of the founding members of the club, Charles' brother John Forster, Alfred Mackenzie (Honorary Secretary) and John Pardoe.

John Pardoe is probably less of a mystery as he was preparing to leave the vicarage in Leytonstone in July 1864 to be ordained as a curate in the town of Hitchin in Hertfordshire (more of John Pardoe in the story of Hitchin FC later). However, as for John Forster and Alfred the answer may never be known. The Forest Club did continue to play during the 1864-65 season, including one game against the Wanderers, but as no detailed match reports have yet been discovered for these matches the destinies of these two players remain unresolved. Suffice it to say that John Forster Alcock was starting to disappear from the Association football scene and his younger brother Charles was taking over his mantle.

And so, at the long-awaited A.G.M of the Football Association on 22nd February 1866, Charles William Alcock (aged 23, now married and father to a four-month-old baby, William Edward Forster Alcock) was duly elected to the FA Committee. Arthur Pember was re-elected as President but Ebenezer Cobb Morley had to step down as Honorary Secretary because of business pressures and, whilst he would stay on the committee, his place was taken by Robert W. Willis also from the Barnes Football Club.

Whilst the newly formed committee only consisted of seven individuals and the meeting room was quite sparse, there were some momentous decisions taken with regard to the laws of the game. Firstly, a tape was to be introduced across the top of the goalposts at a height of eight feet and now a goal could only be scored by placing the ball under this tape. Apparently, in a game at Reigate Priory, a goal had been scored when the ball had passed through the posts at a height of at least ninety feet. This goal had been given at the behest of the crowd who were certain it passed between the posts. However, the committee adjudged this goal to be most 'unsatisfactory' in terms of the spirit of the game.

The next key change was to the offside rule and perhaps Harry Chambers, of the Sheffield Football Club, had finally been listened to. The committee deliberated abolishing the offside rule altogether but finally settled on a player being onside *'unless there are at least three opponents between him and their own goal.'*

The third key change was abolishing the rule concerning a free kick being awarded if the ball was caught in the air. This was another step towards the game being played with the feet only. The committee hoped that these rule changes would encourage more clubs to adopt their rules and join the Association.

William Chesterman: Honorary Secretary of Sheffield FC (1857-1889) - possibly the saviour of the Football Association.

Mr. William Chesterman, the Honorary Secretary of the Sheffield Football Club, had felt that these changes, if adopted, would bring the two associations rules closer together and he wrote that despite the fact that Sheffield FC would not be able to send a representative to the meeting, he proposed a match should be arranged between the Sheffield Club and a representative side from the London Clubs playing to the new Football Association rules.

The invitation was accepted and a date fixed for the match to be played in London on Battersea Park on 31st March 1866. The game would be played to the new Association rules and would last 90 minutes, starting at 3.00 p.m. and finishing at 4.30 p.m. The Sheffield side was apparently going to be chosen from 23 different clubs in the Sheffield area. In reality the players would mainly be drawn from Sheffield FC However, a date had been set and the world's first representational match was about to take place.

"I thought you said it would be warm down south! This is more like a walk up on the top of Howden Moors. The cold wind could blow you inside out." exclaimed the youngster, Arthur Wightman.

Harry Chambers looked up at the ominous grey-black clouds scurrying across the skyline. "I know lad. Last time I was down in the Capital playing football it was cold and wet but that was at the beginning of January not at the start of the Great British Summer."

"Still, the trip down from Sheffield was incredible. I'd never been on a steam train before. It would have taken us days by horse-drawn buses and we did it in only five hours. Mind you, I got my face covered in soot when we went through those tunnels near Welwyn. Luckily I'd packed some handkerchiefs in my suitcase to clear my eyes."

"What did you think to King's Cross station and the Metropolitan Underground railway that brought us down to Paddington ?"

Arthur looked at Harry, glassy-eyed; "I've never seen so many people in my life. How do they get all those people onto the trains? And the smell and the noise! Those street vendors near the metro and the gentlemen in top hats walking around with placards on their backs. I've never seen anything like it. I thought Sheffield's Victoria station was the grandest building I'd ever seen but Kings Cross is like a glass cathedral in comparison. Mind you I didn't like going underground, it doesn't seem natural, does it? All dark in those carriages with only those smelly gas lamps to see the person across from you and the steam outside and all around. It was like being in one of those scary new submarines. I don't mind saying I was scared witless. I'm glad you were there Harry. I really am. What stories I can tell the lads when we get home. They're not going to believe a word of it."

The eleven Sheffield players had exited Paddington station and stacked their luggage onto the horse drawn omnibus that would take them down across the Albert Bridge to Battersea Park. William Chesterman, the captain, made sure everybody was on board and then found himself a seat near to Harry and Arthur. "So, we're playing to the London Football Association rules today lads."

"I know," Harry replied dubiously, "I'm still not sure the lads have all got the hang of their offside rule yet. We've only had a week to practise it and I'm sure I see some of them looking around the field and counting three opponents before they pass. It's an improvement on their last rule but we still don't like it."

"I understand Harry but I see this as a chance of bringing the two sets of rules together. If this is a success and we can get a return match with them they'll soon see the error of their ways when they play the game under Sheffield rules. The London Association aren't exactly setting the footballing world alight at the moment and their membership has been dwindling. They've already made three changes that have brought their rules nearer to ours. It's only a matter of time."

The Prince Albert pub, 85 Albert Bridge Road, Battersea – c. 1890

The horse-drawn omnibus pulled up outside the Prince Albert pub opposite the gates to Battersea Park. The landlord, George Mellish, had given the eleven Yorkshiremen permission to use his pub as a changing room, anticipating a good return on his generosity after the match. He was sure the men from the north would sink a few pints of his best stout after the game.

It is interesting to note that today's game was to be played by eleven players on each side (at this time the laws of the game did not specify the size of each team, but the game had gravitated to eleven as being the ideal) Also, the ground in Battersea Park would be 120 yards long and 80 yards wide. As the match was to be played on the cricket practise ground, the park-keepers were not too strict on football being played over the cricket square and so a decent size pitch could be marked out. In fact, Charles Alcock's new team the Wanderers had played matches here against the Civil Service; the only issue was making sure the match finished before dusk when the park keepers locked the gates.

Today's game was to last 90 minutes, from 3.00 p.m. to 4:30 p.m. (the laws did not specify the length of a match and there was no provision for half-time, sides would change ends when a goal was scored) Knocking-on with the hand was still allowed but not to score a goal. Also, for the first time the size of the ball was stipulated and this would be a 'Lillywhite number 5' It was agreed that this was the perfect size to play football.

And so, the two sides took to the field. The Sheffield team looked defiant in their scarlet red jerseys. The London XI ran out in their all-white kit which was a brilliant contrast to the green turf and the grey of this gloomy day. The Sheffield lads looked at each other and smirked:

"All white? We'll soon have those pretty southern boys covered in mud. There won't be an inch of white showing come 4.30 p.m."

Harry Chambers had given his team-mates a run down on the five players he knew from the match he'd played in two years ago (The President's XIV v. Secretary's XIV).

"The London lads are led by two stalwarts of the game. Don't be fooled by their age. Although Ebenezer Cobb Morley is 34 and Arthur Pember, their captain is 31, between them they have created the Football Association and the new rules. Both are born leaders and fitness fanatics. Morley set up the Barnes Football Club and, as they are located near the River Thames, all the players are keen rowers. Ebenezer even has a gym set up in his house to make sure he keeps his fitness levels up. Arthur Pember is also as fit as a fiddle and has recently led mountain expeditions up Mont Blanc in France. So, as a leader of men, it really is no surprise that he is the President of the FA, the creator and captain of No Names Kilburn and the London Captain today.

As for the younger lads, Charles Alcock is a fantastic dribbler and he will take any opportunity to have a shot at goal if you let him. Make sure you close him down and stop him in his tracks. He scored two cracking goals in that last FA match. He's probably being playing football as long as anyone as both himself and Charles Tebbut (26) both started out in the Forest Club. It goes without saying they know their own game.

Last but not least, is Alfred Joseph Baker from the No Names Kilburn club and who at 20 years old is one of the youngest members of the side but watch out he's also one of the quickest. He is a renowned sprinter and one of the fastest Londoners over 100 yards. You'll know when he's off on one of his runs as he bends his body forwards and he's off like a shot. Make sure you drop back a couple of yards to stop the ball getting through to him."

The Sheffield XI were as prepared as they could be and at 3.15 p.m. William Chesterman met Arthur Pember in the middle of the pitch for the toss of the coin. The umpire flicked the silver shilling piece (current value 5 pence) into the air and as it spun William called 'Tails'. As the coin landed on the turf, William could see the words 'ONE SHILLING' surrounded by laurel branches and topped by the Royal Crown.

A Victorian shilling piece (1866)

Sheffield had won the toss and William immediately chose to play from the western goal so any wind would be in their favour. Arthur Pember therefore kicked off and immediately the London side took charge of the game with some brisk play. After only a quarter of an hour, a quick break by the Londoners resulted in a shot on goal sailing through the posts of the Northerners. It was none other than the old fox, Ebenezer Cobb Morley, who turned away in celebration.

"I told you we needed to keep an eye on the old boy, that shot came from nowhere." shouted Harry Chambers.

Alex Dixon, Sheffield's goalkeeper, shrugged his shoulders and put his hands up in the air. "We can't get used to this enormous goal, Harry. That would never have been a goal in Sheffield, I would have got my hand to it. Perhaps you and I need both need to drop back into the goal area to help cover any shots from different angles?"

The two sides immediately changed ends and the wind picked up and rain started to fall again. It seemed that everything was conspiring against the Northerners as either the heavy rain or skin tingling hail blew into their faces. During the next few minutes Sheffield managed to protect their goal but J.A. Barnes of London managed to score a touchdown on one side of the Sheffield goal.

This match saw the debut of one 19-year-old Arthur Fitzgerald Kinnaird playing for the London team. Arthur had come in as a last-minute replacement for his fellow Etonian, Quintin Hogg of the Wanderers. Charles Alcock had first played against Arthur in January 1866 when his Wanderers side came up against the Old Etonians and then met him again in two goalless draws when he was the guest player for the Harrow Chequers and the Civil Service. Charles was so impressed with the youngster he had no hesitation in putting him straight into his London side. Although Arthur was not to make his debut for the Wanderers until the following season, this was to be the start of the career of probably the most successful footballer of the Victorian era.

John Biddulph Martin, from the Wanderers Club, was having a fine game and he went on an amazing run and passed the ball through to Charles Alcock who shot and scored.

"OFFSIDE!" shouted the umpire.

"DAMNATION!" screamed Charles who suddenly realised he was the first player to fall foul of the new offside rule as there were only two Sheffield players between him and the goal.

The game carried on with great vigour and a few 'awkward kicks were taken and given.' Also, some of the knock-ons with the fist were flying very close to Sheffield and London noses. It wasn't long before John Biddulph Martin managed to force over another touch-down for London. He was having a fine game and just ten minutes later he got his team's second goal. The Sheffield team were starting to look despondent as the teams changed ends for the second time. The Yorkshiremen were looking at their first defeat following successive victories over Lincoln and Nottingham.

The rain was relentless and the pitch was starting to cut up quite badly. Luckily the renowned Kings Road Cricket Club only used this section of Battersea Park for practice. During one particular extreme downpour, the experienced Charles Tebbut of the No Names Kilburn Club (but originally a player of the Alcock brothers' Forest Club) succeeded in scoring another touch-down for the Londoners. It was all one-way traffic now with the vociferous Battersea Park crowd urging their team on and with ten minutes to go John Biddulph Martin scored a fourth touch-down to go with his goal.

The Londoners then asked William Chesterman if he wished to call an end to proceedings as there was no sign of any let up in the weather. However, the Sheffield Club wished to carry on to the bitter end and the game finished up as two goals and four touchdowns to nil, in favour of the Londoners.

As the players marched off to the changing room, some of the Londoners were feeling battle weary and bruised having been severely kicked and knocked about. The Sheffielders, in contrast, retired with no injuries. Maybe they weren't quite the 'Gentlemen' their nickname led us to believe. (iii)

The two sets of players then caught carriages alongside the River Thames to their post-match dinner held at the Albion Tavern and Hotel, 26, Russell Street, Covent Garden. The Tavern was directly opposite the Drury Lane Theatre and was a regular host to the visiting celebrities who plied their trade behind the footlights. It's certain that an occasional star of the stage would have walked along the passageway outside their dining room. After an agreeable evening, William Chesterman and Arthur Pember toasted each other's sides and then Arthur raised his glass of claret to the sky and made a toast to football and their new starlet and leading light himself, Charles Alcock.

Secretly, the Northerners were angry at having been beaten playing to unfamiliar rules and on top of that not all of them had been properly adopted. They couldn't wait for the return match in Sheffield, where they could get their revenge. Amazingly, it would be nearly five years before the two sides would meet again. (iv)

An early photo of a group of Sheffield Footballers (c. 1875) in their scarlet jerseys and white knickerbockers. It appears that a couple of stalwart female players have tried to infiltrate their way into the back row of the team.

LONDON XI V. SHEFFIELD XI

Saturday 31st March 1866
Battersea Park, London
(Kick-Off : 3.15 p.m.)

LONDON XI (2, 4 T.D'S)
White Jerseys & White Shorts

Arthur Pember (captain)	No Names Kilburn
Charles W. Alcock	Wanderers
Alfred J. Baker	No Names Kilburn
J.A. Barnes	Barnes FC
Robert D. Elphinstone	Civil Service
Arthur F. Kinnaird	Wanderers
John Biddulph Martin	Wanderers
Ebenezer Cobb Morley	Barnes
D. M. O'Leary	Barnes
Charles M. Tebbut	No Names Kilburn
Robert W. Willis	Barnes FC

SHEFFIELD XI (0, 0 T.D'S)
Red Jerseys & White Shorts

William Chesterman (captain)	Sheffield FC
W. Baker	Sheffield FC
Harry W. Chambers	Sheffield FC
J. Denton	Sheffield FC
A. A. Dixon	Sheffield FC
F. Knowles	Sheffield FC
J. Knowles	Sheffield FC
John C. Shaw	Hallam & Sheffield FC
B. Shepherd	Sheffield FC
J. D. Webster	Sheffield FC
Arthur Wightman	Sheffield FC

Goals, London: E.C. Morley (1), J.B. Martin (1)
Touch-Downs London : Barnes (2), Tebbut (1), Martin (1)

Author's Notes:

(i)   As reported in Bell's Life – 23ʳᵈ January 1864

Barnes FC No Names Kilburn HM War Office (Civil Service) Crystal Palace Forest Club, Leytonstone	Forest School Sheffield FC Royal Engineers Uppingham School

(ii) In C.W. Alcock's own words in 'The Association Game'

'…the transmutation of the Forest chrysalis into the resplendent butterfly – the Wanderers, a name to conjure with in the early days of the Association game.'

(iii) The match reports of 'Sheffield versus London' vary in their detail and conflicting statements are made in the 'Bell's Life, and 'Sporting Life'. I have, therefore, taken the details of the match predominantly from the match report published in The Field on Saturday 7ᵗʰ April 1866. This match report appears as a cutting in Arthur Kinnaird's football scrapbooks and, if there were any obvious errors, he tended to correct them in pencil in the margin. There were no such corrections to this report. This was also the match where it is purported that the Sheffield XI headed the ball, much to the amusement of the Battersea crowd who had never come across this spectacle. I have not come across any written evidence of this so have omitted it from the match report.

(iv) The return match between Sheffield v. London was played to Sheffield rules at Bramall Lane on the 2ⁿᵈ December 1871. The game wasn't sanctioned by the FA as they would only play to their own rules. It fell to none other than Charles William Alcock to extend an olive branch to the Northerners and he took an unofficial London side up to Sheffield to continue the links between the two clubs. The Yorkshiremen ran out 3-1 victors. Previous attempts had been made to play the game and in fact 'The Sportsman' advertised the fixture to be played in Sheffield on the 19ᵗʰ January 1867, but unfortunately the rules could not be agreed and the game didn't go ahead as planned.

Chapter 8: The Youdan Cup

The World's First-Ever Football Knockout Competition
(16th February to 9th March 1867)

Upon returning from London in 1866, the Sheffield Football Club continued with their campaign to take football and the Sheffield rules to the wider world by playing inter-county matches. Apart from London they played teams from Lincoln, Nottingham and Manchester. They hadn't enjoyed the game in Battersea Park and they were still focused on driving a game which would be played with the feet and not the hands. In the Sheffield rules, the knocking the ball on with the hand they had witnessed in London, was completely prohibited and the penalty for doing so was a 'free kick'. The only time the hands could be used was when taking a 'throw in' and when a 'fair catch' was made.

When the Sheffield footballers regrouped at the start of the 1866-67 season a plan was formed to start a Football Association and consequently, in January 1867, the Sheffield Football Association was formed, consisting of fourteen clubs and between 1,000 to 1,200 members. Most of the cricket clubs in Sheffield had started a football club to partake in the new winter sport of football. They had no prejudices and were happy to adopt the playing rules of the Sheffield Association. No decisions were taken with regard to making any further changes to the Sheffield rules as the committee had decided to wait for the next annual meeting of the London Football Association to be held on the 26th February 1867.

William Chesterman walked up the creaky wooden stairs to the upper floor meeting room of the Freemasons Tavern. It was 8 p.m. and as he took his seat, he was surprised to see that there were only five other attendees, representing just three other clubs, sat around the giant oak table. Arthur Pember, Ebenezer Cobb Morley and Robert Graham were attending on behalf of Barnes Football Club. Charles Alcock was there representing the Wanderers and Walter Cutbill was present on behalf of Crystal Palace. This was probably the lowest point of the London FA's short existence and to make matters worse Arthur Pember proceeded to resign as President. He revealed his plans to move to the United States of America and his desire to become an investigative journalist in New York. Also, James Turner of Crystal Palace would not be standing for re-election as Treasurer. The London FA's future lay in tatters. Ebenezer Cobb Morley had managed to resolve his business affairs and was willing to stand again as President but his question was, was it worth it?

'I'm very discouraged at the paucity of attendance this evening. I remember that at the commencement of the Association in 1863, we had a crowded room, and much more enthusiasm was displayed by those who attended in the interest of the pleasant pastime of football than has ever been shown since. The only way I can account for it is the supposition abroad that the Football Association has accomplished the objects for which it was established, and that there consequently is no further need of its services. We should seriously consider this night whether it is worthwhile to continue the Association or dissolve it. If after further discussion they considered they had made the rules perfect, what was the utility of meeting again to do nothing?"

Strong words indeed, from a man who had devoted so much time and energy to the Association's cause. Whilst the Association seemed to have fallen to its lowest ebb there were three critical factors that would ensure the future of this world-famous institution.

The first was William Chesterman himself, who despite having his proposed rule changes turned down (the introduction of the rouge system (i), a one man offside and a free kick for handball) was surprisingly supportive of the London FA and encouraged them to continue, diplomatically stating,

"...the alterations we propose are not of much consequence. We will be guided by the result of tonight's meeting's deliberations and we will give all our attention to the superior alterations that the London representatives might make."

Secondly, a letter was received from Arthur Kinnaird, now at Cambridge University, who was obviously keen to continue his links with the FA following his inclusion in the London side for the representative game against Sheffield. Arthur would join the Committee the following season and go on to serve the FA up until his death 55 years later. He was considered to be the first football star and appeared in nine FA Cup finals winning five.

The third factor was Charles Alcock himself. That evening he was elected onto the FA Committee and immediately started to have an influence. His (The Wanderers) proposal to abolish the system of touchdowns and replace it with a goal-kick to the defending team was immediately accepted. His reasoning had been that it encouraged far too much play down the sides of the pitches and if the FA were serious in expanding its remit, then this change would entice back the public schools. His response to the future of the Association was short and succinct,

"In 1860 only two clubs played foreign matches (Presumably his Forest Club and Mincing Lane?), *while the matches played in London last year (1866) amounted 122, exclusive of public-school matches."*

The inference was obvious, the burgeoning game needed an administrator and that administrator needed to be the London Football Association. Charles was now fully aware of the formation of the Sheffield Football Association and the strength of their membership. The 24-year-old Charles had also had a career change from marine insurer to sports journalist and as such was also aware of other goings on 'Up North'. It was probably Charles who had edited the details of the report of the FA meeting in 'The Sportsman' newspaper on the 28th February 1867, just two days after the meeting had been held. Below this report were two detailed match reports containing the heading;

'YOUDAN'S FOOTBALL CUP'

Thomas Youdan was an Irishman, who fled to Sheffield at the age of eighteen, following the Potato Famine. He started work as a silver stamper, but soon found himself running a successful pub and from his profits he soon expanded into the entertainment industry opening the renamed music hall, the Surrey Theatre, which offered cheap entertainment to the people living in the tenement slum area of Sheffield. Despite some horrendous setbacks during the Great Sheffield Flood of March 1864 and a subsequent fire in 1865 which burned down his music hall, Thomas was not a man to be beaten and from the compensation he received he opened the Alexandra Theatre and Opera House. In January 1867, Thomas offered a mouth-watering line up that would set your imagination running and which would soon relieve you of your hard-earned shilling (5p), sixpence (2.5p) or threepence (1.25p)

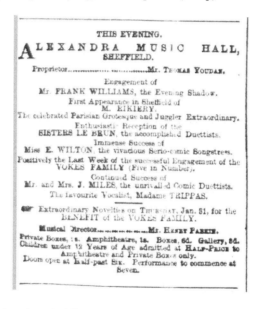

An advert for Thomas Youdan's Alexandra Music Hall
Sheffield Independent - Thursday 31 January 1867

Who had come up with the idea of a knockout football competition was unknown but it must have been the brainchild of one or two individuals on the Sheffield committee? Perhaps the Sheffield representatives had overheard Charles Alcock talking of his exploits in the Harrow Cock House Cup competition over a glass of claret at the post-match celebrations. Whatever, the Sheffield Association had stolen a march on their London counterparts and I'm sure the idea rankled with Charles. This would be something he would be sure to rectify in the years that followed.

Thomas Youdan initially offered the design of his Cup to the general public. Anybody could submit ideas to the Sheffield Daily Telegraph for a prize of one sovereign (£1). A couple of designs were chosen and these were amalgamated into the final design. Unfortunately, the manufacturing process was too long for the finished Cup to be ready for presentation and so a silver claret jug was offered instead. Also, a second trophy was to be offered to the runners-up funded by the gate admission money from the final matches. Thomas Youdan probably saw this as an opportunity to promote his new theatre through the universally popular sport of football and by sponsoring the cup he knew he would gain publicity across the city. However, Thomas was also a charitable man and he often made numerous donations to the poor and elderly and also to the soup kitchens in the city. He would have been more than happy to contribute to something that encouraged the physical well-being of the people of Sheffield.

Twelve Sheffield clubs were to compete. The Sheffield Football Club declined entry as they were embarking on their series of inter-county matches and would be indisposed on the proposed dates. The following rules appeared in the local press:

Every game to commence punctually at three o'clock. Waiting for players not allowed. *Feb. 16th, 1867. FREDK. CORBETT, Hon. Sec.*

- Matches to be played under Sheffield Rules.
- Matches to start at three o'clock, with two umpires and one referee.
- There will be 12 players on each side.
- Games will last ninety minutes. If the scores were tied, up to one hour of extra-time would be played, with the first team to score during this period being declared the winner. (GOLDEN GOAL RULE)
- If scores were still tied after extra-time, the match would be replayed.

The draw was made and the following games took place:

NORTON 2 (6) v. UNITED MECHANICS 0 (0) at Norton.
MACKENZIE 1 (1) v. GARRICK 0 (0) at The Orphanage.
HALLAM 2 (2) v. HEELEY 0 (1) at Hallam.
NORFOLK 2 (4) v. FIR VALE 0 (0) at Norfolk Park.
BROOMHALL 0 (2) v. PITSMOOR 0 (0) at Ecclesall Road.
WELLINGTON 0 (0) v. MILTON 2 (5) at The Orphanage.

Goals scored, Rouges (i) in brackets.

And so began the world's first-ever knockout football competition and 'KNOCKOUT' was the right word. These were the first football matches where a prize was at stake and the competitive level was high. The adrenalin was flowing and games saw rough play with excessive 'charging' of opponents. Consequently, in the Norton v United Mechanics game John Hadfield, an accomplished athlete, dislocated his shoulder. He didn't realise this and carried on playing in agony. At Norfolk Park, in the Norfolk v. Fir Vale match, a young gentleman was thoroughly 'pumped out' when the game was at its fiercest. He fell to the ground completely exhausted and had to be helped up by his fellow team-mates. On account of the rough play in the first round, the committee added a new rule that *'the referee shall have power to award a Free Kick to the opponents of any Club, which makes more than three fouls or kicks-out, when the ball is being thrown in, if he (the referee) considers those fouls or kicks-out to be intentional.'*

Despite the new rule, rough play continued in the second series of matches played on Saturday 23rd February 1867.

NORFOLK 1 (0) v. BROOMHALL 0 (0) at Norfolk Park.
MACKENZIE 0 (1) v. MILTON 0 (0) at The Orphanage.
NORTON 0 (0) v. HALLAM 0 (0) at Norton (after 1 hour of extra time was played!)

One young player for the Mackenzie team named Mr. Green, who was a well-known pedestrian (the Victorian name used to describe a person engaging in competitive running or walking) was another to break his collarbone whilst charging an opponent of the Milton team. After the game a collection was made for Mr. Green

81

at Mr. C. Webster's, the Mackenzie club-house, and apparently it raised enough money for his immediate needs. Also, a weekly payment would be made to him to cover his loss of wages whilst off work.

Despite the fact the football at its outset had set its stall out to be a less violent than the public-school versions of the game and a gentler game than rugby, it seemed as though the added elements of competition and reward had brought the game back to its roots. The clubs immediately recognised this and the following report was made in the Sheffield Daily Telegraph on Saturday 9th March 1867.

The Norfolk, the Milton, and the Mechanics' Clubs have already taken steps for apportioning some of their resources to recoup, as far as pecuniary help can do it, these unfortunate young men for the suffering and loss which have followed their earnest efforts in support of the honour of their respective clubs, and to win for them a trophy of which any club might well feel proud.

The Cup games themselves had caught the public's imagination and a crowd of nearly a 1,000 watched Norfolk's victory at Norfolk Park. This was surpassed by nearly 3,000 spectators witnessing the epic two and a half hour 0-0 draw between Norton and Hallam at Norton. This would turn out to be a world record attendance for a football match. (ii)

Replay: Monday 25th February 1867.
HALLAM 0 (1) v. NORTON 0 (0) at Hallam?

In the replay Hallam scored a rouge after an hour's play. In so doing they scored the world's first-ever golden rouge (goal) and proceeded to the final.

And so, the excitement continued and we were down to three remaining clubs (an odd number) to compete for the Youdan Cup. A further draw was made which resulted in the following tie played at the Brammall (iii) Lane Cricket Ground on Saturday 2nd March 1867. Admission: 3d. (1.25 pence), Ladies: Free.

HALLAM 0 (4) v. MACKENZIE 0 (0)

Norfolk Football Club were awarded a walkover (bye).

The contestants of the world's first-ever Football Cup Final were decided and the Hallam and Norfolk football clubs would meet on Tuesday 5th March 1867 which was Shrove Tuesday. This was the day when most of Sheffield's work-force would have a day's holiday. Thomas Youdan's instinct to finance this tournament had been proved correct again and it served as the perfect promotional tool for his theatre. The spectators the games had attracted had ensured that his name would be known all around the city of Sheffield. To ensure the maximum return on his investment, the third match of the series and the final game would be played at Brammall Lane where there was a magnificent grandstand which could house a large number of the spectators. It had also been decided that a 'play-off' match for second place would take place, with the admission money going towards a second trophy; a double handed goblet surrounded by athletic figures.(Value £2, 10 shillings)

YOUDAN CUP FINAL

Tuesday 5th March 1867 – Brammall Lane Cricket Ground

HALLAM FC 0 (2) v. NORFOLK FC 0 (0)

The Hallam and Norfolk clubs met at Brammall Lane yesterday to play off for this prize. The sides were very equal, both as to ability and size. Nothing was got up to half time, but after changing ends and a short time before time was called, Hallam scored a rouge, the touchdown being cleverly made by Ash, who is a fine sprinter. This riled their opponents, as they only had a few more minutes to play. Norfolk went in a 'burster', and the players were floored in all directions. In doing this, they exposed their goal, and a player to whom they have awarded the sweet name of 'Treacle' secured a second rouge for Hallam, immediately after which time was called. As a whole, the match was a capital one and were they to play again, Hallam would only just have the call for choice. All played well, but more particularly Dale. Donovan, and Ash. A vast concourse of spectators witnessed the match. We should think upwards of 2,000.

(Sheffield Independent - Wednesday 6th March 1867) (iv)

'PLAY-OFF' for 2nd Place

Saturday 9th March 1867 – Brammall Lane Cricket Ground.

NORFOLK FC 0 (1) v. MACKENZIE FC 0 (0)

And so, the Youdan Cup (vi) had been a resounding success. Apart from the large number of spectators the competition had introduced:

- Referees to adjudicate when the umpires could not agree.
- Extra-time – Norton v. Hallam – 23rd February 1867
- The Golden Goal – Hallam v. Norton - 25th February 1867.
- The walkover (bye)
- A 'Play-Off' for second place.
- The beginnings of the creation of a Player Benevolent Fund (v)

The only downside, apart from the number of injuries were the lack of goals. Only ten had been scored in the thirteen matches played in the tournament. Seven were goalless, of which six were decided by rouges. Only one goal was scored after the first round. Maybe there was an argument for increasing the size of the Sheffield goals after all?

Still, the blueprint for a successful Football Cup competition had been written and maybe somewhere in the dark offices of 'The Sportsman' newspaper in Central London, Charles Alcock sat and read the match reports coming from the north of England with great interest. Here was proof that a Cup competition could spread the popularity of the game. The 24-year-old, recently married and now father to a one-year-old son (William) no doubt filed this in his memory bank.

He'd only recently joined the ranks of the FA and his time would come!

HALLAM FC V. NORFOLK FC
YOUDAN CUP FINAL
Tuesday 5th March 1867
Brammall Lane Cricket Ground, Sheffield
(Attendance 2,000; Kick-Off : 3.00 p.m.)

Scorers for Hallam: H. Ash, 1 rouge; 'Treacle?', 1 Rouge

HALLAM FC 0, (2 ROUGES)
Blue Jerseys

J.C. SHAW (Captain)
H. BRAMWELL
G. ELLIOTT
H. ASH
W. ADSETTS
J. DALE
J. BRADBURY
G. JONES
T. ARMITAGE
J. BOWNES
S. GILBERT
A. HOBSON

NORFOLK FC 0, (0 ROUGES)
Colours unknown

J. ROBERTS (Captain)
T. SANK BELL
J. PASHLEY
J.P. DONOVAN
H. CAWTHORNE
T. GOODWIN
C. GRAYSON
C. MARSHALL
J. WILDBLOOD
G. RODGERS
G. PROCTOR
J. SIMMONITE\J. PRING

Author's Notes:

(i) The rouge came from the Eton Rules field football. Sheffield had adopted the four-yard-wide goal with a further two 'rouge' flags another eight yards either side of the goal through which a ball could be kicked and if touched down, a rouge was scored. The rouge was to be used as a match decider should the scores be level at the end of a game. This system would be in play for the forthcoming Youdan Cup.

(ii) This attendance would remain a world record for a football match for ten years and would not be exceeded by the FA Cup until 1878.

(iii) Bramall Lane was originally spelt Brammall with two 'm's.

(iv) The match details reported for the final were sparse compared to some of the reports of the earlier games. This was probably due to the final being played on a national holiday.

(v) The committee of the Sheffield FA had obviously put a framework together to give some sort of guarantee for player welfare. A benefit society for players came into its own during the following season. There were reports that players were contributing to this fund through their clubs but the monies available were obviously not enough for the number of claims. Fund raising events had to be staged to supplement the benefits. Thomas Youdan assisted with this, putting on theatrical evenings at the Alexandra Music Hall dedicated to the fund, as well as a Town v. County football match staged at Bramall Lane. By the end of the 1869 season, it seems that funding for injured players was discontinued.

(vi) The Challenge for the Youdan Cup was intended to be continued the following year but for some reason it never took place. However, a second cup, The Cromwell Cup, was provided by Thomas Youdan's stage manager at the Alexandra Theatre in 1868, the wonderfully named, Oliver Cromwell.

Chapter 9: 'Look, No Hands!'

The Birth of FOOTball & the First-Ever International
ENGLAND v SCOTLAND
Saturday 5ᵗʰ March 1870

It was the turn of the decade. A time for great excitement and the emergence of new ideas. Britain was now the supreme industrial powerhouse of the world and its empire stretched far and wide. Victoria was Queen and William Ewart Gladstone was Prime Minister. New inventions and new opportunities arose every day. Nothing was impossible.

In London the world's first underground passenger 'tube' railway had been built through 'Tower Subway' under the River Thames. It wasn't a commercial success but the principle of travelling underground and under a river had been successful and would pave the way for the expansion of the existing London Underground.

Intrepid passengers travelling in a horse drawn carriage being pulled under the River Thames. The young boy to the right looks suitably frightened!

In 1863, a 3.75-mile section of the Metropolitan District Railway line had been opened to connect the Paddington and King's Cross stations. It was a great success and more expansion of the line soon followed to Hammersmith and Kensington Olympia. The initial lines were built using a 'cut and cover' method but the 'tube' technique meant that the expansion could now take place almost anywhere in the Metropolis. For the Victorian footballer this meant they now had a means to avoid the severe traffic congestion of the multitude of carts, cabs and omnibuses that were constantly blocking London's main roads.

In the world of football, Charles Alcock had just celebrated his 27th birthday and the also birth of his second child, Elizabeth Maud Alcock and his wife was pregnant again with their third child. Despite his increased family responsibilities, Charles continued to play football two or three times a week in the winter and then played cricket in the summer.

He didn't shirk in his administrative duties either and at the first A.G.M of the new decade he was appointed Honorary Secretary and Treasurer of the Football Association, taking over from Robert Graham of Barnes FC This would be an appointment that would last for 25 years and during his time in the post Charles would revolutionise the game we know and love today.

This first meeting set the scene for things to come and sometime after 8.30 p.m. on Wednesday 23rd February 1870, in the Freemasons Tavern on Great Queen's Street, Lincoln's Inn Fields, handling the ball was abolished forever.

The far-reaching proposal contained just eleven words; '.. *that handling the ball under any pretence whatever shall be prohibited*'

This was unanimously agreed by the clubs who were present and the motion carried, along with changing ends at half time if no goal had been scored. (i)

Three proposals for the abolition of the use of hands had been made to the committee, but it was this simple one line proposed by the Upton Park Football Club, that was accepted by a majority. In the other two proposals, made by the Wanderers and the Civil Service, it was suggested that a throw in be awarded to the opposing team from the spot where the ball was handled. The Nottingham Club went on to suggest a place kick should be awarded for any infringement of handling the ball. However, the awarding of any penalty for handball was not agreed, possibly because it would take a while for the players to adapt from their previous style of play.

The Civil Service went one step further and suggested that the goalkeeper should be the only one who could handle the ball. Such was the variety of use of goalkeepers in games, it was felt necessary to add the definition of a goalkeeper into the laws. (ii) A further memorandum would be added, again proposed by the Nottingham Club, that *'handling is understood to be playing the ball with the hand or the arm'*

This meeting was far more cordial than previous meetings of the FA and reflected its growing membership (circa 34) with representative clubs both from both the capital and the provinces.

In attendance that day were the

Amateur Athletic Club	(1868)
Wanderers	(1859)
Clapham Rovers	(1869)
Harrow Pilgrims	(1864)
Gitanos	(1864) *
No Names Kilburn	(1863)
Brixton	(1867)
Barnes	(1862)
Hampstead Heathens	(1868)
Upton Park	(1866)
Nottingham (County)	(1862)
Lincoln	(1861)
Newark	(1868)
Royal Engineers	(1863) sent apologies
Civil Service	(1862) sent apologies
Crusaders	(1859) sent apologies *

Although not mentioned in the press reports, representatives of other clubs were also elected to the committee of the Football Association which, including the President and Secretary/Treasurer, was now twelve strong. These included:

Crystal Palace	(1861)
Sheffield	(1857)
Old Etonians	(1864) *

* Not members of the FA

Just prior to this meeting, another historic event had been due to take place. On Saturday 19th February 1870, the first-ever football international was scheduled to be played at the Kennington Oval between an English XI and a Scottish XI. The suggestion to play the match at The Oval must have been driven by Charles Alcock, as his Wanderers side had now started to play their home matches at the home of the Surrey County Cricket Club rather than Battersea Park. Whoever had suggested the match was unknown. However, the new FA Committee included five members of Scottish descent. As the 1869-70 season was coming to a close and most clubs were beginning to organise their end of season athletics meetings, it was decided to stage the event prior to the commencement of the cricket season.

Kennington Oval, circa 1850

As it happened Saturday 19th February 1870 saw one of the most severe frosts ever witnessed with temperatures as low as minus 18 degrees Fahrenheit (-28 degrees Celsius). A topical Victorian newspaper entitled 'The Era' reported it as follows;

'THE WEATHER has been intensely severe throughout the last week, and navigation has been forced to be suspended on the Thames owing to the floating ice, and all building operations are at a stand-still. The frost has interfered with the proper working of the telegraphs and caused great

inconvenience to commercial men, whilst, owing to the tempestuous weather in the Channel, all communication with the Continent was cut off for two days.'

In sport all horse-racing and dog-coursing was postponed and the practice sessions for the forthcoming boat race between Oxford and Cambridge had to be cancelled. A cricket match took place on the ice at Cambridge, with good scores being recorded by both sides. This was probably a result of playing the match with no bails on top of the stumps due the bitingly cold north-easterly wind constantly blowing them off.

Inevitably the first meeting of England v. Scotland had to be postponed and a new date was set for Saturday 5th March 1870. This was fortuitous in many respects, the main one being that the new rules concerning 'no handling' and 'half-time' had been introduced. This would be the first game of true football, as we know it, ever to be played.

"Is everybody here yet?" Charles Alcock looked nervously at his watch. The game was due to kick-off at three o'clock and already a large crowd had amassed behind the roped off area of the cricket ground where the match was about to be played.

" Not yet," replied James Kirkpatrick, the captain of the Scotland side, "with the selection of players from different clubs arriving from all areas of the Capital, there's bound to be a few delays." (iii)

"It was ever thus," bemoaned Charles, "maybe we need to adopt the rules of the Sheffield FA where there is no waiting for players and kick-off is always bang on time. Mind you, I suppose this is an historic occasion for football and the crowd won't mind waiting for a few minutes longer."

It was a bright spring day and there was a strong easterly wind blowing from one end of the ground. An expectant crowd of nearly 400 (iv) lined the pitch and from the accents that were being bandied about there seemed to be a fair few supporters in favour of the Scottish side. Charles looked out of the cricket pavilion windows. He could see the two towering gasometers of the Phoenix Gasworks over in the distance dominating the skyline. There was a small tent set up for the ladies present and on either side of him there were at least fifty carriages, parked in front of the Kennington Oval Rackets Court.

At the eleventh hour the Scottish side had to bring in two replacements as Lord Kilmarnock was called up for duty by the Royal Horse Guards and one of their other talented players, Ferguson, had to withdraw. Their places were taken by George Kennedy of No Names Kilburn and Alexander Morten of Crystal Palace. Mind you, the Scottish side were not understrength at all and they could boast a Parliamentary 'back two', with none other than the Right Honourable John Wingfield Malcolm, M.P. for Boston in Lincolnshire and the son of the current Prime Minister, William Gladstone Junior. With John Malcolm measuring six-foot-five in height and Willy Gladstone being over six feet tall and both gentlemen sporting bushy beards, it was thought they should strike fear into the hearts and minds of the young English forwards. (v) The reporter of none other than the Daily Telegraph didn't hold back in his assessment of the strength of the Scottish side.

'The disproportion between the two teams was somewhat striking, as the 'canny Scots' were, to all appearances, a more powerful body than the less stalwart Englishmen; and the gigantic form of the worthy member for Boston (John Malcolm) towering like a veritable 'King of men' over his fellows, suggested a preponderance of strength in favour of the sons of Wallace and Bruce.'

Eventually all the players arrived and it was time for the two captains to lead the teams out onto the pitch. As the players clattered down the pavilion steps, all they could see were row upon row of top hats, bowler hats and a few cloth caps surrounding the roped-off pitch. There was a pervading smell of tobacco smoke floating across the ground in the spring air. Apart from the ladies, nearly all the menfolk seemed to be puffing on a cheroot or drawing on a pipe and blowing the smoke up into the air.

A silver shilling was tossed up into the air which fell in favour of the Scots and their captain, Jimmy Kirkpatrick, chose to play towards the western goal with the strong wind behind him. It was just after 3.15 p.m. when Charles Alcock 'the English Commander' kicked off and 'sent the ball well into the quarters occupied by the Scottish Chieftains'. I wonder if Charles knew that he had taken the first offensive kick in a fierce rivalry that would last for centuries.

Despite the new FA Rules, the tactics of the teams hadn't changed and the formations tended to be attack minded with a goalkeeper, one back, a midfielder and eight forwards rushing the ball 'en-bloc' towards the opponent's goal. It is not clear from the newspaper reports of the time, whether the Civil Service's proposal that the goalkeeper could handle the ball *for the protection of his goal* had been approved in the FA's AGM held on 23rd February 1870. The Scottish press, however, reported the rule's adoption in their match reports that week. (vi)

The English were favourites to win but having lost the toss, and given the fact that they were now playing into an unusually strong wind, they struggled to get the ball forward and threaten the Scottish goal. Dribbling proved to be difficult on the greasy pitch which was still wet from the heavy rain of the previous two days. Try as they might the English forwards, Alcock, Baker, Nash and Vidal were constantly frustrated by the two colossi, Gladstone & Malcolm and Alexander Morten, the goalkeeper. All three were magnificent in defence.

After three-quarters of an hour there was still no score, so according to the new rules of the Association, ends were changed and the match restarted. There was no half-time break. With the wind behind them, the English started to get on top and it looked as though a goal would be inevitable. In expectation, the English supporters had surrounded the rear of the Scottish goal at the northern end of the ground. Surely the English would score. However, inexplicably Charles Alcock, as captain, had allowed his goalkeeper to join in with the attacks. This tactic immediately backfired as the young Scot, Robert Crawford, took aim with a long side-kick and the ball flew into the English goal. Whether this was a fluke as reported in the Victorian press is arguable. It could be said that this was a great piece of speculative skill on behalf of the 17-year-old. Whatever the reason, it was a goal and the Scottish supporters went wild and with fifteen minutes remaining the English had it all to do.

The sides changed ends again and despite playing against the strong wind the English took to the field with renewed energy in an attempt to make amends for their misfortune. Time was running out, when Alfred Baker, a renowned sprinter, burst down the side of the pitch and scored a wonderful equaliser.

'Tumultuous applause' echoed around the Kennington Oval ground and within seconds the timekeeper called "Time" and the match was over. The first football international in the world had ended, 'honours even', in a one-all draw.

ENGLAND V. SCOTLAND

Saturday 5th March 1870
Kennington Oval, London
(Kick-Off : 3.15 p.m.)

ENGLAND (1)
White Jerseys & White Shorts

Charles W. Alcock (captain)	Old Harrovians
Edward E. Bowen	Wanderers
Alfred J. Baker	No Names Kilburn
William C. Butler	Barnes FC
William P. Crake	Harrow School
Evelyn Freeth	Civil Service
Edgar Lubbock	Old Etonians
Alexander Nash	Clapham Rovers
Guilio C.T. Smith	Crusaders
A. H. Thornton	Old Harrovians
Robert W. S. Vidal	Westminster School

SCOTLAND (1)
Blue Jerseys & White Shorts

James Kirkpatrick (captain)	Civil Service
Robert E. W. Crawford	Harrow School
William H. Gladstone M.P.	Old Etonians
George C. Gordon	No Names Kilburn
Charles R. B. Hamilton	Civil Service
William A. B. Hamilton	Old Harrovians
Arthur F. Kinnaird	Crusaders
William Lindsay	Old Wykehamists
John W. Malcolm M.P.	London Scottish Rifles.
Alexander Morten	Crystal Palace
Kenneth A. Muir Mackenzie	Old Carthusians

**Goals : Robert Crawford (Scotland)
: Alfred Baker (England)**

*Note: Player's teams are as listed in the Press. A lot of the Wanderers
players were listed as playing for their old school sides.*

Author's Notes:

(i) The Wanderers proposal was to:

'Add to Law III.- In the event, however, of no goal having fallen to either party at the lapse of half the allotted time, ends shall then be changed.'

(ii) The proposal from the Civil Service carried the clarification:

'That such prohibition, however, do not extend to the post of goal-keeper*, who shall be allowed to use his hands for the protection of his goal. In the event of the infringement of this rule by any player, the ball is to be taken into touch in a line with the spot where such infringement took place, and thrown in by one of the opposite side.

*Definition of terms — Goal-keeper — The goal-keeper shall be the player who, for the time being, occupies a position between the goal-posts for the defence of his goal.

(iii) All the Scottish players selected for the match had some sort of Scottish heritage but had been raised south of the border. Whilst this would be acceptable today and constitute an international side, the FA and most football historians deem this match and the four that followed as being 'unofficial' or 'pseudo' internationals. Despite the FA's desire to play a pure international, it must be remembered that in 1870 there was only one Scottish club that played Association football and that was the Queen's Park Club in Glasgow. The predominant sport in Scotland at this time was the rugby version of the game. There was also the issue of the cost of organising a Scottish team to travel to London or vice versa. The logistics of organising the eleven-a-side match with players emanating from within the capital had already proved challenging. Whilst this may remain an unofficial international it must be stated that the game attracted great interest both north and south of the border and the match was widely reported in the English and Scottish press. As already mentioned, it even made page 2 of the Daily Telegraph & Courier (London) with the title;

INTERNATIONAL MATCH AT FOOTBALL.

(iv) The crowd number is taken from the Leeds Mercury (Tuesday 8th March 1870) which stated:

'.. took place at the Surrey cricket ground, Kennington Oval, on Saturday last, in the presence of an assemblage of spectators computed to number upwards of 400 persons.'

(v) The average height of a Victorian Englishman was 5'6" and the range of heights would have been between 5'3" and 5'9". Players such as the Parliamentarians, William Gladstone Junior at just over 6'0" and John Malcolm at 6'5" were unusually tall for the period.

(vi) The match reports in the Scotsman and Glasgow Herald (Monday 7th March 1870)

'the laws of the Football Association, it may also be remarked, are essentially different in their composition and aims to those lately fixed by the leading clubs of Scotland; and in elucidation of some of the technicalities of the English code, it will be as well to explain that the use of feet forms the essence of the laws which guided the present contest; that handling was strictly prohibited, except in the liberty granted to the goalkeeper alone to make usage of his hands in defence of his goal; and that the specialities of the rugby game, which to some extent has been adopted in Scotland are entirely eschewed in the rules of the English Association.'

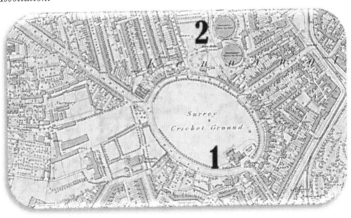

Surrey Cricket Ground: The Kennington Oval, showing the pavilion to the south (1) and the two gasometers (2) to the north of the ground, c. 1871

Chapter 10: The 'Little Tin Idol' is born.
The Birth of the Football Association Challenge Cup
(November 1871 to March 1872)

"It is desirable that a Challenge Cup should be established in connection with the Association for which all clubs belonging to the Association should be invited to compete." – C. W. Alcock (July 1871)

On the 26th October 1870, Florence Caroline Alcock was brought into the world. She was Charles and Eliza's third child and as a consequence their expanding family had moved south from Islington to the more spacious Grassendale House on Rosendale Road in the small village of West Dulwich. Was it any coincidence that Charles would now be in striking distance of both Battersea Park and the Kennington Oval, the new home of the Wanderers?

The Alcocks had engaged two au pairs to assist them with their nursery duties. A Theresa Steinwitch, aged 27, from Bavaria in Germany and Frances Galier, aged 25, from Limerick in Ireland. This was probably a wise move by Charles, as with five ladies and one young boy in the house, he was still planning on a busy football season ahead. On the 2nd July 1871 he wrote a letter to the Field newspaper.

THE FOOTBALL ASSOCIATION.

Sir,—I shall be glad if you will allow me a few lines in your paper to notify to all whom it may concern that the two matches annually played between England and Scotland have already been already fixed for the coming season. The first will take place at The Oval on Saturday, Nov. 18, 1871 and the return on Saturday, Feb. 24, 1872. at the same ground. The committee are desirous of making this announcement as early as possible, in order to afford Scotch players, the fullest opportunity for competing, as well as to prevent the secretaries of association clubs from making arrangements that may clash with the international contests. The committee have also decided on accepting the challenge of the Sheffield Association to play a home-and-away match during the season, the first to take place at Sheffield.

A Challenge Cup of the value of £25 will be given for annual competition among the clubs playing Association rules, and the committee invite any suggestions from those interested relative to the arrangements necessary for the satisfactory accomplishment of this object.

Charles W. Alcock, West Dulwich, Surrey, July 28th.
Hon. Sec. of the Football Association.

So, as well as arranging some further internationals against Scotland and agreeing to play matches home-and-away against Sheffield, in the last paragraph Charles alluded to some kind of Challenge Cup competition also being arranged. Whose idea this was is not clear but Charles would have been inspired by memories of his Cock House Cup Final at Harrow and also by the success of the Youdan and Cromwell Cups in Sheffield. Challenge Cups were not new in 1871. In fact, they were awarded for all sorts of sports from athletics, swimming, shooting, sailing, rowing and even croquet. A Challenge Cup was exactly that. The winner of the Cup would be challenged by all the other competitors each season. These competitors would play in a knock-out competition to earn the right to play the current holder in the final.

The curious thing was that, despite having made an announcement about the cup in the July, the organisation of the silver Challenge Cup competition didn't take place until the October. A second meeting was hurriedly arranged to discuss the format of the tournament on Monday 16th October 1871 at the offices of Charles' Sportsman newspaper at Boy-Court on Ludgate

Hill at 5.30 p.m. and all the captains of the Association Clubs were urgently invited to attend.

The following proposal was put forward at the meeting;

'That a Challenge Cup be given for annual competition, open to all clubs belonging to the Football Association.'

An objection was immediately raised against *'the establishment of the Cup this season, owing to the difficulty of deciding the ties, in consequence of most of the fixtures of the several clubs having been already made.'*

Charles was not one to have his project stopped in its tracks and the proposal, seconded by a Mr. Morton Peto Betts, was carried unanimously. A Mr. Douglas Allport, of the Crystal Palace Club, then resolved that a sub-committee be appointed to frame a code of rules to be submitted to the approval of a second general meeting.

This sub-committee consisted of:

Charles W. Alcock (Wanderers)
Reginald H. Birkett (Clapham Rovers)
James Kirkpatrick (Civil Service)
James Powell (Barnes Club)
Alfred Stair (Upton Park)

A lot of the Provincial clubs present immediately declined the invitation to enter the FA Cup, citing the distances they would have to travel to London in order to play their ties. Fifty clubs were eligible to enter, but only twelve chose to do so: Barnes, Civil Service, Clapham Rovers, Crystal Palace, Hampstead Heathens, Harrow Chequers, Harrow School, Lausanne, Royal Engineers, Upton Park, Wanderers and Windsor Home Park. Before the First Round draw took place Harrow School, Lausanne and Windsor Home Park all withdrew, reducing the number of entrants to nine. Four further clubs then agreed to enter, taking the number of clubs up to thirteen. This included Scotland's leading club, Queen's Park, who were excited by the prospect of a Cup competition. This enthusiasm may have been due to the fact that they only had a couple of teams to play against in Scotland and this tournament would give them an opportunity to spread the word of Association football north of the border. The follow up meeting of the FA took place quickly and the clubs reconvened in the offices of the Sportsman the following Monday 23rd October 1871 at 5.30 p.m.

Everything seemed to be happening in haste. Had someone forgotten all about the Cup during the summer months or were the Football Association being pressed into action because of the successes of the newly formed Rugby Football Union? The R.F.U had been formed with 21 clubs on the 26th January 1871 and by 25th March they had played their first official rugby international in front of a crowd of 4,000 spectators at Raeburn Place, Edinburgh. Scotland won the match scoring two tries and a goal to England's single try. Not only that, but the newly formed R.F.U. had then met up and agreed the first laws of the game which were approved in June 1871. Football needed to get a move on if they were to spread the gospel far and wide and Charles Alcock knew that the FA Cup was the vehicle to do this. The FA's plans to introduce the Challenge Cup needed to go ahead this season, whatever.

After a quick ratification of the rules and a few minor amendments, Ebenezer Cobb Morley stated that the new rules for the competition would be sent immediately to the printers for circulation amongst the members of the Association. These were as follows;

RULES FOR THE COMPETITION 1871-2

1. The Cup shall be called the **Football Association Challenge Cup.**

2. The Challenge Cup shall be open to all clubs belonging to the Football Association and shall be competed for annually by **11 members of each club**.

3. Each club desirous of competing shall give **notice** of such desire to the Secretary of the Football Association on or before the 15th day of August in that season in which such club proposes to compete.

4. No individual shall be allowed to play **for more than one competing Club,** but the members of each representative team may be changed during the series of matches, if thought necessary.

5. The **duration** of each match shall be one hour and a half.

6. The Committee shall divide the Clubs who shall enter for competition of the Challenge Cup into **couples**, which couples shall play one match each, and the winners of the matches so played shall, in like manner, be divided couples, and each such couples shall play one match, and so on until there shall be one couple left, which last couple shall be the holder for the current year.

7. The Committee of the Football Association shall have the power to draw the ties in such competitions in such manner as they think fit, either by lot or otherwise, and to make such other arrangements as they may deem necessary.

8. In the case of **Provincial Clubs,** it shall be in the power of the Committee to except them from the early tie drawings,

and to allow them to compete especially against Clubs in the same district, except in the case of the final ties.

9. In the case of a **drawn match**, the Clubs shall be drawn in the next ties, or shall compete again, at the discretion of the Committee.

10. In the event of a team **refusing to play again**, or failing to play-off the tie in which it has been drawn within the stipulated time, it shall be adjudged to have lost the match.

11. The **holder** of the Cup shall be liable to play only the winner of the trial matches.

12. When the **Winners** of the Cup shall have been associated by such matches as aforesaid, the Secretary of the Football Association shall hand over the Cup to such winners on their subscribing a document to the following effect :- We A.B., the Secretary of the Club, and C. D., E. F., & G. H., members of and representing the said Club, having been declared the winners of the Football Association Challenge Cup and the same having been delivered to us by J. K., the Secretary of the Association do hereby on behalf of the said Club, and individually and collectively engage to return the same to the said J. K., on or before the first day of February next, in like good order and condition, and in accordance with the conditions of the annexed rules, to which also we have subscribed our respective names.

13. The holders of the Challenge Cup shall hand it over to the Secretary of the Football Association, on or before the **first day of February** in each year, unless the holders shall have won the Cup three years in succession, when the Cup shall become the absolute property of the Club so winning it.

14. The ties shall be played off **within a month** after the publication of the ties in such papers as the Committee may think fit, such publication to be deemed sufficient notice of the drawing.

15. The Secretary of each winning Club shall**, within seven days** after the date of the match, send notice of the result, in writing, to the Secretary of the Football Association.

16. The ties in the final two drawings for the season 1871-72 **shall be decided in London,** upon a ground which shall be hereafter chosen by the Committee. In subsequent competitions, the holders of the Cup, shall have choice of grounds, subject to the approval of the Football Association.

17. In addition to the Cup, the Committee, will present to the winners of the Final, **eleven medals or badges, of trifling value.**

18. The Committee shall appoint **two umpires and a referee** to act at each of the matches in the final ties. Neither the umpires nor the referee shall be members of each of the contending Clubs, and the decision of the umpires shall be final, except in the case of the umpires disagreeing, when an appeal shall be made to the referee, whose decision shall be final.

19. All questions of eligibility, **qualification of competitors**, or interpretation of the Rules, shall be referred to the Committee of the Association, whose decision shall be final.

20. The President and Treasurer of the Football Association, shall be, for all intents and purposes, the **legal owners** of the Cup, in trust for the Association.

21. The Committee of the Association shall have the power to alter or add to the above rules as they from time to time shall deem expedient.

Note: The Laws of the Game the Football Association Challenge Cup ties shall be played under are those as defined in Appendix 7 of this book.

Shortly after the discussion concerning the rules to be adopted, it was at around 6.00 to 6.30 p.m. when the first FA Cup draw in football's short history took place. It probably didn't constitute as an exciting a draw as we witness nowadays. There would have been no long drawn-out, one hour build-up, for the purposes of the media. No star guests would be present to pull the black porcelain balls out of the velvet bag. The thirteen clubs which had already declared their intention to play were drawn with the following result:

The Wanderers v. Harrow Chequers

Barnes v. Civil Service

Crystal Palace v. Hitchin

Donington Grammar School v. Queen's Park

Royal Engineers v. Reigate Priory

Upton Park v. Clapham Rovers

Hampstead Heathens (a bye)

FA Committee recognised the lack of enthusiasm for a Cup competition this season and in order to encourage more teams from the provinces outside London to participate, the following rule was introduced.

"In the case of provincial clubs, it shall be in the power of the committee to except them from the early tie-drawings, and to allow them compete specially against clubs in the same district, except in the case of the final ties."

However, the Football Association needed an immediate response from the Secretaries of clubs wishing to enter and they had to declare their intentions, at once, to Mr. C. W. Alcock, Hon. Sec. of the Football Association, Grassendale House, West Dulwich, Surrey.

Given the rushed introduction of the tournament and the fact that it would cost any entrant one guinea to play (to help fund the £25 it would cost to manufacture the cup), perhaps it was understandable that there was no flood of applications to Charles William Alcock. In fact, only one other provincial club declared their intention to play and that was the Great Marlow Club from Buckinghamshire. Bearing in mind that the Club had only just been formed the previous season, (22nd November 1870) this was an ambitious step for the small provincial club to take.

Charles William Alcock the great administrator, sat in the offices of the Sportsman newspaper

As the draw for the First Ties had already been made it meant that the only opposition that the new entrant, Great Marlow, could face was the Hampstead Heathens who were based in the heart of the City of London. It was therefore not surprising that suddenly Great Marlow's local neighbours, the Maidenhead Football Club (recently formed in September 1870), entered the fray. Given the new FA rule concerning provincial sides being allowed to play each other, the two newly-formed clubs, who were only six miles apart, were subsequently drawn together. This was allowed despite the fact that Maidenhead Football Club were not even a member of the FA at the time they entered the competition.

Maidenhead FC v. Great Marlow
Hampstead Heathens (a bye)

And so, the draw for the First Ties was complete. The clubs now had one month within which they had to agree a date and a location for their games to be played. Oh, and pay the one guinea (£1 1s. 0d.) entry fee of course!

The world's first FA Cup would feature just FIFTEEN teams.

Chapter 11: The Fifteen Teams

Metropolitan Clubs

Barnes
Civil Service (War Office)
Clapham Rovers
Crystal Palace
Hampstead Heathens
Harrow Chequers
Royal Engineers
Upton Park
Wanderers

Provincial Clubs

Donington School (Lincolnshire)
Great Marlow (Buckinghamshire)
Hitchin (Hertfordshire)
Maidenhead (Berkshire)
Queen's Park (Glasgow, Scotland)
Reigate Priory (Surrey)

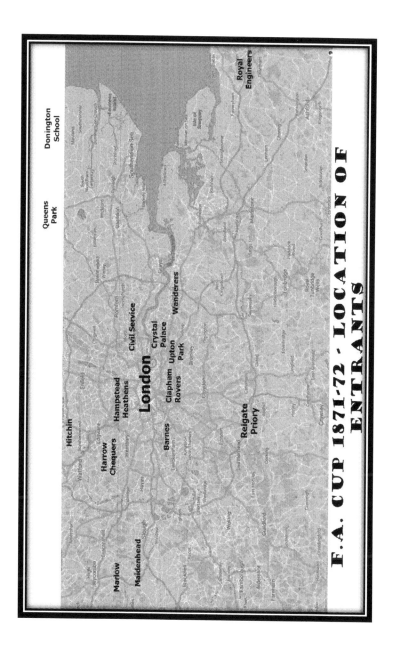

F.A. CUP 1871-72 - LOCATION OF ENTRANTS

BARNES FOOTBALL CLUB

Founded: 1862
Secretary: Mr. James Powell
Colours: Blue & white hooped shirts and socks, white shorts
Ground: Field next to the White Hart pub

The district of Barnes lies six miles to the south west of Central London, in what is known as the Barnes loop, south of the River Thames. Barnes Football Club was created from the well-established rugby, cricket and rowing clubs in the area. The athleticism of their members means they should put up a good fight against any opposition. A founder member of the FA, the club can boast the current FA President, Ebenezer Cobb Morley, as one of its former players so they'll be keen to put in a good showing in this new 'showcase' tournament.

CIVIL SERVICE FOOTBALL CLUB

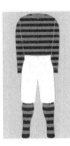

Founded: 1862*
Secretary: Mr. J.H. Giffard
Colours: Blue & orange hooped shirts and socks, white shorts
Ground: Lillie Bridge and Kennington Oval

Currently the Civil Service play both the codes of Football Association and those of the recently formed Rugby Union. The club can claim to be one of two, along with Blackheath, who are founder members of both associations. Let's hope they don't over stretch themselves on the field of play or forget which code they're playing. Formerly known as the War Office, the Civil Service will be making sure they draw on their knowledge of the country's 'DEFENCE'.

CLAPHAM ROVERS FOOTBALL CLUB

Founded: 10 Aug. 1869
Secretary: Mr. C.C. Tayloe
Colours: Cerise & French-grey halved shirts, white shorts & black socks
Ground: Clapham Common

Another club formed to play both codes of the game. When originally founded, Clapham Rovers would play football one weekend and rugby the next. They play both codes each weekend now. Reginald Birkett, their captain, was on the FA subcommittee that agreed the rules for this first competition so they should be well rehearsed in the Association code. The club have also played on Tooting Bec and Wandsworth Common so fingers crossed the chosen eleven turn up at the right ground.

CRYSTAL PALACE CLUB

Founded: 1863*
Secretary: Mr. D. Allport
Colours: Blue & white jersey, blue serge knickerbockers & socks
Ground: Crystal Palace cricket ground

The Crystal Palace Club have been founded by the existing members of the cricket club and local dignitaries to provide a continuation of sporting activities during the winter months. Playing on the same ground and under the g(l)aze of the magnificent glass structure of the Crystal Palace, the new footballers will be hoping not to make a 'Great Exhibition' of themselves as they enter this first-ever FA Cup.

DONINGTON GRAMMAR SCHOOL FC

 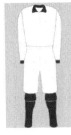

Founded: May 1870
Secretary: L.S. Calvert or E. Morris
Colours: White with blue trim, white shorts , blue socks
Ground: School premises

Donington Grammar School, near Spalding in South Lincolnshire, is the only school team to enter this year's FA Cup competition. Their Headmaster Mr. William J.R. Constable has taken on a new drill master at the school at the cost of three shillings a week and it is hoped that his newly-trained schoolboys will be able to teach the older teams they face a lesson. Mind you with four daughters and three sons to his name, William can almost put out a team of Constables himself.

GREAT MARLOW FOOTBALL CLUB

Founded: 22 Nov. 1870
Secretary: Mr. Charles Miller Foottit
Colours: Dark Blue & white hooped shirts, blue serge shorts & socks
Ground: Alder /Crown Meadow

Formed only one year ago, Great Marlow FC already has 60 members and they are looking to make their presence known in the game of football by entering in the first-ever FA Cup. The Buckinghamshire side hold their meetings in the pretty riverside surroundings of the 'Complete Angler' Hotel on the River Thames and they will be hoping to land themselves a 'big fish' to play against in the tournament.

HAMPSTEAD HEATHENS FC

Founded: June 1868
Secretary: Mr. J. Percival Tatham
Colours: White with blue binding, blue cap
Ground: Hampstead Heath

The 'Hampstead Heathens' get their name from a phrase used by the literary critic David Masson who was referring to a circle of authors living on Hampstead Heath in the early nineteenth century that included the poet, John Keats. The Club would like to stress that their name comes from their locality and not from them being irreligious in any way. On the contrary, they will be praying for a good run in this first-ever tournament.

HARROW CHEQUERS FC

Founded: 1865
Secretary: Mr. M.P. Betts
Colours: Blue and white cheques
Ground: Lillie Bridge, West Brompton, mainly a ground used for rugby in 1871

Named for its association with Harrow School, the club is predominantly made up of 'Old Harrovians', a name they will subsequently adopt in later years. Their current ground is at Lillie Bridge (not far from Chelsea's current Stamford Bridge ground) and just opposite Brompton Cemetery. They will be hoping that their FA Cup First Round hopes are kept 'alive' and they do not play like the Chelsea Pensioners, who live just down the road at the Royal Hospital.

Founded: Oct 1865
Secretary: Rev. John Pardoe
Colours: Black and magenta hooped shirts and socks, white shorts
Ground: The cricket ground, Hitchin Hill

Another football club formed by some of the playing members of Hitchin cricket club such as the Reverend John Pardoe (of Forest Club fame) and Cecil Frederick Reid. Hitchin FC played their initial matches at Dog Kennel Farm in Charlton, before moving to their current location at the cricket ground located on Hitchin Hill. So, let's hope it's not a case of 'Who let the dogs out?'. Mind you with three members of the clergy playing for the club, Hitchin FC will treat the opposition with the greatest respect.

MAIDENHEAD FOOTBALL CLUB

Founded: Sept. 1870
Secretary: Mr. Ernest Donajowski
Colours: Black and red hooped shirts and socks, white shorts
Ground: York Road, Maidenhead – Half a mile from train station

Another team that has been in existence for only 12 months is Maidenhead FC with the club's first match having been played on 17th December 1870 against Windsor Home Park at Bond's Meadow, near Maidenhead Bridge. The club soon found a home at the local cricket ground and played their first match against their local rivals Great Marlow on 16th February 1871. The tree-lined setting was so picturesque they have remained there ever since.

QUEEN'S PARK FOOTBALL CLUB

Founded: July 1867
Secretary: Mr D. N. Wotherspoon
Colours: Blue jerseys & reversible blue & red cowls
Ground: Queen's Park, Glasgow

Queen's Park Football Club are one of the few clubs playing Association football in Scotland. Their appearance in this first-ever FA Cup has been greatly welcomed as it offers the first opportunity of a match between a team from north of the border and one from south of Hadrian's wall. It will be interesting to compare the two styles of football and I'm sure their match, whomever they draw, will be of great interest to the general public and should draw a great crowd.

REIGATE PRIORY FOOTBALL CLUB

 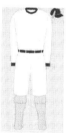

Founded: 1871*
Secretary: Mr W. B. Richardson
Colours: Dark blue cap, belt and stockings, white jersey & knickerbockers
Ground: Priory cricket ground – 5 minutes' walk from the train station

Reigate Priory FC is a new football club, situated 20 miles south of London, in the county of Surrey. Reigate Priory have only recently requested membership of the FA and it could well be that their first-ever match will be played in the FA Cup. Another picturesque ground situated in the grounds of the old monastery and one that will remain their home for the next 150 years.

ROYAL ENGINEERS A.FC

Founded: Oct. 1867
Secretary: Mr Edmund W. Cresswell
Colours: Jersey, nightcap and stockings, blue & red hooped shirts
Ground: Chatham Lines, Kent

The Royal Engineers Association Football Club represent the Corps of the Royal Engineers, known as the 'Sappers' of the British Army. Their barracks are situated in Chatham, Kent. Their captain, Captain Francis Henry Marindin, has been newly elected onto the Committee of the FA and he will no doubt be making sure order is maintained at all times. He shares the footballing captaincy duties with Capt. William Merriman and merry men is something they all hope to be, come the end of the tournament.

UPTON PARK FC

Founded: Dec. 1866
Secretary: Mr Alfred Stair
Colours: Scarlet and black hooped shirt and stockings, white shorts
Ground: Upton Park, West Ham

Upton Park FC play at West Ham Park and are not be confused with the modern-day West Ham FC who played at Upton Park. Confusing I know, but there was some later connection between these two sides through the Thames Ironworks. Upton Park FC play in the once palatial grounds of Upton House (now called Ham House), previously owned by the famous Quaker family, the Gurneys, and lately is the seat of Thomas Fowell Buxton M.P.

WANDERERS
1859

Founded: 1864*
Secretary: Mr. C. W. Alcock
Colours: Orange, violet and black shirt and stockings, white shorts.
Ground: The Oval, Kennington Park

Founded in 1864 by none other than the 'omni-present' Mr. Charles William Alcock. The Wanderers evolved from the 'Forest Club' team, formed in 1859 by Charles and his brother John Forster Alcock, after leaving Harrow School. Finding the cost of renting their own pitch prohibitive the 'Wanderers' took to the road and played on various pitches such as Battersea Park, before finding their new home at 'The Oval' cricket ground in Kennington Park.

Author's Notes:

* Foundation dates as supplied by the Club's Secretaries to the Charles Alcock Football Annual (September 1871) for the season 1871-2. As will be seen by the dates on the Clubs' badges these dates would often be inaccurate and were dependant on the knowledge (or lack of) of the Clubs' Secretaries at the time.

The Clubs' badges I have used to represent the Football Clubs are the oldest I can find and do not all date from 1871. Some are of modern design. For example, the Barnes Club badge belongs to the new fledgling Barnes FC. – supplied with kind permission of the Club (See Chapter 27)

All kit images are 'Copyright Historical Football Kits and reproduced by kind permission.'

***

The fourteen clubs drawn to play each other in the FA Cup First Round Ties (Hampstead Heathens had a bye) set about agreeing the date and location of their seven fixtures. According to Rule 14 of the 'Rules of the Competition' they had a month within which they had to agree the fixture. This may seem like a lot but it must be remembered that this was an age before the advent of the telephone and all communications would have been made by post or telegram. Four of the fixtures were agreed and were set to be played on Saturday 11th November 1871. However, the other three fixtures had not been agreed within the month they had been allotted. The following announcement was made in the 'Field' on the 25th November 1871.

ASSOCIATION CUP TIES. – In consequence of the Royal Engineers and Reigate Priory Clubs being unable to fix a day for their match before the 24th inst., the Reigate Priory club has retired in favour of the Royal Engineers. The Harrow Chequers have also been compelled, for the same reason, to make way for the Wanderers. The second ties will be drawn on Wednesday evening next.

Donington Grammar School (circa 1871-72). The Headmaster W.J. R. Constable can clearly be seen towering over his pupils. The drill master engaged to improve the athleticism of the boys is standing on the right.

There was no news concerning the Queen's Park versus Donington School match but they were subsequently both allowed 'byes' into the second round. So, immediately the first FA Cup would now be contested by thirteen clubs. What does seem strange in this sequence of events is that on making the draw for the first ties and with the FA modifying the rules of the competition to try and include as many provincial clubs as possible, this had largely been ignored. Was it any surprise that the two clubs that had been drawn against arguably the two strongest teams in the competition, then withdrew? Both had only just recently been formed.

Reigate Priory played their first practice match on Saturday 5th November 1870. They played on the cricket pitch in the grounds of the Priory and this beautiful location is one where the club still plays today, making it one of the oldest grounds where football has been played continuously in the world. It is not to be confused with the Reigate Football Club which began life around 1865 and which played a match on Reigate Hill against the Wanderers in December of that year. This team seems to have folded around the same time as Reigate Priory FC commenced at the new ground. A Walter B. Richardson of Reigate FC seemed to be instrumental in setting up the new side.

Reigate Priory Football Club. - On Saturday last the members of the above commenced practice in the cricket ground, when there was a pretty good muster. Mr. E. C. Hanbury and Mr. Walter Richardson were captains of the sides, and the game was kept with unabated vigour for two hours, during which time Mr. Hanbury's side obtained three goals, and Mr. Richardson's two. Considering it was the first practice, the rules of the game were well followed, and judging from the appearance of the players it was precious hot work. As shinning and tripping are forbidden, the disagreeables of the game are dispersed, and only a healthful exercise is enjoyed. Surrey Advertiser (12th November 1870)

One of Reigate's first competitive matches was a derby match played against local neighbours, the Redhill Football Club, on 28th January 1871. However, it seemed as though the club weren't up to speed with the current rules of the Football Association as Reigate won by one goal and two touch-downs to Redhill's one touch-down. Other home and away matches were arranged with new clubs such as Horsham but this was in no way adequate preparation for a match against the mighty Royal Engineers. It would appear from the Royal Engineers fixture list that the only Saturday game that they could make was Saturday 11th November like the others. They played matches against East Kent (4th), Royal Military Academy (18th) and Barnes (25th). However, on the 11th November Reigate Priory had scheduled their first match of the season against Windsor Home Park;

'A match will take place on Saturday (this day) between the Windsor Home Park Club and the Reigate Priory Club, play to commence at a quarter past 3.' – (Eton and Windsor Express - Saturday 11th November 1871).

It is surprising that neither club could rearrange one of their fixtures, but maybe this reflected the status of the new competition or maybe it reflected the disparities between the two sides.

It was a similar case for the Harrow Chequers. Whilst they had been founded in January 1864 as the Harrow Chequers, in 1869 they then became the Harrow Pilgrims. Now, as recently as the 25th October 1871, they were only just in the process of reforming as Harrow Chequers when they entered the FA Cup!

HARROW CHEQUERS CLUB – A meeting for the purpose of formally reviving this club will be held at the Pall Mall restaurant on Wednesday evening next at six o'clock, when all Old Harrovians are invited to attend. (The Sportsman - Saturday 21st October 1871)

Could this be seen as a move by one Charles William Alcock to bolster the entrants to the new FA Challenge Cup competition by involving his old school club? We shall never know the reason for their entry and subsequent withdrawal from the competition, but suffice it to say that on Saturday 11th November, with both clubs having a free Saturday, the Wanderers played out a one all draw with the Royal Engineers at The Oval, with Morton Peto Betts (A Harrow Chequer) captaining the Wanderers team!

THE FA CUP

1871-72

Chapter 12: The First FA Cup Game?
Match 1: Hitchin FC v. Crystal Palace Club
FA Cup First Ties
Saturday 11th November 1871
(Kick-Off 3 p.m.)

It was Sunday the 5th November 1871, traditionally Guy Fawkes night, and the Reverend John Pardoe sat at his writing desk in the study of his pretty cottage, 'The Elms' in the tiny village of Little Wymondley, Hertfordshire. He was trying to find the right words for that night's sermon. He looked out from the window and stared vacantly across the neatly mown lawn but the right words just wouldn't come into his head. All he could think about was football and the visit next Saturday of the great Crystal Palace Cub. It was the first tie of the new Football Association Challenge Cup and he wondered how his small-town Hitchin side would fair against 'The Palatials' from the City of London.

John Pardoe's cottage 'The Elms', Little Wymondley.

Of course, he was no stranger to playing against Crystal Palace. Having formed the Forest Club with the Alcock brothers in 1859 and then having made an appearance in that first reported match against them on the 15th March 1862. John was well accustomed to playing against big sides. Mind you, that was nearly ten years ago and the thirty-two-year-old played a more administrative role in the Hitchin club now. Even so, he was still nervous for his side, his baby.

As he made his evening walk up to Saint Ippolyts-cum-Wymondley church (i) on top of the hill in the hamlet bearing the same name, all was quiet in the centre of Hitchin town. Of course, John realised that the annual fireworks procession had been postponed until tomorrow (Monday) on account of it being the Sabbath. The Hitchin fireworks display was a sight to behold with upwards of 10,000 people flocking into the town, by coach and train, and packing the Market Square. Hitchin was famed for its fireworks and its annual torchlit procession which:

'.. *featured upwards of 200 young men dressed in every conceivable form of masquerade, many of them on horseback, and carrying different coloured torches, headed by a brass band, in a van illuminated by Chinese lanterns, making a circuit of the Market Square, and the midst of the moving lights, a complete shower of rockets discharging coloured balls, and they will then form some idea of what was to be seen this occasion.'*
(Hertford Mercury and Reformer - Saturday 11th November 1871)

John's thoughts soon turned back to his evening service and somehow, he managed to get through his sermon without mentioning sport or football. However, he did take the liberty of mentioning the time, date and location of the FA Cup match to his congregation at the end of the service. Whilst his fellow Harrovian, Charles Alcock, had gone onto pastures new in 1864 with his Wanderers side, John Pardoe had also left Leytonstone during the same year and was ordained as the curate of Hitchin on the 3rd July 1864.

John was keen to get to work and to get to know his new parishioners and it wasn't long before he had joined the Hitchin Cricket Club. Imagine his surprise when he came across a fellow Harrovian, Cecil Frederick Reid, son of a local Hitchin brewer, who had been born at 'The Node' in Codicote, just seven miles south of Hitchin. Although Cecil was three years his junior, they had come across each other during their time at Harrow between 1855 when Cecil started and 1858 when John went on to study at Cambridge. Both talked about their footballing exploits and Cecil explained

121

how he was good friends with Charles Alcock, being the same age and having joined the school at the same time. Consequently, Cecil, after leaving Oxford, had gone on to play for the Old Harrovians and then just recently he'd been asked if he wanted to play for Charles Alcock's Wanderers side. This was an opportunity he could not turn down and he was due to start playing for them this winter in their first match of the 1865-66 season on 28th October 1865 against the Civil Service at Battersea Park.

"That's a shame", said John, " I'm looking to start a Hitchin Football Club up this winter and it would have been great to have you play for us."

"Maybe sometime soon," replied Cecil. "I'm happy to get a team together from my contacts in the Wanderers and come up and play you when you are ready."

"That would be marvellous, Cecil. We may be able to get a side together early in the New Year and it would be great to have some stiff opposition for the team to play against."

It wasn't long before John had persuaded some of his cricketing team-mates to join him in setting up Hitchin Football Club, and in November 1865 the club was formed with John standing as its first Secretary. The Hertfordshire Express of Saturday 25th November 1865 contained a small paragraph which read as follows:

'A meeting of gentlemen convened by private circular, was held in the National School Room on Friday evening for the purpose of establishing a football club. Hubert Delme Radcliffe Esq. presided and about 25 gentlemen were present. The establishment of such a club was unanimously agreed to, the subscription to be two shillings and sixpence per annum, members to be admitted by ballot. Hubert Delme Radcliffe was chosen as President and the Rev. John Pardoe as Secretary, a committee of five gentlemen were also appointed, and rules agreed to. The President announced that F.P. Delme Radcliffe would allow the club to play the games in any part of the park they chose to select, and also that his name might be put down for an honorary subscription of one guinea. It was arranged that the club should commence playing at the close of the cricket season in each year and continue to its opening, and to meet for play on Saturday afternoons at half-past two o'clock, the opening game to be played that day.'

Instantly, John set about teaching his new-found pupils the laws of Association football. Then, he got back in contact with Cecil

Reid who, true to his word, said he would get a side together. Both Cecil and another Harrovian, Robert Dalrymple Elphinstone, of the Civil Service (who had played in the original London XI versus Sheffield XI) selected their own eleven and travelled up to Hitchin by train from King's Cross. It was the 24th February 1866 and despite their inexperience, the newly formed 'Hitchinites' carried off a marvellous first victory winning by two goals to one. The side featured three Lucas's, a Radcliffe (any relation to the President?) and Francis Shillitoe (another future Wanderers player). The goals for Hitchin were scored by none other than John Pardoe himself and a Mr. Conder, whilst Robert Elphinstone managed to score the goal for his London side. Hitchin Football Club were up and running.

Hitchin in those days was a small market town that had been built on farming and wool production. However, it was also renowned for its malting and brewing. In fact, the town's reputation for excellent barley malt and sumptuous grapes prompted Queen Elizabeth I's reputed retort to a Spanish nobleman who was extolling the virtues of his country's vineyards; *'My Hitchin grapes surpass them, or those of any country'.*

The town was also developed as something of a health resort with its clean air and the spa springs at Charlton. The inns prospered and direct coach services were established to London and other surrounding towns. The key landowners were the Radcliffes at Hitchin Priory who, as we know, were to play a key part in the 'Hitchinites' development. In the first part of the 19th century a gas works, a lavender distillery and a pharmaceutical factory were opened, In the 1820's a 'New Town' was developed on Hitchin Hill. The arrival of the Great North Railway in 1850, with a station built to the north-east of the town, boosted the town's economy and an imposing Corn Exchange was built in the Market Place to facilitate the sale of grain and malt to its new markets in the Capital and the Midlands.

Apart from the Wanderers, Hitchin Football Club's early matches in 1866-1868 tended to be against the public-school sides, such as the Old Harrovians and Old Etonians. This was due to the lack of local clubs available to play in Hertfordshire. However, as the popularity of Association football began to spread across the country, future matches were played against newly-formed clubs such as St. Albans Pilgrims, Welwyn, the Clapham Common Club and Clapham Rovers. These early matches were played at Hitchin's home ground, Dog Kennel Farm near Charlton, (one mile outside of Hitchin) until the end of the 1868-69 season. Then at the annual meeting of the club on 30th September 1869, at the Sun Hotel, it was stated that;

'This season, (1869-70) with the permission of the cricket club, the football club will shift the locale of their play to the cricket ground It was determined that for the future members wear a uniform cap, and claret (black?) and magenta were fixed as the colours of the club.'
(*Hertfordshire Express and General Advertiser - Saturday 9th October 1869*)

On the 5th February 1870 they managed to arrange a fixture against the newly formed Hornsey Football Club, whom they despatched 2-1. This was one of the Club's first reported matches to be played at the Hitchin cricket ground.

In the summer of 1871, when Hitchin submitted their entry for the Charles Alcock Football Annual for the 1871-72 season, the ground declared was the cricket ground on Hitchin Hill. This would be the venue for the first-ever FA Cup game against Crystal Palace.

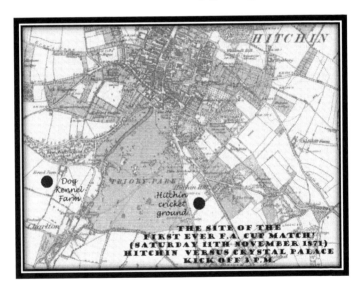

The location of the first-ever FA Cup match to be played ?
Hitchin cricket ground, Hitchin Hill, Hertfordshire.

"Morning lads, it's an early start today, we're away at Hitchin in the First Tie of the FA Cup. We can't afford to be late to the game and this is a competition that I want us to do well in."

Douglas Allport (ii) was quite excited about today's game as he talked to his team on the platform of Sydenham station. It was a grey, dank morning and the magnificent structure of the Crystal Palace could just be seen still sparkling under the low-lying clouds that seemed to be draped over its shoulders. The Crystal Palace team were catching the 7.28 a.m. Brighton to London train where they would disembark at London Bridge station. It was then a walk and a short metro journey across the city to King's Cross station.

"This is wonderful," piped up the youngster, Freddy Heath. "It reminds me of my first game for the Palace last season. Remember when we got the train down to Chatham to play the Royal Engineers? Let's hope the result is not another nil-nil draw."

"We should be okay today, Freddy," replied his captain confidently, "we've got a good team. Although I believe one of the old Wanderers players, Cecil Reid, is captaining their side."

"We'll be fine," said Freddy. "They'll need to watch out for our speed and our excellent dribbling."

Douglas Allport smiled, 'Ah, the exuberance of youth' he thought to himself. However, he also thought his team had a good balance of youth and experience. Apart from himself (33), Alexander Morten (39) and James Turner (31) the rest of the team were all under 25 and keen and hungry to play football. Alexander and James were also very experienced players and both were excellent goalkeepers. 'Alec' Morten had already had a distinguished playing career, starting off with No Names Kilburn in 1863-66 before moving to play for Crystal Palace from 1865 onwards. He also made many appearances for the Wanderers during this time and according to the Charles W. Alcock's Football Annual, he was probably the best goalkeeper in the world:

'Toujours prêt is his motto when between the posts, in which position he is without a rival, never losing his head, even under the most trying circumstances. (Charles Alcock Football Annual 1873)

We have already seen that he played in the first unofficial England v. Scotland international on the 5th March 1870 and amazingly he would then go onto play for England in an official international in March 1873 at the ripe old age of 41.

However, today Douglas would turn to his loyal servant James Turner to play in goal. James had been with the club from the beginning and played in their first match against the Forest Club back in March 1862. His involvement as the Treasurer of the FA (1864-67) meant he was selected for the President's XI to play alongside Alec Morten against the Secretary's XI in that historic match in January 1864.

The Crystal Palace players boarded the train at King's Cross and Freddy piped up again; "Are we travelling First Class, sir?"

"No, lad. We will be travelling 2nd class but under a covered carriage, so you won't get covered in soot when we go through the tunnels at Welwyn. We'll arrive early in Hitchin and then we can have a light lunch before making our way to the ground. We'll have to hire an omnibus as the cricket ground is just over a mile from the railway station, but we should get there well before kick-off."

The 'Palatials', as they are sometimes known, are a team made up from the upwardly mobile members of London Society. There are stockbrokers, merchants, architects and accountants but also a coal merchants' clerk and an assistant draper. There should be no excuse for not 'capitalising' on their professional experience.

The Palace players sat in the cricket club dressing room and changed into their serge blue and white hooped shirts, serge blue shorts and socks. Once they were all changed, they looked a formidable outfit, as impressive as the Crystal Palace building itself.

The Hitchin players were already changed into their strips. They had also got to the ground early. There were a few nerves around the Hitchin dressing room as they listened to the city voices of their London opponents echoing through the corridor of the cricket pavilion. In particular, the teenagers Henry Baker (17) and Ernest Woodgate (18) were showing some signs of tension. Their captain, Cecil Frederick Reid, could see that they were worried and immediately sought to reassure them.

"Don't worry lads, you'll be fine. Once you're out on the pitch all those nerves will go away and you'll be able to play your usual game. I've played in enough big matches to know that whatever the reputation of a side, if we play together like we do in training and we stick to the rules, we will do well."

William Tindall Lucas, the other old head in the side, nodded in agreement. William was a respected banker in the town and someone the local lads could look up to and to have a player of Cecil Frederick Reid's calibre to lead the team was perfect. The younger players had all heard of Reid's Brewing Co. Ltd as they were one of the top four brewers in London (later to be merged with Watney to become Watney, Combe and Reid in 1898). Pubs bearing that name can still be seen in London today, producing their own version of their popular, dark porter beer.

Apart from the Reverend John Pardoe, who would be cheering from the side-lines, there were two other members of the cloth taking to the field for Hitchin, the Reverend Charles Baker and the Reverend William Haselrigg. So, will God be on their side?

In addition to the clergymen, there were the two Baker brothers (army lieutenants), a brewer (Cecil Reid), a banker (William Lucas), an attorney (Francis Shillitoe), a maltster (William Hill), a gun salesman (Thomas Mainwaring), a young farm labourer (Ernest Woodgate) and the son of an auctioneer (George Jackson). All bases were covered. It started to drizzle as the players took to the field and they could feel it was greasy underfoot.

"This might suit us, lads," shouted Cecil. "The Palace won't find their usual dribbling game as easy on this surface!"

Palace won the toss and played with a slightly favourable breeze behind them. This meant that Hitchin had the honour of kicking off the first-ever FA Cup game (iii), bang on three o'clock.

The first half was very even, with most of the play taking place in the middle of the field. There were a couple of enterprising attacks by Palace's Tommy Spreckley and Wally Baker but these were admirably repelled by the Reverend Charles Baker. Perhaps he'd said an extra prayer that morning?

As no goal had been scored by half time, ends were changed in accordance with the new rules. The second half went pretty much as the first, apart from the last few minutes when, with the wind behind them, Hitchin seemed to have the better of the game. Time was called and the crowd of 500 or so spectators cheered in unison, their voices echoing across the fields of the adjacent Priory Park. Hitchin had emerged undefeated against the mighty Crystal Palace and they would now advance to the draw for second ties of the Football Association Challenge Cup

The Crystal Palace men played well together, and were more conversant with the rules than their opponents, who, however, played up with great spirit, W. T. Lucas, W. G. Haselrigg, and G. Jackson being conspicuous forwards; while for the Palace, besides those mentioned, Bouch and Soden were always well on the ball, and Cockerell, at half-back, rendered valuable assistance. (Sportsman – 15th November 1871)

HITCHIN FC V. CRYSTAL PALACE CLUB
FOOTBALL ASSOCIATION CHALLENGE CUP
FIRST TIE
Saturday 11th November 1871
Hitchin Cricket Ground, Hitchin Hill
(Attendance 500/750 ; Kick-Off : 3.00 p.m.)

HITCHIN FOOTBALL CLUB (0)	CRYSTAL PALACE CLUB (0)
Black and magenta hooped shirts and socks, white shorts	Blue & white hooped shirts and socks, blue serge shorts
Cecil F. Reid (captain)	Douglas Allport (captain)
William T. Lucas	Alexander Morten
Francis Shillitoe	John Cockerell
William Hill.	Alfred J. Heath
George D. Baker.	William Bouch
Henry E. Baker	Charles E. Smith
Rev. Charles A. Baker.	Frederick B. Soden
Rev. William Haselrigg.	Henry Daukes
Thomas. C. Mainwaring	Walter C. Foster
George Jackson	Thomas F. Spreckley
Ernest Woodgate.	James Turner

Author's Notes:

(i) The Reverend John Pardoe is shown on the 1871 census as living at the Elms, New England (Wymondley) with his mother, Frances and a nineteen-year-old servant girl, Alice Gray. His occupation is the curate of St. Ippolyts church and he assists the Vicar Fenton J.A. Hort in his duties. In 1870, Fenton J. A. Hort was appointed a member of the committee at Cambridge University, responsible for revising the translation of the New Testament, and for ten years this was one of the most exacting demands on his time. He returned to Cambridge a year later (1872), when he accepted a fellowship and lectureship at Emmanuel College. During this time his assistant, John Pardoe, took over most of his ministerial duties.

(ii) Crystal Palace's captain Douglas Allport was closely involved in the inauguration of the FA Cup, proposing the FA sub-committee that drafted the rules for the cup competition.

(iii) I have based my assumption of this match being the first FA Cup match ever to take place on the following evidence.

The Upton Park and Clapham Rovers tie kicked off at 3.30 p.m. (as reported in the Sporting Life – Wednesday 15th November 1871 and the Field – Saturday 18th November 1871)

Maidenhead versus Marlow kicked off at 3.20 p.m. (Maidenhead Advertiser – Saturday 18th November 1871)

Barnes versus Civil Service would have kicked off around 3.00 p.m. but there may have been a slight delay due to the Civil Service waiting for players to turn up from other parts of London, as they ended up with less than eleven players.

I have therefore selected the Hitchin versus Crystal Palace game as the first match to kick-off followed by Barnes versus Civil Service.

Chapter 13: 'Oarsmen v. The Admiralty'
Match 2: Barnes FC v. Civil Service FC
FA Cup First Ties
Saturday 11th November 1871
(Kick-Off around 3 p.m.)

No visit to Barnes would be complete without making a stop outside the home of the Honorary Secretary and future President of the Football Association, Ebenezer Cobb Morley. His house is located at No. 26, The Terrace, overlooking Barnes Railway Bridge and the silky River Thames. As we know, this is the historic location where Ebenezer transcribed the first thirteen rules of Association football.

Old Barnes Bridge in 1849. Ebenezer's house at No. 26, The Terrace and the White Hart Inn are on the left side of the River Thames, just beyond the rail bridge.

Ebenezer Cobb Morley was born in Hull on August 16th 1831. He trained as an articled clerk to a solicitor and at the age of 27 he moved to Barnes. Initially, he stayed in rooms at the White Hart Inn directly overlooking the River Thames. He didn't wander far and quite soon he bought his house at No. 26, The Terrace, just a hundred yards down the road and he remained there until his death in 1924 at the ripe old age of 93. He would have been dismayed to learn that in future years his treasured home would pass into the hands of the Welsh pop singer Duffy (2011) and then four year later it would collapse when under the ownership of the Phones 4u boss, who was having the basement enlarged to house a cinema, wine cellar and gym.

No. 26, The Terrace, Barnes
Home to Ebenezer Cobb Morley for 66 years.

Ebenezer Cobb Morley was sports mad. He was a keen rower and founded the Barnes and Mortlake Regatta in 1862, which continues to this day. He hunted with foxhounds and even had his own pack of beagles. He had a gym built at home to keep fit and luckily for him his house didn't collapse on this occasion. On top of this he played football on Barnes Common and then went on to form Barnes Football Club with his friends and fellow rowers at the White Hart Inn in 1862. According to an 1870 newspaper article, Barnes FC was *'generally considered as an offshoot of the London Rowing Club.'*

Barnes' home games were played five minutes from Ebenezer's house at Limes Field in Mortlake, just along from the White Hart Inn and across from the Castelnau House. This was confirmed by none other than Robert George Graham, who played for the

Barnes Football Club between 1865 and 1869, and was Honorary Secretary of the FA from 1867 until 1870 (i):

'John Johnstone, the owner of Pretender (a racehorse that had won the Epsom Derby and the 2000 Guineas at Newmarket in 1869) *, ... placed his field, opposite his residence, Castelnau House, at its disposal for matches and the club's athletic sports.'*

'The Limes' and Castelnau House on the banks of the River Thames painted by JMW Turner whilst on an extended visit in 1827.

***

It was Friday and the midday diners were heading to the White Hart Inn for lunch on its terraces overlooking the beautiful River Thames. Today, it didn't look its immaculate Victorian self. The Inn was in the process of having its outside walls refurbished and consequently was covered in scaffolding and tarpaulins. Everybody was seated outside and wearing face masks until they were escorted to their tables. These being the Covid-19 rules that had to be adhered to during this crazy pandemic. I queued up with them, not to dine, but hopefully to get a look inside this wonderful Victorian pub. I was particularly interested in seeing the Morley Room on the first floor, where Ebenezer Morley and his fellow oarsmen would meet to discuss various sporting matters and the team selections for

133

the boating regattas, the athletics and of course the football team. It would have been in this very room that the Barnes team would have been selected for their first-ever FA Cup match.

The Manageress of the pub was very accommodating and left me on my own to venture up to this historic location. As I looked around and peered out of the sash windows that afforded beautiful views of the Thames, I could imagine these young Victorian sportsmen, strong in body and mind, discussing the issues of the day. I could imagine Ebenezer Cobb Morley banging on the table to bring order to the over exuberant chatter going on in the room. The expectant players looked up and studied him with piercing eyes, trying to ascertain if they would be playing in the forthcoming Cup Challenge match.

'The Morley Room' – White Hart Inn – Home of Barnes Football Club.

As I looked around the Morley Room with its leather armchairs and formally laid out tables, I took a look at the numerous old photographs that were strategically placed on the surrounding walls. There were old photos and paintings of the annual Oxford and Cambridge boat race that would pass the pub on its final one mile stretch to Chiswick. There were old photos of the White Hart Inn and of the town of Barnes in Victorian times but not one photo of the great man himself.

Upon leaving I thanked the Manageress and delicately pointed out the error of their ways, after all it being 2021, it was the 150th anniversary of their first FA Cup game. She replied politely that there might be some old football photos downstairs, in the basement, if I wanted to have a look. There wasn't and I don't think Ebenezer would have found it that amusing to be portrayed next to the ladies' and gent's loos!

***

"Are these all the players you've got?" demanded Percy Weston, the captain of the Barnes team. "I've almost got as many players from my family in my team as compared to the number in yours."

This wasn't quite true, but there were three Weston brothers in the Barnes team and the Civil Service had only managed to gather eight players so far. John Hardinge Giffard, their captain was most apologetic as he explained:

"Well, there may be a couple more on the way, but we do get problems like this every week and we quite often have to play short-handed. We've also got another team playing Clapham Rovers to the rugby code this afternoon and we've lost one of our better players, George Gordon, to the rugby lot. You know he played for England against Scotland in that first-ever unofficial international. Also, we've lost Evelyn Freeth, our other England international, an outstanding back, who played in that game as well. So, you can see what we're up against."

Mind you, both John Hardinge Giffard and the Scot, Jimmy Kirkpatrick, had already played a number of games for their second team, the Wanderers, this season. This meant that so far, the Civil Service hadn't managed to field a full side. This showed the issues with playing football within the Civil Service as they struggled to split their resources between the two codes. The rugby team had also played two players short against the Clapham Rovers XV.

No further players from the Whitehall offices turned up so the Civil Service would have their backs up against the wall today. John and Jimmy, along with Charles Trollope, were all clerks to the

Admiralty and they would need all their skills in Royal Navy strategy to repel the Barnes forwards.

The two sets of players got changed in the White Hart Inn and made the short 100-yard walk down Mortlake High Street to the pitch on Limes Fields. Both teams looked surprisingly the same in their hooped shirts and white shorts, the only difference being Barnes played in blue and white hoops and the Civil Service in blue and orange. They marched through the rows of lime trees and onto the pitch where Percy Weston won the toss. Consequently, the Civil Service now had to play into the wind with just eight players. It just wasn't their day. Apart from the clerks from the Admiralty the Civil Service team was bolstered by other clerks based in the Home Office and also a probate clerk, who might be needed by the end of day's play.

A map of Barnes and Mortlake c. 1870 showing the White Hart Inn (1), Ebenezer Cobb Morley's house (2) and the location of the football pitch, opposite the Limes and Castelnau House.

The Barnes team was very young indeed and apart from Robert Wills (28), the Club Secretary, the average age of the team was below twenty. Percy Weston, their captain, was only 19 and whilst

136

his elder brother Edward was 22, Vincent the youngest brother would not celebrate his 16th birthday until three days' time. (ii)

Also, it might be of interest to an arborist that five members of the Barnes team lived at the Cedar Houses and were playing at the Limes Field.

The match kicked off and the youngsters of Barnes soon found out that the depleted Civil Service weren't going to give in easily as they were extremely efficient in the defence of their goal.

The very experienced John Giffard and Jimmy Kirkpatrick marshalled their troops expertly and after 45 minutes the youngsters had not been able to penetrate the Civil Service goal. So, at half time ends were changed and now the Service had the wind behind them.

The play continued in much the same vein as before with no lack of effort on either side. There was some argument about the new 'no handling' rule, as the young Barnes team seemed to think you could still punch the ball with your fist. The Civil Service team knew this to be cheating but even the two umpires couldn't agree.

'Oh, for a referee!'

Eventually fortune favoured the Barnes team and their captain Percy Weston scored what was said to be a 'fluky' goal with his toe,

'..with the apparent collusion of two Civil Service backs, who shall remain nameless.' (Sportsman newspaper – Saturday 18th November 1871)

Whether there would have been any collusion by the Civil Service to gift a goal to the Barnes Football Club seems strange, given the efforts they had gone to in the first half. Still, betting did take place on the results of these matches, so who knows?

Anyway, this first goal seemed to knock the 'wind out of the sails' of the Admiralty and soon their goal was breached again when Arthur Dunnage, a medical student from Kingston-upon-Thames, scored the decisive goal for Barnes underneath the tape of the Civil Service goal. Soon, darkness began to descend on the banks of the River Thames and the final score of Barnes 2, Civil Service 0, meant the young oarsmen were through to the next round.

BARNES FC V. CIVIL SERVICE FC
FOOTBALL ASSOCIATION CHALLENGE CUP
FIRST TIE

Saturday 11th November 1871
The Limes Field, Barnes
(Kick-Off : around 3.00 p.m.)

BARNES FC (2)	CIVIL SERVICE (0)
Blue & white hooped shirts and socks, white shorts.	Blue & orange hooped shirts and socks, white shorts.
Percy Weston (captain)	John H. Giffard (captain)
Edward C. G. Highton	William C. Butler
Charles J. Morice	A. B. Bateman
William R. Collins	James Wearne
Edward. T. Weston	Charles W. A. Trollope
Arthur R. Dunnage	Henry C. Houndle
Vincent E. Weston	William H. White
W. Bruce	James Kirkpatrick
Robert W. Willis	
Henry E. Solly	
Frederick C. Clarkson	

Goal scorers: Barnes:
Percy Weston (1), Arthur Dunnage (1)

Author's Notes:

(i) At the Football Association A.G.M. on the 23rd February 1870, Robert Graham was replaced by none other than Charles William Alcock., who took on the joint roles of Honorary Secretary and Treasurer. During 1868, Robert Graham had attempted to increase membership by writing to every known club in the country. He was successful and his action increased the membership of the FA to 30 clubs. However, this did not prevent the Association from running out of money, with the officers having to cover expenses out of their own pockets. At this time the annual subscription to the Association was fixed at 5 shillings. However, an analysis of the annual accounts (many thanks to Phil Martin) shows that only 40 - 50% of the members were actually paying up.

It must be remembered that these were young men who were trying to administer a fast-growing national game and debt collection had to be by letter or personal contact at matches. Robert Graham was only 23 when he took on the dual role of Secretary and Treasurer and whilst he was a promising business man (he would go on to be a stockbroker and Company Director), maybe finance wasn't his strong point.

Even in 1870, the omnipresent Charles Alcock found the joint roles too much of a responsibility as he tried to advance the game nationally. What they needed was a safe pair of hands, an experienced accountant, and in February 1871 they found the right man, Alfred Stair of Upton Park Football Club.

Alfred had joined the Civil Service in 1864 in the Treasury, and he would go on to become the Principal Accountant in 1887 and then Assistant Account-General in 1889. He would then serve as Accountant and Comptroller-General of Board of the Inland Revenue from 1900–1910. He was the perfect man for the job and it was his proposal that the subscription for entry to the FA Cup should be one guinea to pay for the Cup, which would cost between £20 - £25.

(ii) Vincent Edward Weston, at the tender age of 15 years 362 days immediately set a record for the youngest player in a Cup match.

Chapter 14: 'The Battle of the Brewers'
Match 3: Maidenhead versus Great Marlow
FA Cup First Ties
Saturday 11th November 1871
(Kick-Off 3.20 p.m. ?)

The plaque outside York Road, Maidenhead

I looked up at the blue circle plaque that stood fixed to the white breeze-block wall in front of me and I could feel 150 years of football history oozing out of the concrete terraces. What sights and smells this small parcel of land in front of me would have witnessed. From top hats and long coats to baseball caps and bomber jackets. From pipe smoke to cigarette smoke and 'vapes'. From Brylcreem and Bovril to Deep Heat and Burgers, York Road would have seen them all come and go, along with heart-bursting cup victories and heart-breaking relegation defeats. This is the inevitable journey through history for all true football fans and every winter for the last 150 years the gates would have opened, or the turnstiles clicked, to the tune of every expectant 'Maidonian' or 'Magpies' supporter.

Maidenhead Football Club were formed in September/October 1870, with Joseph Henry Clark (a future Vice President of the Football Association) becoming the club's first President. Ernest Donajowski became the club's first Honorary Secretary and Fred Nicholson, the first Treasurer.

'We congratulate the town on one of its recent innovations, namely a Football Club. The idea was mooted some two months since, by a few young men who are fond of the game; and now appears to be firmly established. and we hope will continue to flourish. The number of members increase weekly, and there are usually 25 or 30 out at practice. The Association rules are adopted and as soon as the members become acquainted to them, we anticipate some good games.' (Maidenhead Advertiser - Wednesday 14th December 1870)

One of the Maidenhead's major benefactor's, William Nicholson, also took a great interest in sports in the town. William was a keen cricketer and footballer and was a member of the Maidenhead cricket team of 18 players which beat an all-England Eleven brought down by John Wisden, in 1853, in a two-day match played at Kidwells Park. Although he was now fifty, he still put in an occasional appearance for the football club. His sons, Frederick and Robert were also keen footballers, in particular, Fred who was a reliable goalkeeper and outfield player. Both were to make an appearance in this season's FA Cup. William had studied chemistry at Radfield College and upon qualifying he put his newly learned skills into concocting the ever-popular potion 'beer'. He opened the Pine Apple brewery on the site of an old pub in the centre of the town and, by 1871, he was employing 22 men and 2 boys.

Maidenhead's first games were organised against the new local side Windsor Home Park and an opening 0-0 draw at home and a narrow 1-0 away defeat was an impressive opening start for the newly-formed club. Their first home game was played on a meadow lent to them by Mr. Bond, down on the Thames by Maidenhead Bridge, and opposite the infamous Skindle's hotel.

However, for their second home game, Mr. Durrant and the cricket club committee allowed them to use their ground at York Road for their fifteen-a-side game against local rivals Marlow. It was Thursday 16th February 1871 and the new game of football created a great deal of interest in the local community and drew a crowd of 'over a thousand people' with a number of local dignitaries watching on in fascination as Maidenhead ran out 2-0 winners.

***

Unfortunately, due to these Covid-stricken times, Maidenhead supporters could not be at York Road to witness their historic 150th anniversary match against Stockport County on Tuesday 16th

February 2021, when true to form, a mind-blowing football occasion produced a mind-numbing 0-0 draw. Instead, the occasion was streamed live on the internet and for £10 you could witness the historic event unfold.

7:05pm – Q&A with the manager Alan Devonshire (ex-West Ham)
7:20pm - Happy Anniversary York Road: Video Messages
7:30pm - Unveiling of the 150th Anniversary Plaque
7:35pm - Match Coverage Begins

The 150th Anniversary mural at York Road, Maidenhead.

As I stood and looked around this antiquated, but traditional football ground, it was difficult to imagine the sound of leather on willow, as a local cricketer hit an enormous six over the row of trees lining the canal. This quintessential English scene would sometimes be interrupted by the sound of a passing steam train's whistle on its long journey from Paddington to Bristol on the tracks of the Great Western Railway. In the south-west corner of the ground stood the rustic cricket pavilion. It was a beautiful sight with its thatched roof perched on top of an architectural masterpiece of Swiss design (i)

This would be the same scene, ten months later, when the 'Maidonians' drew the 'Marlovians' in the first-ever FA Cup.

It was November 1871 and the players and committee of the Great Marlow team sat around the large table in the Coffee Room of the Complete Angler Hotel. (ii) The club had been formed in this very room almost one year ago to the day on the 22nd November 1870, around the same time as the Maidenhead Football Club had been formed.

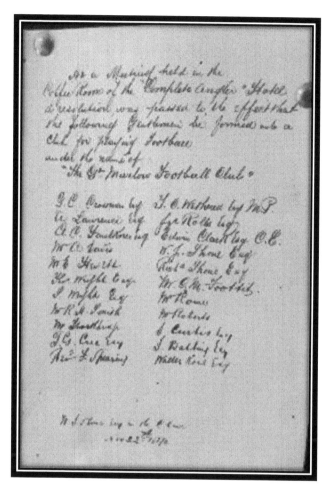

Minutes of the 'Great Marlow Football Club' - 22nd November 1870 as pinned on the Clubhouse wall - reproduced with the kind permission of Marlow Football Club

At a meeting held in the Coffee Room of the 'Complete Angler' Hotel, a resolution was passed to the effect that the following Gentlemen be formed into a club for playing football under the name of:

G. C. Crossman Esq.	T.O. Wethered Esq. M.P.
A. Lawrence Esq.	Jack Rolls Esq.
A. C. Faulkner Esq.	Edwin Clarke Esq.
Mr. A. Davis	W. J. Shone Esq.
Mr. E. Hewett	Richard Shone Esq.
Thos. Wright Esq.	Mr. C. M. Foottit
J. Wright Esq.	Mr. Rowe
Mr. R. H. Smith	Mr. Roberts
Mr. Stockbridge	J. Curtis Esq.
J. G. Cree Esq.	J. Batting Esq
Rev. F. Spearing.	Walter Rose Esq.

W. J. Shone in the Chair – Nov. 22nd 1870

The beautiful setting for 'The Compleat (Complete) Angler Hotel, by the River Thames, venue for meetings of the Great Marlow Football Club.

Mr. Thomas Owen Wethered, the President, looked sternly across the table at the Captain of his side, Alfred Faulkner and his right-hand man, the Secretary of the club, Charles Miller Foottit. Thomas was a well-respected pillar of society in Great Marlow, being the current owner of his family brewing business, Thomas Wethered & Sons Ltd, which was renowned for its beer throughout England. Not only that, but Thomas was also the Conservative M.P. for Great Marlow, a man whose views were to be respected.

144

"Right then, gentlemen, we have been drawn against our usual adversaries in this new FA Cup competition and we need some plan as to how to beat them. I'm not getting beaten by my main competitor, Nicholson's brewery. Have you got any ideas?"

Nicholson's Brewery (Maidenhead) v. Wethered's Brewery (Marlow)

"We have just the solution," replied Alfred Faulkner, "do you remember Cuthbert Ottaway who played cricket for us in the summer whilst still at Oxford University? Well, both he and his friend Cecil Clay have agreed to turn out for us against Maidenhead."

Thomas nearly choked on his own beer. This was a major coup indeed. Cuthbert was a renowned sportsman and had represented Oxford in five different sports, something no other scholar had ever achieved before. Ottaway was a dazzling forward and his speed and skill at dribbling was renowned.

"Well maybe we'll actually be able to turn the tables on them and beat them this Saturday. They're getting a bit over-confident now and their supporters are starting to call them 'The Invincibles' on account of being undefeated so far this season. We've agreed to play the match at their cricket ground again, so it would be nice to beat them on their own patch."

Alfred looked around at his players; "Right, kick-off is scheduled for 2.30 p.m. so as we are all travelling from different places, please don't be late. If you are going to arrive by train the ground is about a ten-minute walk from the station. After our great victory against Windsor Home Park in our first match let's keep up the good play. The best of luck to all!"

***

Unfortunately, the Marlow players didn't plan their journey to York Road very well and it was twenty past three before all were present and even then, there was a delay as Great Marlow FC had turned up with twelve players, and consequently one had to sheepishly return to the pavilion and collect his overcoat and wear it whilst the match was finally started. Thomas Wethered was not impressed.

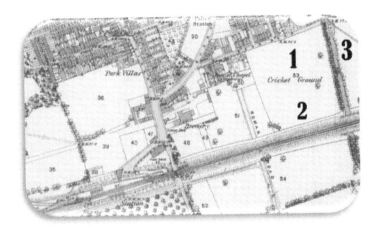

Map showing the location of the Maidenhead Cricket Ground (1) on York Road, bordered by the railway on one side (2) and the canal (3) on the other.
(CIRCA 1875)

Maidenhead won the toss and chose the goal at the railway end of the ground, deciding to play uphill for the first half. Was this a deliberate new tactic, knowing the opposition may well tire when ends were changed for the second half?

The match report published in the Maidenhead Advertiser is such a fascinating insight into Victorian sports writing, I thought I would let local reporter Harry Andrews take up the story:

'On the ball being kicked off Maidenhead went in with a rush, and quickly got it nearly up to their opponent's goal; then Marlow pulling themselves together, worked down to the railway, and had the best of it for some little time, capital dribbling play being noticed at frequent intervals by Rev. E. Leigh for Maidenhead, and Mr. Ottaway for Marlow; just then Maidenhead made a grand effort, worked the ball up slowly but surely in the right direction, the

146

principal part of the play being done by Young (who showed splendid form throughout the match), and though repeatedly spoiled in his attempts, at last saw an opening; and made a good try at goal, only missing his mark by a yard or so.

The hardest work up to this time, besides that mentioned, had been done by Monnington, Lloyd, Richardson, Goulden and Hebbes for Maidenhead; and by Wright, Crossman, Ottaway, Clay and Batting for Marlow, with an occasional long kick from Vardy and Faulkner respectively, also a run up by Carter from (the) Maidenhead goal to the middle of the field, and a fine run neatly down nearly the length of the ground, by Bevan, interspersed by some very clever dodging by Austen Leigh and Price; the latter playing very carefully and neatly, and once bringing the ball with judgement to within a yard or two of the dreaded posts; also Richardson by a similar bit of play immediately after. Just before half-time, Tindall made a fine run down for Marlow, and being backed up with spirit just then, and the red and black men being rather winded; a near shave of the local goal was the result, but a miss is as good as a mile.

Ends being changed and play resumed, Marlow led off well at first, but were soon penned; and then Austen Leigh getting possession of the ball began the finest run down of the match, cleverly passed Faulkner, who presented a seemingly impassable barrier, and gradually working it down to within a trifle of goal, and , well backed up all this time by his own side, made his effort as straight as possible; but the goal keeper sending it back, it was met by Young (who) again wriggled (if we may use the word) up to the front, and then successfully kicked between the posts, amidst loud cheering.

Being then kicked off afresh, Ottaway considered it was his turn for a bout, and kept the ball, by some beautiful play to himself for a considerable time till Lloyd took it away from him, and with the help of Carter, brought it down until they got it behind the goal, this keeping Marlow on the 'qui vive', and also on the defensive, giving them very little breathing time; for hardly had they got it back into the middle after this when Young determined to keep up the charter while he was about it, 'persuaded' it in and out amongst sundry obstacles, and again made for the right spot – counting a second goal for Maidenhead.

Marlow, thinking this was no joke, led off with a will, looking like mischief, and soon got up to the neighbourhood of the tree, but Lloyd making another little arrangement on the quiet, with his leathern friend, accompanied it down the whole length of the field, making one believe he was going into the Navy instead of the Army, so well up was he in his navigation. This fine bit of play was soon followed by another on the part of Hebbes, who had a capital try at goal; the ball only just clearing the top of the left post; also, an attempt by Carter, and some very active business on the part of F. Nicholson, who had been keeping goal all the early part of the game.

147

Marlow now tried all they knew to wipe off part of their defeat, and just before time was called, and when all the players were scattered about the field, they made a first rate rush up the centre of play, and would very likely have gained a goal, if they had backed up better. Time being soon after called, this spirited match came to an end.

We should have been glad to particularise more fully some of the individual play of the Marlow men, but did not know who they were at the time.' (iii)

And so, Maidenhead Football Club went through to the draw for the second ties of the Football Association Challenge Cup.

Marlow Football Club hold the record for the greatest number of applications submitted for entry into the FA Cup, applying in every tournament and playing in all but one (Season 1910-11), when it is believed their application was a couple of days late. They made an appeal to the FA but unfortunately this was turned down and they couldn't take part. (iv)

Maidenhead Football Club have also entered into every FA Cup competition bar one (1876-77) when they declined to enter on financial grounds.

'the committee had not considered it advisable to enter for the Association Cup this year, thinking it better to save the expense and to keep disengaged for the other matches.' (Maidenhead Advertiser - Wednesday 18th October 1876.)

Entrants in the first
FA Cup competition -
1871/72

FA Cup mural painted on canal side of Maidenhead's York Road ground.

148

MAIDENHEAD v. GREAT MARLOW

FOOTBALL ASSOCIATION CHALLENGE CUP
FIRST TIE

Saturday 11th November 1871
York Road, Maidenhead
Attendance: 1,287 (v), (Kick-Off : 3.20 p.m.)

MAIDENHEAD FC (2)	GREAT MARLOW FC (0)
Black and red hooped shirts and socks, white shorts	Dark blue & white hooped shirts, blue serge shorts & socks.
William Goulden (capt)	Alfred C. Faulkner (capt)
Rev. Arthur Austen-Leigh	S. Wright
Thomas N. Carter	Cuthbert J. Ottaway
James Lloyd	Cecil Clay.
John W. Monnington	Tindal
George Young	John Batting
Frederic Price	J. Stockbridge
Charles A. Vardy	J. D. Crossman
Frederick W. Nicholson	Bevan
George H. Ebbes	Thomas Kedge
William C. Richardson	Charles Nichol

Goal scorers: Maidenhead : George Young (2)

149

Author's Notes:

(i) Unfortunately, this beautiful structure burnt down in March 1892. The pavilion was situated close to the train line and a spark from a passing G.W.R. engine set fire to the thatched roof, setting the whole building ablaze. A week later the Maidenhead cricket and lawn tennis club was wound up.

(ii) Nowadays spelt 'Compleat Angler Hotel' but in the newspapers of the day such as 'The Windsor and Eton Express' and on the Ordinance Survey map of 1875 it is described as 'Complete Angler Hotel'.

(iii) It is interesting to note that about six of the Marlow players, who played in the FA Cup match that day, weren't reported in any of the teams that played during the rest of the 1871-72 season. Maybe because of the result, or maybe as with Cuthbert Ottaway (more of him later) because of their ability.

(iv) Source – Minutes of Great Marlow Football Club by kind permission of Terry Staines, Chairman.

(v) Match attendance comes from an internet source which cannot be verified. It would not be unreasonable to assume it is correct, given that over one thousand spectators were quoted as having been present at the first match at York Road.

Chapter 15: The First FA Cup Goal?
Match 4: Upton Park versus Clapham Rovers
FA Cup First Ties
Saturday 11th November 1871
(Kick-Off 3.30 p.m.)

"King Henry VIII used to go hunting from here you know. Yes, the Royal hounds were kept in kennels at the back of the pub and the King himself would come up and follow the chase into Epping Forest. It's rumoured that King Henry granted his Master of the Hounds the privilege of making some money from the sales of refreshments to travellers that passed this way. That made 'Ye Olde Spotted Dog' the only pub in the land to have a licence direct from the Crown. So, we're rubbing shoulders with Royalty today, lads!"

The Spotted Dog pub; 212, Upton Lane, Forest Gate, E7.

Francis Wilton was a local lad having been born in Stratford in the east end of London and lived all his life in the area. He lived in Romford Road now, just around the corner from 'The Spotted Dog' pub and he knew his local history. His two friends and fellow Upton Park team-mates, Tommy Kitson and Henry Compton, looked on in awe. They were both next door neighbours on the Ilford Road only a short walk from here and they had no idea of the pub's history.

"Well, all I can say is that I hope our play gets the Royal seal of approval this afternoon. We're going to have to play well to beat the Clapham Rovers."

Henry Compton was only 18 and although he didn't know much about local history, he did know a lot about football and he read all the match reports in the London press.

"That Reginald Birkett, their captain, is one hell of a player. He can play according to both the Association football and Rugby codes and he's extremely good at both. On top of that they've got Alex Nash. You know, he was selected for England in that first international match against Scotland, so we're going to have to watch him."

Conrad Warner, the Upton Park captain joined the conversation to reassure his young player; "Don't worry son, we've got some great players as well. They've only scored a couple of goals in five or six matches this season so they're not exactly on fire. We've got a better record so far and what about our 2-1 victory over the almighty Wanderers at The Oval the other week? That was pretty special, wasn't it?"

The youngster perked up immediately. "You're right, Sir. That was a great day and I scored a goal. I've never seen so many spectators. It will be good to be playing at home for the first time this season. All the lads from the cricket club will be coming down to support us."

Tommy Kitson got up from his wooden chair in the Upton Park team changing room. The Spotted Dog pub was only a few minutes' walk from West Ham Park where today's match was due to be played. He walked down the corridor and peered into the adjoining changing room, left empty for Clapham Rovers and shouted:

"There's nobody here yet and it's nearly three o'clock. If they don't turn up soon, they'll have to award the game to us and we'll be through to the next round. Mind you, if they take much longer to get here, we'll be playing most of the game in the dark." (i)

Reginald Birkett, the Captain of the Clapham Rovers, was still waiting for his team outside Plaistow station on the London, Tilbury and Southend Railway line. He'd given the team strict instructions of how to get to West Ham Park after the home game against Windsor the previous Saturday. It was now quarter past two and there were still a couple of players missing. One of them was Alex Nash who would be making his 1871-72 debut for the team today. He'd had to write a letter to Alex to inform him of the plans for today's match so he was just hoping he'd received it. Having played for England under the new rules, Alex was key to Reggie's plans for this first-ever cup match. Another missing player was the 19-year-old Jarvis Kenrick, a promising half-back, who had to travel from his home town of Caterham in Surrey. Jarvis had only missed one match for the Rovers this season and that was because it was a mid-week match on a Wednesday. Eventually everybody arrived but they were now half an hour behind schedule and they headed straight to The Spotted Dog pub to get changed.

The now 'Rotting Dog' – Upton Lane - May 2021

I stood outside The Spotted Dog pub. It's still there, on the corner of Upton Lane, but what an eyesore. This Grade II listed building with over 500 years of history has just been left to fall into disrepair and will soon be derelict. All the windows are boarded up and the paint is flaking from the white wooden fascia. Surely something could be done to restore this important London site with its historic links to Royalty, sport and football?

I walked to the end of Upton Lane and turned right onto Ham Park Road. I tried to imagine the 22 players in their colourful football shirts, covered by their long overcoats, clattering down the road in their football boots 150 years ago. It was only a short five-minute walk to West Ham Park. (Also known as Ham Park or Upton Park) As they approached the entrance, they would have seen the nurseries to their left which are still in the same location today. Upton Park Football Club were due to play Clapham Rovers on the cricket pitch in the north-east of the park. (ii)

Permission had been granted for the South Essex Cricket Club (formerly Upton United C.C.) to play there by Thomas Fowell Buxton, Esq., M.P. in 1862. The Buxton family were keen cricketers and owned Ham House and its 77-acre grounds.

Upton House c. 1780, subsequently renamed Ham House

When the cricketers turned to playing football in the winter of 1866, Thomas and Lady Buxton naturally granted them the rights to also play football in the park. The club was originally formed in December 1866 (iii) as the South Essex Football club by Horace Augustus Alexander, its first President Frederic Barnett and most certainly a young Alfred Stair (who had now just recently become the Treasurer of the Football Association in February 1871).

The South Essex Football Club played its first match (14-a-side) at Upton Park on Saturday 2nd March 1867 against a London Hospital side. The match ended up as a no score draw. By the time of their next match on Saturday 6th April 1867 they had changed their name to Upton Park Football Club. They were still finding their way however and a six-nil drubbing by the Forest School showed they still had a lot to learn.

By the time of their second season 1867-68, the Upton Park Club had reached the lofty heights of playing a match against none other than the mighty Wanderers. The match report of the game played on 16th November 1867 showed that the club had flirted with the rugby code of the game for a while but after this match they were firmly committed to the rules of Association football. I've no doubt that the representatives of the Wanderers Club (Charles W. Alcock didn't play that day) ensured they chose the right code of the game.

The Upton Park ground sounded idyllic:

'.. a ground endeared to myriads of cricketers by memories of the hard hitting and the long scores which have been made on its well-levelled turf, of pleasant matches judiciously enlivened by the occasional introduction of ambrosial claret cups quaffed under the shade of the grand old trees, opposite to which the well-known stripes of the Cricket Company gracefully wave in the breeze.
(Field - Saturday 23rd November 1867)

Clapham Rovers were formed on the 10th August 1869. (For more details see Chapter 16.) At this very first meeting they agreed to play under both codes of football with Association rules to be played one week and rugby the next. This earned the Rovers the nickname of the 'hybrid' club.

The members of the newly formed Clapham Rovers club were mainly professional gentlemen, solicitors, architects and commercial clerks. The Upton Park team also came from a similar background and today's side contained eight clerks either from the world of insurance, shipbuilding or the London Stock Exchange plus a solicitor, a civil engineer and an artist/wood engraver, W. B. Gardner, who made printed images for the Victorian newspapers such as 'The Graphic' and 'The Illustrated London Times'.

And so, the 'Battle of the Clerks' eventually kicked off at the rather late time of 3.30 p.m. Conrad Warner, Upton Park's goalkeeper and captain, shouted across the field to his counterpart, Reggie Birkett.

"Now, remember which code you are playing today, Reggie. There's to be none of that handling nonsense at any time during the match. Make sure your players know the rules. Alfred Stair, who's on our committee got the 'no handling except for the goalkeeper' rule passed at the recent FA Committee meeting and it's now in your rule book. Make sure your players are all aware, won't you?"

"Certainly, old chap. Don't worry, we've been practising the new rules ever since we received our printed copies at the beginning of the season. Some of our team are young enough to have only played to the Association rules so they've never handled the ball. Besides, our rugger team are miles away today and playing the Civil Service back on Clapham Common. "

For the first quarter of an hour the match was pretty even with no advantage being gained by either side. Then suddenly the young Jarvis Kenrick, assisted by some good play by George Holden, an occasional captain for the Rovers, succeeded in getting a shot in on the Uptonians goal. The ball flew under the tape and the goal was greeted by loud cheers from his team-mates. It was one-nil to the Clapham side and the 19-year-old had scored the first-ever goal in FA Cup history! Or had he?

The history books credit Jarvis Kenrick as the scorer of the first FA Cup goal but, given the match didn't kick-off until 3.30 p.m., had the first goal been scored in one of the other first tie games? According to the match reports in the sporting press, Jarvis' goal was scored somewhere between the 15th and 20th minute (iv) so around 3.45 – 3.50 p.m. A study of the other 'first tie' matches show:

Hitchin v. Crystal Palace (k.o. 3 p.m.) was a nil-nil draw so can be discounted.

Maidenhead v. Great Marlow (k.o. 3.20 p.m.) George Young scored for Maidenhead just after half time so somewhere around 4.05 - 4.10 p.m. Again, this goal can be discounted.

Barnes v. Civil Service (k.o. 3 p.m. ?) The first Barnes goal was scored by Percy Weston just after half time. and would place the time of the goal at around 3.45 p.m. In other words, around the same time as Jarvis Kenrick's goal for Clapham Rovers.

There are two factors to consider:

The kick-off time of the Barnes v. Civil Service match is not quoted in the Sports Press. I have assumed that, due to the Civil Service turning up with only eight players, the kick-off may have been delayed until after 3 p.m. whilst they waited for other players to turn up.

If Jarvis Kenrick's goal was scored after 15 minutes and not twenty minutes, then the time of the goal would be around 3.45 p.m. In my research, I have found three match reports quoting the time of the goal as after a 'quarter of an hour' and one quoting 'twenty minutes'. (iv)

So, on balance we can assume that Jarvis Kenrick scored the first-ever FA Cup goal – JUST!

Nineteen-year-old Jarvis Kenrick of Clapham Rovers, scorer of the first-ever goal in FA Cup history.

After Jarvis' first goal, and despite the changing of ends, the heads of the Upton Park players seemed to go down. Despite the efforts of their captain, Conrad Warner, Francis Wilton and Edward Curwen, they just could not lift their side and, fifteen minutes later, A. Thompson scored a second for Clapham. The game then continued at a slow pace and as darkness crept in, Jarvis Kenrick nipped in to score another with ten minutes to go. The final score was 3-0 to the Rovers.

What had happened to the Uptonians? This was completely out of character. Maybe it was the delayed start that had caused them to be sluggish when taking to the field. Hanging around in the changing rooms for half an hour can't have helped. What is certain is that they never conceded three goals again that season. In fact, in the match reports I unearthed, they don't appear to have conceded another goal in the 1871-72 season, finishing it undefeated.

UPTON PARK v. CLAPHAM ROVERS
FOOTBALL ASSOCIATION CHALLENGE CUP
FIRST TIE

Saturday 11th November 1871
West Ham Park,
Attendance: 1,500, (Kick-Off : 3.30 p.m.)

UPTON PARK (0)	CLAPHAM ROVERS (3)
Scarlet and black hooped shirt and stockings, white shorts.	Cerise & French-grey halved shirts, white shorts & black socks.
Conrad Warner (capt)	Reginald H. Birkett (capt)
Walter Freeth	Jarvis Kenrick
Milner Jutsum	Robert A. M. M. Olgivie
Francis Wilton	R.W. Dent
Thomas Kitson	George Holden
Henry Compton	Alexander A. E. Nash
Edward Curwen	Andrew J. Nash
William B. Gardner	P. St. Quentin
Alexander M. Jones	A. Thompson
Frederic Barnett	Charles C. Tayloe
Charles E. Wilson.	Charles F. Wace.

Goal scorers: Clapham Rovers : Kenrick (2), A. Thompson (1)

Author's Notes:

(i) In November, the sun starts to set at around 4.15 p.m. with dusk and darkness falling at 4.52 p.m. Therefore, any matches kicking off at 3 p.m. and lasting one and a half hours with no half-time break would finish at around 4.45 p.m., just minutes before total darkness. It must be remembered that in Victorian England, whilst there was gas street lighting in London, light pollution was significantly less than today and football matches played in parks would usually end up being played in total darkness at dusk.

(ii) Upton Park Football Club played on the areas marked as cricket grounds 1,2 or 3 on the map below (PITCH). There is a reference to the 'pavilion end' in a match against the Wanderers. (Field - Saturday 23rd November 1867). This would suggest the pavilion (3) was visible from that goal. The pavilion is the large circular area situated just north of Ham House. All of these pitches are in the area of the park nearest to 'The Spotted Dog' pub (1) and the nurseries (2).

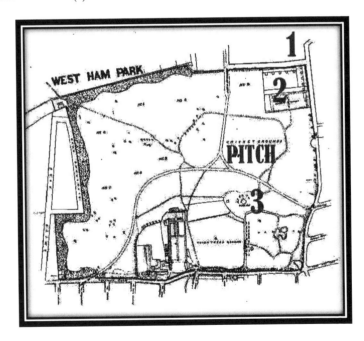

Map of West Ham Park – circa 1908

(iii) *SOUTH ESSEX FOOTBALL CLUB.*

We are happy to have to record the formation of another new arrival into the now rapidly-increasing list of football clubs playing in the neighbourhood of London. The little Stranger whom we are so glad to welcome into the football ranks is one formed from the South Essex Cricket Club, and having for its practice ground that famous park belonging to Lady Buxton, Upton, so well-known to all cricketers, either supporters or opponents, of the Cricket Company. The club, we believe, owes its existence to the indefatigable Alexander, who, no doubt, tired of the calm which always follows the storm of cricket, and sighing, like his ambitious ancestor, for worlds to conquer, has introduced the game of football into the neighbourhood Upton, with the praiseworthy intention of imitating in the football he exploits of the South Essex Cricket Club in the cricket world. We wish the South Essex Football Club every success, and to the members, 'Here's their good health, and their wives and families, and may they all live long and prosper. (The Sportsman - Tuesday 18th December 1866)

(iv) Match reports showing the time of Jarvis Kenrick's goal for Clapham Rovers.

For the first quarter of an hour the home team played up well together, and the game was very even. At length, after a good rush of the Rovers, Kenrick by a first-rate piece of play, succeeded in getting the first goal. (Sportsman – Wed. 15th November 1871)

The ball was started at half-past three, and the game kept up with great spirit all through. After about twenty minutes, the forward play of Holden and Kenrick, which was very good, was rewarded with a goal, which fell to the share of the latter player. (Sporting Life – Wed. 15th November 1871)

During the first quarter of an hour the play was very even, the Uptonians playing very well together. At last, Kenrick, by a good piece of play, obtained a goal for the Rovers, (The Field – Saturday 18th November 1871)

At 3.30 the game commenced, and was kept up with great spirit for a quarter of an hour, when Kenrick landed the leather safely between the posts, this success being greeted with cheers by his fellow players. (Bell's Life – Sat. 18th November 1871)

(v) Attendance taken from 'The Victorian Football Miscellany' by Paul Brown (page 59)

Draw for the Second Ties

THE ASSOCIATION CHALLENGE CUP
(Wednesday 29th November 1871)

The second ties in the competition for the above Cup were drawn yesterday (Wednesday) evening, with the following result :

Barnes Club plays Hampstead Heathens.

Crystal Palace Club plays Maidenhead Club.

Hitchin Club plays Royal Engineers.

Wanderers Club plays Clapham Rovers.

Donington Grammar School plays Queen's Park Club, Glasgow.

In the last instance the two clubs, being unable to arrange a date for deciding their first tie owing to the short notice received, were permitted to be included in the second drawing.

The methodology of the Second Round (Ties) draw seems to defy the FA's own rules for the competition in that Rule 8 allowed provincial teams to be drawn together. Poor old Donington School from Spalding in South Lincolnshire were left to sort out their match against Queen's Park in Glasgow and, due the prohibitive costs (around £2 a student) and the time that would be taken up travelling to Glasgow, they decided to scratch from the competition.

The other provincial clubs that came close to one another, Hitchin and Maidenhead, were not drawn together. Maidenhead Football Club were drawn against a London club (Crystal Palace) and Hitchin Football Club, although drawn against another provincial side (Royal Engineers) they were based in Chatham, on the other side of London. A neutral venue was eventually agreed and the match was to take place at The Oval, a venue half way between the grounds of the two clubs.

Chapter 16: 'Clapham Rovers are not Common at all'
Match 5: Clapham Rovers versus Wanderers
FA Cup Second Ties
Saturday 16th December 1871
(Kick-Off 3.00 p.m.)

Clapham Common was once a waste land just to the south of the River Thames. Clapham itself was a small village and home to a few farmers who grazed their livestock on the common land and gathered brushwood for their fires. The Common was noted for its excellent gravel and pits were dug to excavate it for building the roads in the Capital. In the 18th century a wealthy local resident, Christopher Baldwin, led an initiative to improve the Common by levelling, filling the ditches and planting trees. Soon the Common was being used for different types of recreation including horse-racing and cricket.

Clapham Common, where cattle, sheep and football all lived side by side.

The many gravel pits became ponds and on one of these the American statesman and scientist Benjamin Franklin experimented with the properties of oil on the surface of water. With the advent of the trains the village quickly expanded into a suburb of London as well-to-do people realised, they could commute into the city.

Grandiose houses were built all around the Common but it remained a rough place, frequented at night by robbers. By the time of the FA Cup in 1871, horses and sheep still grazed freely on the Common and no doubt pitch inspections had to take place before the numerous rugby and football matches took place every week.

The location of the football pitches is not clear but a map of the Common around 1871 shows the majority of the common was covered in trees and ponds, apart from the area to the north-east which was clear and suitable for recreation to take place.

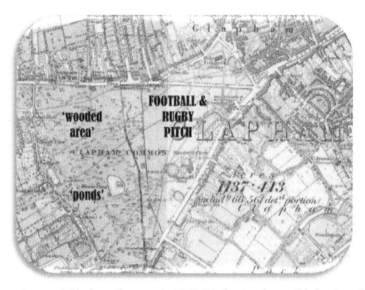

A map of Clapham Common in 1868-71 showing the possible location of the football and rugby pitches.

As already mentioned, Clapham Rovers were formed at a meeting arranged by a Mr. W. E. Rowlinson and a Mr. Robert Seymour Whalley on the 10th August 1869. They are not to be confused with the Clapham Common Club (C.C.C.), formed in 1865, who were also playing on the Common at that time.

It seems that there was a preponderance of players at this time living around Clapham who all wanted to play football or rugby. It appears that the Clapham Rovers team may have been formed after a fun match played on Boxing Day, 26th December 1868, on the Common when a newly named Clapham Rovers side took on a team called the Universal Humbugs. What is noticeable from this match is that it featured two of the Tayloe brothers. John Edward Tayloe, the current captain of the Clapham Common Club, played for the Universal Humbugs side and Edward Tayloe captained the Clapham Rovers side.

Clapham Rovers first match appears to have been a game against the local grammar school on the 6th March 1869, a game which they easily won by one goal and three touch downs to nil. John Tayloe captained the side. What had happened? Had there been a falling out between the Tayloe family and the Clapham Common club or was this just a natural creation of two sides due to the volume of players available to play the game? What we do know is that the Tayloe brothers never played for the C.C.C again and by 1871 the club had disappeared from the football scene.

After their official formation in August 1869, the club opened the 1869-70 season with a warm up game on the 18th September 1869 between Mr. Tayloe's side, which featured all three of the brothers John, Edward and the youngest, Charles, against Mr. Greenhill's side, which contained a certain Mr W.E. Rowlinson, the club's first President.

The following Saturday, 25th September 1869, the club's first official game was against none other than the mighty Wanderers side, captained by Charles William Alcock himself. The Rovers were fortunate to win the toss and with the wind behind them, John Tayloe scored their first official goal. Not only that, but they then held on for a one-nil victory, a result that shocked the Wanderers team, even though the Wanderers had had to play with just ten men. And so, the Rovers were up and running and the football world had better watch out for these new kids on the block.

And so, two years later the two sides were drawn against each other in the Second Tie of the Football Association Challenge Cup. Since that first game, the sides had met four times, with three further victories falling to the Rovers and one scoreless draw. Charles William Alcock was determined to rectify this sequence of results. He was not prepared to be defeated in HIS club's first appearance in HIS first FA Cup tournament. His team selection was to feature a lot of players with connections to his old school at Harrow. Firstly, there were three players from the Harrow Chequers side that had scratched from the first tie of the competition. Morton Peto Betts, William Parry Crake and the Reginald Courtenay Welch all went to the school and had played for the Chequers and the Old Harrovians. Then at the last moment, due to the absence of two of his players (i) he had to call on the services of another two of his Harrow School contacts. The first was the 19-year-old Percy Temple Rivett Carnac, who had just left Harrow School, and was a regular in the Harrow School XI. The second was another youngster, the 20-year-old Reginald Courtenay Welch, an able cricketer and goalkeeper with a good eye for the ball.

Charles Alcock had chosen his side wisely as within the next twelve months, nine of them would play for England in the future internationals against Scotland. He had given his team strict instructions to catch the train from Ludgate Hill to the Clapham and North Stockwell station (now Clapham High Street) and then to walk directly to the ground. They were to arrive already changed into their kits under their long overcoats as there were no changing rooms available today. (ii)

Travelling on the train in Victorian London was quite an experience and I let Stella, 'The Woman About Town' (iii) in the Sporting Times, give you a flavour of the journey.

'I wish some means could be adopted upon the metropolitan lines for letting us know where we are. The porters are in an evident league to keep us in the dark on this head. Their sharp, cockney explanations are even more unintelligible than the normal words of command of a parade ground, or the voice of a penny boat's captain in a thick fog. The train draws up, two or three strong-lunged officials jerk out something simultaneously, which might as well – or even better – be Greek. For, in these days of advanced education someone might understand that, and before you have time to discover what is meant by the discordant sound the train is off again. The porter fiend especially enjoys himself when he has a chance of rattling off a long list of names. Often have I listened in amazement to his wonderful garrulity as he runs the names of a dozen stations one into another, finishing off with a high staccato note which makes one jump almost as much as the slamming of the carriage doors, which the same gentle individual in velveteens indulges in.

"Sproadncrossbumsydpidandgringe train!" this is what I heard one say at London Bridge only yesterday. It's better than a double acrostic. (iv) What we want is to be independent of these vocal Bradshaws. And it can be so easily done, and so cheaply. Why does not every metropolitan railway follow the example of the North Kent line, which has the name of the station on all the lamps in and about the platform? It is thus visible by day and night from any part of the train.

And now I have begun grumbling with the railways I could go on for columns. Where are the ladies' carriages that no train should be without? Why have I not, when I travel, the right and chance of being without male society if I wish? Men can be alone – they have their smoking carriages; then why not women also? This is the sort of women's rights that Miss Becker should howl for. Where, too, now that the cold weather has come, are the foot warmers? How is it that a first-class carriage is as drafty in winter as it is stuffy in summer? Why can't we take our railway tickets at authorised offices about London, just as we book places for the opera? Why must we all crowd and crush, and lose our change and temper getting tickets at a little pigeon-hole with a rude clerk behind it, just three minutes before the train starts? Oh, if I were only at the Board of Trade, wouldn't I initiate railway reform!'

(Sporting Times – 2nd December 1871.)

Was it any wonder that not all the Wanderers team arrived on time?

On Saturday last these clubs met for the second time this season, the occasion being the second round in the competition for the Association Challenge Cup, the draw for the ties having thus pitied two of the strongest clubs in London against each other. An even contest was generally anticipated, and these expectations were more than realised, as the match was from first to last maintained with great equality although the result was a victory for the Wanderers. Owing to the late arrival of some of the latter, the game, instead of being commenced half-past 2, was delayed until 3 o'clock, and. consequently, during the last quarter of an hour was sustained in almost total darkness. Both sides were strong, although at the last moment the Wanderers were compelled to fill the places of A. C. Thompson and R. H. Benson with others of their body. At 3 o'clock the ball was kicked off by S. Baker on behalf of the Clapham Eleven, and for some little time there was no noticeable inequality, the well-concerted rushes of the Clapham forwards being ably repelled by the efficient play of the Wanderers' half-back (E. Lubbock). Meanwhile the Wanderers' forwards had been working with praiseworthy energy, and at last, after some brilliant dribbling by Crake, a chance of a kick at goal was offered to the Hon T. H. Pelham, and steadying himself cleverly for the shot, the latter by a neat kick secured the fall of the Clapham goal. Ends were consequently changed, and the fight again resumed with unabated vigour by both parties. Again, the equality that was visible at the outset was the prominent feature of the play, and until the end there was indeed, no sign that it was likely to be disturbed. Once, in turn, was each goal seriously threatened, by Alcock on the one hand, and on the other by the Rovers, after really splendid run down by G. Holden; but Birkett and Welch were each equal to the emergency, and the danger averted.

167

Thus, In the absence of any score to the Rovers, when time was called at half-past 4 o'clock, the Wanderers remained in the possession of a well-earned victory, after one of the most pleasantly contested games of the season. For the Rovers Ogilvie, Kenrick. and Holden were certainly the most prominent representatives of Clapham, and Kenrick throughout was especially useful. For the Wanderers A. G. Bonsor deserves especial praise, and M. P. Betts worked as hard as he charged.

(Bell's Life – Saturday 23rd December 1871.)

The Wanderers were in the draw for the Third Ties.

CLAPHAM ROVERS v. WANDERERS
FOOTBALL ASSOCIATION CHALLENGE CUP
SECOND TIE

Saturday 16th December 1871
Clapham Common,
Attendance: ?, (Kick-Off : 3.00 p.m.)

CLAPHAM ROVERS (0)	WANDERERS (1)
Cerise & French-grey halved shirts, white shorts & black socks	Orange, violet and black shirt and stockings, white shorts
Reginald H. Birkett (capt)	Charles W. Alcock (capt)
Jarvis Kenrick	Charles W. Stephenson
Robert A. M. M. Olgivie	Edgar Lubbock
Thomas S. Baker	Reginald C. Welch
George Holden	Morton Peto Betts
C. L. Huggins	Edward E. Bowen
Andrew J. Nash	Alexander G. Bonsor
P. St. Quentin	William P. Crake
Robert S. F. Walker	Thomas C. Hooman
C. C. Harvey	Percy T. Rivett Carnac
Charles C. Bryden	Thomas H. W. Pelham

Goal scorers: Wanderers: Thomas H. W. Pelham (1)

169

Author's Notes:

(i) A. C. Thompson and R. H. Benson were replaced by Reginald Courtenay Welch (reserve) and the Harrow youngster Percy Temple Rivett Carnac. The original team for the match against Clapham Rovers had been published by Charles Alcock in the Sportsman – Saturday 16th December 1871.

(ii) The travel instructions given here were issued to his team when playing at Clapham Common against the C.C.C. on the 20th March 1869. The team were told to catch the 1.17 p.m. train from Ludgate Hill to Clapham and North Stockwell for a 2.30 p.m. kick-off. As the journey takes at least half an hour followed by a fifteen-minute walk, the players must have arrived already changed for the match. The fact that the players were given Ludgate Hill as their departure point shows that a lot of the Wanderers players were living north of the Thames rather than near their adopted ground at the Kennington Oval. I must admit this itinerary for the players was very tight time wise and left no margin for error. I am not surprised that not all of the Wanderers team arrived at 2.30 p.m. for the original kick-off.

(iii) I came across Stella's weekly column in the Sporting Times completely by accident. Her views on Victorian society and the events and fashions of the time are worthy of a book or a Netflix series on their own. I would urge anybody who is interested in finding out what life was like for a young woman in the Victorian era to read her racy columns (Sporting Times 1871-1874)

(iv) 'acrostic' is a poem, word puzzle, or other composition in which certain letters in each line form a word or words.

Chapter 17: 'This Pitch isn't Big Enough for the Both of Us!'
Match 6: Crystal Palace versus Maidenhead
FA Cup Second Ties
Saturday 16th December 1871
(Kick-Off 3.15 p.m.)

CRYSTAL PALACE

Situated about halfway between Sydenham and Anerley station, on the right side of the railway from London to Croydon, the site of the Crystal Palace on the summit of Penge Park, is one of the most beautiful in the world. Standing on the brow of the hill, some two hundred feet above the valley through which the railway passes, the building is visible for many miles in every direction. But when the train approaches the spot where the brilliant and fairy fabric, in the midst of the most enchanting scenery, is revealed suddenly to the eye, the impression produced elicits our warmest admiration. The models of the diluvian and antediluvian extinct animals, the Irish elk with its magnificently branching antlers, the Iguanodons, the Megalosaurus &c. &c., in the foreground among the Geological Islands and Lakes; the cascades and terraces, the luxuriant foliage, flower beds and fountains, ascending up to the splendid and unrivalled fabric of glass which rears its radiant and glittering bulk upon the Surrey hill, form a coup d'oeil of wonderful beauty, magnificence, and grandeur, the view of which we may envy the Brighton Railway traveller who enjoys the sight daily, in virtue of his season ticket.

BRADSHAW'S HANDBOOK – 1863 (i)

"Hey Dad, apparently we're going to be playing our next cup game at the Crystal Palace in London. It sounds like something from a fairy-tale, you know, like the tower in that story about Rapunzel, the girl with the long golden hair."

Henry Hebbes put down the sack of coal he was filling and looked over to his twenty-year old son in admiration. George was a hard-working lad and he was sure he would make a success of his coal and corn merchant's shop, as soon as it was his time to take over the family business. But for now, it was time for him to enjoy the success of his footballing career with the Maidenhead Club. George had played in most of the club's matches so far this season and, as they were undefeated, he would no doubt play in the second tie of the Association Challenge Cup.

The south entrance of the Crystal Palace during The Great Exhibition of 1851 - when Britain showed what it had to offer the world.

"The Crystal Palace is a sight to behold, son. Make sure you go up and have a good look at it when you get there. I remember it being built for the Great Exhibition in Hyde Park before we moved out of London to Burnham (5 miles from Maidenhead) when you were five years old. I can remember the Christmas of 1854 when a gigantic Christmas tree was placed in the central transept covered in Chinese lanterns and flags of every nation. It attracted over 10,000 visitors in one day. I believe there is going to be an exotic cat show this year, featuring 350 different animals. Your mother and I are going to close the shop early and we intend to come down on the train to give you, our support."

By the look of it the match had created great interest throughout the Berkshire town:

The second ties for the Association Cup were drawn the other day, when the opponents of Maidenhead appeared to be the Crystal Palace Club; and it is arranged to meet on the Palace grounds next Saturday, at 3 o'clock. We believe a good team has been chosen for Maidenhead, and such is the great interest taken by the town in the club that many have expressed their determination to go and see the match, and if need be, give their young townspeople a cheer of encouragement, as the undertaking is no slight one; yet, after seeing their determination against Oxford, we anticipate they will not lie easily beaten at the Crystal Palace. (Windsor and Eton Express - Saturday 16th December 1871)

The Maidenhead team met on platform 2 of the brand-new Maidenhead Junction station, built by the Great Western Railway on its Bristol to Paddington line. (ii) It had only been opened six weeks previously and it now meant that the journey from Maidenhead into Central London could be done in an hour-and-a-quarter. As the 11.35 train pulled into the station, the team piled into the second-class carriages, full of excitement and expectancy for the game ahead. All the talk was of the match and the visit to the magnificent Crystal Palace. William Goulden, the captain, tried to calm his team down. William was only twenty-six years old himself, but he was already a schoolmaster, choirmaster and organist at the All-Saints School on Boyne Hill in Maidenhead. He was described as 'a sturdy player with just the voice for a captain' and he used this to share his thoughts with his excited team.

"Let's hope the pitch is in good condition today. Crystal Palace had to abandon their game against the Civil Service last Saturday because of the severe frost and snow. We must be made of sterner stuff as we managed to play our practice match between our members from Bray and Cookham, despite losing a few players who went off skating."

"Yes," replied Freddy Nicholson, "we even got my dad to step in and play. He did alright despite the fact that he was fifty this year. He really enjoyed it despite the cold."

"Indeed, our vice president played well. We might need him again today. I haven't heard from young Freddy Price. I'm not sure if he managed to get the time off from Philberd's School. I did write to his headmaster to tell him about the importance of the game but

173

didn't hear anything back. It will be quite a blow as Freddy is a great dribbler with the ball."

"Don't worry Dad. I've had a word with our Robert. He's brought his kit and he's willing to stand in if Freddy doesn't turn up."

Robert Nicholson was really a cricketer, that was his game, but with his family's enthusiasm for this new sport, he was quite often cajoled into playing for the Maidenhead team.

"Great. Now remember lads when we get to Paddington we need to stick together as we have to get across the city on the Metropolitan Line to Mansion House. (iii) From here we'll have to walk to London Bridge to catch the London, Brighton and South Coast Railway down to the Crystal Palace station. The football pitch is on the cricket ground on the east side of Crystal Palace Park. I believe the Kent County Cricket Club play a couple of matches there each summer."

The young George Hebbes couldn't believe his luck.

"This is going to be one of the biggest adventures of my life. To go on the train and then the Underground and then to see the wonders of the Crystal Palace will surpass anything I've ever witnessed before. So far this season we've played all of our matches at home. It will be fantastic to play on another ground."

"Yep, but it's not going to be cheap. This is going to cost the club a pretty packet."

Charles Alfred Vardy stroked his beard and looked thoughtfully across the carriage at his captain. Charles had been instrumental in setting up the Maidenhead Football Club. It was his baby and whilst he was looking forward to the day ahead, he was concerned about the cost to the club. Charles would go on to be a key member of the Committee in future years, becoming the Club Secretary and Treasurer. Also, Charles was right. This would be the biggest one-off expense for the club this season and along with the entry fee into the Cup it would account for over twenty-percent of the members' subscriptions. (vi)

William Goulden was guarded in his reply, "I understand where you are coming from Charles, but we tried to get a date when they could come to play at our ground but given the home fixtures we had already arranged, this was the only Saturday available and the match had to be played at their ground. Mind you, think of the prestige that our club will get from playing this match against this historic club, one of the founders of the Football Association. The match reports will be in all the London papers and it will put Maidenhead on the football map."

As a player Charles Vardy was a no-nonsense full-back. He was 'solid, steady, but alert and ever ready.' In the early days of goalkeeping, the craft of the position had not always been fully developed and the goalkeeper had to rely on competent full-backs to help protect the goal. Charles Vardy was one of these and 'like the last button on the comedian's breeches, the last responsibility rested with him.' Charles was honest and would not stoop to any gamesmanship. Sometimes players would waste time at York Road by deliberately kicking the ball into the canal. Charles would never entertain any such play and he would always honestly protect his goal.

"We'd better win then!" was his brief reply.

***

I made the walk through the upper terraces of the Crystal Palace Park. I tried to imagine this majestic building spanning 563 metres across the top of Penge Peak. There is one cast iron stanchion that is still in situ. It was built by Adam Hart-Davis and his team for the excellent BBC2 series 'What the Victorians Did for Us' but even with this as an excellent pointer, you can't begin to imagine how imposing this structure would have been. The panorama of the Surrey Hills and countryside that unfold in front of you is still impressive despite the expansion of the London metropolis.

I continued down to the lower terraces and past the mighty 'Sphinxes' which still guard the wide stone staircase of the Italian terrace. Here you arrive at what would have been a series of parterres and sunken gardens, watered by the spray of six beautiful fountains that arched 250 feet into the air.

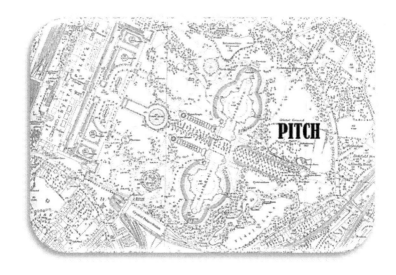

Map of the Crystal Palace Park showing the location of the cricket pitch, the venue for the FA Cup game against Maidenhead (1871)

Today the gardens formed a massive car park as the Crystal Palace Park was being used as a course for a triathlon which was currently underway. I had to wait for the cyclists to pass in front of me before being told to advance by the numerous stewards protecting the route. Soon I passed the statue of the great Joseph Paxton, whose ambitious plans for the Crystal Palace had been approved by the committee for the Great Exhibition of 1851 after rejecting 245 entries. Amazingly Joseph wasn't an architect but a botanist and builder of greenhouses. His ground breaking design, which was based on his glasshouses at Chatsworth, introduced many revolutionary architectural and construction techniques and it was no surprise that in October 1851 he received a knighthood from Queen Victoria.

After passing through a walkway, which takes you through the centre of the dated National Sports Centre (1964), I took a flight of steps that led down to an open expanse of grass. Surrounded by trees, this would have been the original Crystal Palace Cricket Ground and the location of today's match.

Looking out on to the Crystal Palace cricket pitch from where the pavilion &
tents would have been. The location of the Crystal Palace football pitch.

It was the perfect location for a sporting event and the steep
bank along one side gave spectators an elevated view of the action.
It was no surprise that when the FA Cup had to move away from
the Kennington Oval, the venue switched to the Crystal Palace and
between 1894-95 and the outbreak of the First World War, it hosted
21 finals. A crowd of 121,919 spectators watched Aston Villa beat
Sunderland 1-0 in the 1912-13 final.

A panoramic view of the Crystal Palace ground during the 1905 FA Cup
Final. The cricket pavilion is to the right.

"I've never seen anything like it," muttered the young George
Hebbes to his mate, Tom Carter. Tom was also 19 years of age and
lived in the vicarage in the same small village of Burnham and the

two teenagers were in awe of the magnificent building they had just visited.

"It's like something from a dream, or something you'd see in a Punch magazine. I can't believe it's real."

The two boys sat in the cricket pavilion changing rooms with their eyed transfixed on the wall in front of them. The Reverend Arthur Henry Austen-Leigh tried to shake them from their trance.

"Come on boys, you need to focus on the match ahead. This is an important game for our club and we'll need to be at our best to beat the Crystal Palace."

Arthur Henry was the curate at his father's church in Bray, who in turn was the nephew of the famous novelist Jane Austen. Arthur was well-educated and had studied at Radley College and Cheltenham before graduating from Oxford with a degree in law and theology. As well as playing football, he was also a fine cricketer and had played in some important first-class matches for the 'Gentlemen of Berkshire'. He'd even been selected to play for the 'Gentlemen of England' against the 'Gentlemen of Kent and Sussex' at Lords in July 1857. He'd opened the batting and scored 31 before being bowled by Tredcroft. One innings was enough for England who were victors by an innings and 206 runs. He was therefore used to the big occasion and now at thirty-five years of age, he felt he was experienced and well placed to calm his two young team-mates. Just as the calm had been restored, William Goulden came storming into the dressing room:

"Have you seen the size of the pitch? They've just put the flags out and it looks as though it's going to be half the size of ours. They've said it's to protect the cricket square but I'm sure the Palace normally play on a bigger pitch than this. It's only about 100 by 50 yards, whilst ours measures 200 by 100 yards. (v) I know that according to the rules we're at the maximum but there should be a rule for the minimum size or we might as well be playing in a public-school courtyard. On top of that the fog has come down and it's starting to drizzle. Is there anything else that can go wrong?"

As it happened, Freddy Price hadn't turned up so Robert Nicholson would step in to play for the Maidenhead Club as discussed. However, the Palace side were still waiting for their goalkeeper Alex Morten to show and by 3.00 p.m. he still hadn't arrived. The kick-off was delayed but by 3.15 p.m. there was still no sign of him and so it was agreed that play should commence. However, it was now agreed they would just play for an hour-and-a-quarter as by 4.30 p.m. it would be dark.

There was a large crowd assembled around the ground with the majority of the spectators spread along the steep bank on the far side from the pavilion. Some of the dignitaries were stood in their thick coats between the refreshment tent and the flagstaff. As the players made their way down the pavilion steps there was a large cheer from the crowd for both sides. It appears a large number of spectators had travelled down from Berkshire and they made up a significant number of the 1,535 crowd. (iv)

George and Tom were still nervous, despite the reassurances from the Reverend Austen-Leigh. Mind you the grandeur of their surroundings were slightly diminished by the thick fog and drizzle which shrouded the towering Palace.

The ground was 'rather rotten' on account of the recent frosts but the first half seemed to go well for Maidenhead, the 'scarlet and blacks', and they seemed to be coping well with the small pitch. Most of the time the ball was kept up towards the Palace end of the pitch and two close attempts on goal were made by George Young and William Richardson.

Crystal Palace were struggling without their stalwart goalkeeper and Douglas Allport had to play in goal, which meant that the Palace players were playing in positions that they were unaccustomed to. Shortly before half-time Alex Morten finally turned up. Apparently, he *was under impression that the play would not commence until the lamps were lighted.* This was rather strange as, given the time and the weather conditions, it meant the game would have been played in almost total darkness.

With no score at half-time, the teams changed ends and immediately Maidenhead had their best opportunity of the game. If it had not been for a bit of luck and one of the Palace backs just being in the right place at the right time, Palace would have been one-nil down. After this fright and with the return of their goalkeeper, Palace started to take more control of the game.

After an hour had passed there was still no score but suddenly Palace managed to get a throw-in on the right. The ball was thrown to Alfred Lloyd who managed to get on the end of it and breach the Maidenhead goal. One-nil to Palace.

Had the 'Scarlet and Blacks' been undone by the small size of the Crystal Palace pitch? There was never any threat of a goal from a throw-in at the York Road ground. It was too wide. It wasn't long before the Palace scored a second goal with a well-placed long side-kick from William Bouch *'the ball grazing both the tape and goal-keeper's hands.'*

Darkness started to fall and it was getting difficult for the players to see their team-mates. However, both teams continued to play as if there was all to play for and then a few minutes before 'time' was called, a third goal was obtained for the Crystal Palace by Charles Chenery, who had worked hard and unselfishly throughout the match. It was ironic that Charles, who was born in Berkshire, would be the man to kill off the dreams of his fellow county men

Despite the defeat, the Maidenhead club had given a good account of themselves, and as usual Charles Vardy had played well at the back and the Reverend Austen-Leigh, John Monnington and their captain William Goulden, were singled out for their particular praiseworthy play. The press noticed their ability to spread out across the pitch as opposed to the Palace forwards who tended to dribble with the ball in a group rather than play a good cross ball to a team mate as has been witnessed by the Maidenhead forwards.

There was no doubt that the 'Scarlet and Blacks' had been outdone by the size of the pitch which did not suit their style of play. However, the press reported that there may have been two other factors at play:

'..their want of speed may perhaps be the combined result of (usually playing on) a very large ground and long flannel trousers.'

The details of the match were taken from the following newspapers:

The Sportsman - 19th December 1871
Sporting Life - 20th December 1871
The Sportsman - 23rd December 1871
Bell's Life - 23rd December 1871
Bucks Herald - 23rd December 1871
Reading Mercury - 23rd December 1871
The Field - 23rd December 1871

CRYSTAL PALACE v. MAIDENHEAD
FOOTBALL ASSOCIATION CHALLENGE CUP
SECOND TIE

Saturday 16th December 1871
Crystal Palace Cricket Ground
Attendance: 1,535 (Kick-Off : 3.15 p.m.)

CRYSTAL PALACE (3)	MAIDENHEAD (0)
Blue & white hooped shirts and socks, blue serge shorts	Black & red hooped shirts and socks, white shorts
Douglas Allport (capt.)	William Goulden (capt.)
William M. Allport	Rev. Arthur Austen-Leigh
Alexander Morten (GK)	Thomas N. Carter
Henry F. Abell	George Wells
Alfred J. Heath	John W. Monnington
William Bouch	George Young
Charles E. Smith	Charles A. Vardy
Charles C. Armitage	Frederick W. Nicholson
Alfred H. Lloyd	Robert W. Nicholson
Thomas F. Spreckley	George H. Hebbes
Charles J. Chenery	William C. Richardson

Goal scorers:
Crystal Palace: William Bouch   (1)
     Alfred H. Lloyd   (1)
     Charles J. Chenery   (1)

Author's Notes:

(i) The Crystal Palace was a cast-iron and plate-glass structure, originally built in Hyde Park, London, to house the Great Exhibition of 1851. After the exhibition, the Palace was relocated to an area of South London known as Penge. It stood there from June 1854 until its destruction by fire in November 1936. This included the Crystal Palace Park that surrounds the site and which had previously been a football stadium that hosted the FA Cup Final between 1895 and 1914.

(ii) The GWR opened its new station on the main line on 1 November 1871. It was initially called Maidenhead Junction.

(iii) In 1871 the inner circle services began, (Metropolitan Railway and District Railway) starting from Mansion House and travelling to Moorgate Street via South Kensington and Paddington.

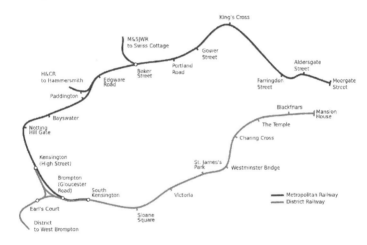

(iv) Crowd number of 1,535 as reported in the book 'The History of the English Football League: Part One 1888-1930' by Michael J. Slade

'..there were very few spectators, the majority of those present having come from Berkshire with the most praiseworthy intention of supporting their playing representatives.' – Sportsman 19th December 1871.

(v) Maidenhead Football Club.

This Club, according to arrangements, met on the grounds of the Crystal Palace on Saturday last, to play off the second ties of the 'Association Cup', when for the first time, we believe, they were defeated. One reason of this result may be attributed to the ground, which was very small, and thus very much cramped the play of team that has been accustomed to play on ground twice the size ; one ground being under 100 by 50 yards, while this one is 200 by 100 yards. The first part of the game looked well for Maidenhead, being nearly successful in gaining two goals, and the ball well kept up to their opponent's quarters. The byes being seven to the other side's two. After the ends had been changed, the game nearly changed entirely in favour of their opponents, with the exception of one good run down, and ended entirely in favour of the Crystal Palace Club. The club were in hopes they could have induced this club to have met them on their own ground, but their engagements are such that they are unable to do so this season.

READING MERCURY – Saturday 23rd December 1871

(vi) On Wednesday May 28th 1872 the Maidenhead Advertiser published an end of season summary for the club which included the match details (players, scores, opposition etc.) of all the games played. Interestingly, they also included their end of season accounts which make fascinating reading and give an insight into the running of an early Victorian football club. I reproduce the Club's balance sheet in full.

MAIDENHEAD FOOTBALL CLUB.

We have today published the balance-sheet and a list of matches played during the past season by our enterprising club (kindly supplied to us by a playing member), and, although a little late in coming out, we hope it may be acceptable to our readers, most of whom have taken great interest in the proceedings throughout. We cannot help congratulating the club on its successes, not only as regards the victories gained, but on its having brought together a number of people in the town, who were before perfect strangers to each other, and also, on its having firmly established, the means of a healthy and invigorating amusement to the inhabitants.

BALANCE SHEET

Receipts

	£	s.	d.
25 Honorary Members	11	10	6
74 Playing ditto ...	13	0	6
99	**£24**	**11**	**0**

Payments

	£	s.	d.
Subscription, Football Association	**0**	**5**	**0**
Newe, Towels,	0	2	4
Cull, Jersey, ...	0	6	0
Biggs, footballs, etc., ...	1	3	7
Expenses to Crystal Palace ...	**4**	**9**	**6**
Rent of ground	3	0	0
Expenses to Uxbridge	1	9	3
Biggs, refilling balls, etc. ...	0	4	0
Burnham, printing, ...	3	12	0
Stamps	0	17	8.5
Sundries	0	3	11.5
Football Association Cup ...	**1**	**1**	**0**
Mr. Hodges,	1	3	0
Use of committee room	0	5	0
Mr. Silver	0	1	6
Matches : Philberds,	0	8	0
Marlow...	0	10	7
Windsor	0	9	3
Uxbridge	0	10	6
Clay's	0	7	0
Cookham v. Bray	0	3	0
Marlow Town ...	0	11	0
Wycombe ...	0	9	9
Crossman's	0	6	3
Swifts	0	6	9
Cookham v. Bray	0	3	3
Crossman's	0	7	9
Balance in hand	**1**	**14**	**1**
	£24	**11**	**0**

Chapter 18: 'Brothers in Arms'
Match 7: Barnes versus Hampstead Heathens
FA Cup Second Ties
Saturday 23rd December 1871
(Kick-Off 3.00 p.m.)

"Is that anybody famous?"

A low voice came from behind me as I stood over the abandoned grave. Nettles and long grass surrounded the oblong grey marble plinth that stretched out before me. A tree had recently been pruned by a chainsaw and the resultant debris had fallen onto the sacred ground below. This simple grave bore two names:

FRANCES MORLEY
15TH AUGUST 1911

EBENEZER COBB MORLEY
20TH NOVEMBER 1924
AGED 93

I turned and looked over to the middle-aged man walking his Labrador through the woods next to Putney Lower Common.

"Do you follow football at all?"

"Of, course. I'm a Queen's Park Rangers fan. Is that somebody to do with football? I walk my dog here most days and I've often wondered who's grave it was?"

"Well actually, this is the grave of Ebenezer Cobb Morley who lived down by the River Thames in Barnes. He was the man that wrote down the original thirteen rules of football in October 1863. I would imagine if this was the man who wrote down the rules of the NFL in America this would be a theme park and they would be charging $30 to get in. But this is England and maybe we forget to protect the roots of our historic game. Even the pub, the White

185

Hart Inn in Barnes, where Barnes FC held their initial meetings, has no photograph of this legendary man on the walls of their Morley Room."

The grave of Ebenezer Cobb Morley and his wife Frances on the edge of Barnes Old Cemetery.

Apparently, the grave had been well-maintained when the FA's Chief Executive, Greg Dyke, had visited it in 2013 on the 150th anniversary of the creation of the FA rules. There were plans to convert the area to a lawn cemetery but these were dismissed as they proved too costly.

It had taken me a while to locate the grave in Barnes Old Cemetery. (i) Initially I had visited the Putney Cemetery with its memorial chapel on Mill Hill Road. I soon realised my mistake and walked the paths through the woods at the rear of the Putney Cemetery and here I stumbled across a number of gravestones well-hidden under some yew trees. I investigated further and disturbed a rat which went scuttling down an overgrown footpath. A green parakeet squawked loudly as it flew overhead, high above the trees. It was as if I was entering a mystical underworld. The graves were all abandoned and covered in green lichen, holly and ivy. A forlorn angel stood alone, arms crossed, her head decapitated by vandals, unable to stand guard and protect their loved one, long departed.

Barnes Old Cemetery – located off Rocks Lane on Barnes Common.

Suddenly, I heard an excited high-pitched shout coming from a distance and through the dense scrub I could see the AstroTurf pitches of the Barn Elms Sports Centre running alongside the cemetery. Appropriately, a football coach was explaining the rules of football to his junior players. Did they realise that the man who'd created them, 158 years ago, was resting less than 100 yards away from their pitch? I wondered if old Ebenezer could hear the coach trying to explain the new offside rule and gently turning in his grave.

***

According to J. Percival Tatham, the captain and secretary of the Hampstead Heathens, the club was founded in June 1868. (ii) The Heathens first recorded match appears to have been played on the 5th December 1868 against the N.N.K. (No Names Kilburn) Club. The Heathens were narrowly defeated by one goal to nil and according to the reporter they only conceded a goal because of a fluke. Apparently, their goalkeeper *had 'lifted his leg instead of keeping it still'* when dealing with an N.N.K. shot and hence they'd lost the match.

In the return match on the 9th January 1869, the reporter of 'The Sportsman' newspaper found the names of the two clubs laughable.

'… and the Hampstead Heathens — what names shall we have next? — have defeated the N.N.'s (North-end Noodles?) by two goals to nothing.

***

The two Tatham brothers, Percy and Sherman, lived at the Mount, close to Hampstead Heath. They had arranged to meet another other local lad, the Scot Alling Erskine, to travel down to Hammersmith station together on the Metropolitan Line. (iii) Here they'd arranged to meet the rest of the Heathens team, including the Leach brothers, Alfred and George, who originated from Londonderry in Ireland, but now lived in St. Pancras. It was the day before Christmas Eve but being a Saturday, they couldn't start to think about the forthcoming festivities. Today was all about football and the Association Cup game against Barnes. As they travelled through the Metropolis, the shops sparkled with bright Christmas decorations festooned around their windows and doors. Brass bands played Christmas carols on street corners and jovial singing could be heard within the taverns of the town. Stella, the 'Woman About Town' from the Sporting Times, described it thus:

'Signs of the coming season are not wanting; muffin bells and hot chestnut trays are everywhere. Already skates have been at a premium. The fruiterers' shops are profusely stocked with furry beasts and feathery birds, which hang in such symmetrical rows. The annuals are upon us in numbers greater than ever. Goose clubs have commenced; pantomimes are in rehearsal; holly has been seen in Covent Garden Market; postmen are already getting more punctual, dustmen more civil; in short, a walk-through London with one eye shut would show one that Christmas is not very far off. (Sporting Times 2nd December 1871)

Percy Tatham did a quick headcount on the platform of Hammersmith station as they waited for the 'down-train' to Barnes and it looked as though they would be playing with ten men again today. One of the three Leach brothers, George, was missing as he was preparing a legal case to be heard in court on Monday. Most of the other players sympathised with this as the majority of them were solicitors or article clerks, mixed in with one banker and a police constable. Still there would be two pairs of brothers playing for the Heathens.

As for the Barnes team they also had two pairs of brothers in their team. Alongside the River Thames in Putney there is a row of attractive houses called The Cedars. At No. 2 lived the two Highton brothers, Edward and Alfred, both of whom were students from a family containing six girls and six boys. Just down the road at No. 24 lived the Weston brothers, Percy, Edward and Vincent, from another big family of eight children. Two of the brothers Percy and Edward would be playing for Barnes in today's match.

And so, around 3.00 p.m. the four sets of brothers stood face to face on the Limes field. Was it a coincidence that the two captains, both called Percy, walked up to the centre of the pitch to make the toss of the coin?

It was The Heathens' Percy Tatham who was successful with his call and he immediately chose the end with a slight breeze blowing behind his team. The Heathens would need all the assistance they could get as they were playing with one man short. The first part of the game was pretty even with the ball mainly being kicked around the centre of the ground. After a while, Barnes finally managed to set up an attack and Arthur Dunnage, a 23-year-old medical student, let fly a good shot which flew dangerously close to the Heathens' goal. This spurred Percy Tatham's Heathens team into action and R. Barker, supported by his team-mates, dribbled the ball towards the Barnes goal, took a shot and the ball flew under the tape. It was one-nil to the ten men of Hampstead.

The sides immediately changed ends and with the breeze behind them, the Barnes club started to set siege to the Heathens goal. Percy Weston was urging his team on. They couldn't lose to the ten men of Hampstead on their own pitch, it would be a disgrace. At first, they were repelled by the good play of the Hampstead full-backs but eventually after 68 minutes the two Highton brothers got the ball into the goal with a lucky bounce off the Hampstead goalpost. Soon darkness fell on the riverside pitch and when 'time' was called the game was still even and so a draw was declared. According to the rules of the competition, the match would have to be replayed.

This would be the first replay in the history of the FA Cup!

BARNES v. HAMPSTEAD HEATHENS
FOOTBALL ASSOCIATION CHALLENGE CUP
SECOND TIE

Saturday 23rd December 1871
The Limes Field, Barnes,
Attendance: ? (Kick-Off : 3.00 p.m.)

BARNES FC (1)	HAMPSTEAD HEATHENS (1)
Blue & white striped shirts and socks, white shorts.	White with blue binding, blue cap.
Percy Weston (capt.)	J. Percival Tatham (capt.)
Alfred C. Highton	Sherman R. Tatham
Edward C. Highton	Charles B. Dimond
C.W.K. Bruce	H. Latham
A. Adams	R. B. Michell
Edward T. Weston	A. Leach
Charles Ommanney	Henry P. Leach
Arthur Dunnage	Harry W. Beauchamp
Todd	R. Barker
L. T. Williams	Alling M. S. Erskine.
Squiz/A.N. Other	

Goalscorers :
Barnes :   Highton   (1)
Hampstead Heathens: R. Barker   (1)

Author's Notes:

(i) Barnes Common showing the location of Ebenezer Cobb Morley's grave **(*)** in the abandoned Barnes Old Cemetery (2) at the left and to the rear of Putney Cemetery (1). It is a place that every football fan should visit to pay their respects to an inspirational man.

(ii) Details taken from the Charles Alcock Football Annual of 1871.

(iii) The Tatham brothers' most direct route to Hammersmith from Hampstead would have been on the Metropolitan Line from Swiss Cottage via Baker Street through Paddington (Bishops Road) and onto Hammersmith.

(iv) The team probably travelled on the London and South Western Railway (L & S.W.R.) from Hammersmith to Barnes, alighting at Barnes station, on Barnes Common. The station at Barnes Bridge would not open until 1916. The team probably then took an omnibus from the station to the White Hart Inn to get changed for the match.

Chapter 19: 'Who Let the Dogs Out?'

Match 8: BARNES v. HAMPSTEAD HEATHENS
FOOTBALL ASSOCIATION CHALLENGE CUP
SECOND TIE - REPLAY
Saturday 6th January 1872
The Limes Field, Barnes
Attendance: ? (Kick-Off : 3.15 p.m.)

It was the first Saturday of the New Year 1872 and the first opportunity for Barnes and the Hampstead Heathens to replay their tied FA Challenge Cup match. This would be the first-ever F.A Cup replay.

Again, the four pairs of brothers would be taking to the field. The Westons & Hightons for Barnes and the Tathams & Leaches for Hampstead Heathens.

It was a damp day and a deluge of rain had fallen during most of the morning. This was no deterrent to either team although only ten Heathens turned up. It was also no deterrent to Ebenezer Cobb Morley's Beagles who went out on a good chase across Putney Heath prior to the match.

THE BARNES BEAGLES.

'These clever beagles, which were formerly owned by Mr. E. C. Morley, of Barnes, who latterly very liberally gave them to the Barnes Football Club, with whose members the pack has been so long associated, held an afternoon meet last Saturday from the Green Man, on Putney Heath, when some capital sport was shown, under the auspices of Mr. J. Powell huntsman, and Messrs. G. B. Yapp and W. Highton as whips. … The run was a most enjoyable one, and the field would have been much larger had not the club been engaged playing an important match the same afternoon.'

(The Sportsman 9th January 1872.)

Ebenezer Cobb Morley rides his horse along the River Thames, close to his home on 'The Terrace' in Barnes.

THE IMPORTANT MATCH

Barnes, having won the toss, selected the upper goal, and play commenced at a quarter past three o'clock. The Heathens, as in the first match, mustered one less than their opponents. Until half time no advantage was gained by either party, though once the Hampstead goal was seriously imperilled by a fine general rush of the Barnes eleven. After change of ends, however, Barnes had the worst of the fight, and, after several ineffectual attempts the Heathens, just at last before time, secured a goal through a good kick from the foot of G.P. Leach. The Heathens thus won by one goal to none, and Barnes were consequently removed from further competition for the cup. For Barnes C. Warren and E. T. Weston played in fine style throughout, being always on the ball; while for the Heathens R. Barker at the side. and .R. B. Michell in the centre, were in great form : and the kicking of S. R. Tatham was as usual noticeable for judgement and accuracy. (The Field – January 13ᵗʰ 1872)

So, the four Heathen brothers were through to the next round of the Cup but unfortunately, the four brothers from Barnes had to go back to the sport of rowing and feeding their beagles.

BARNES v. HAMPSTEAD HEATHENS
FOOTBALL ASSOCIATION CHALLENGE CUP
SECOND TIE - REPLAY

Saturday 6th January 1872
The Limes Field, Barnes,
Attendance: ? (Kick-Off : 3.15 p.m.)

BARNES FC (0)	HAMPSTEAD HEATHENS (1)
Blue & white striped shirts and socks, white shorts.	White with blue binding, blue cap.
Edward T. Weston (capt.)	J. Percival Tatham (capt.)
Percy Weston	Sherman R. Tatham
J. Graham	R. Barker
A. Adams	A. Bird
Arthur Dunnage	Charles B Dimond
H. Ellis	Alling M.S. Erskine
Alfred C. Highton	George P. Leach
Edward C. Highton	A. Leach
Charles Ommanney	James Marshall
Henry Soley	R. B. Michell
C. Warren	

Goalscorer :
Hampstead Heathens: George P. Leach   (1)

Chapter 20: 'A Royal Hitch for Hitchin'
Match 9: Royal Engineers versus Hitchin
FA Cup Second Ties
Thursday 14th December 1871
Rearranged : Wednesday 10th January 1872
(Kick-Off 3.00 p.m.)

THE ILLNESS OF THE PRINCE OF WALES

The country was in shock. Albert, the Prince of Wales, Queen Victoria's son and heir to the throne, was seriously ill and undergoing treatment at Sandringham. The young Prince had been on a trip to Scotland and upon his return he had visited the seat of Lord Londesborough at Tadcaster, near Scarborough, with Princess Alexandra. It was believed that *'he was most probably near Scarborough, a place where there is much fresh air, but a place also perhaps not more free, than other watering places, from a very bad system of drainage.'*

Prince Albert had been diagnosed with typhoid fever, the same disease that had killed his father, Albert the Good. The seriousness of the illness caused an outpouring of grief across the land as the worst outcome was expected. To make matters worse, it was announced that Lord Chesterfield, who was visiting Scarborough along with the Prince, had just passed away with the same disease. The doctor's reports from Sandringham were given by the hour and on Tuesday 12th December there was the hint of some good news.

The Daily News refers with satisfaction to the fact that the Prince was able to take a glass of Burton ale, drinking it with relish, and resorted to the ale again twice within a few hours; but there has been no sleep, and the graver symptoms do not relax.. (Huddersfield Chronicle – 16th December 1871)

Posters announcing the details of the Prince's progress were put up daily on walls all over London and thousands of citizens flocked into the streets to read them. In the provincial towns, plans were made for the cancellation of the Christmas festivities should things take a turn for the worst.

The Royal Engineers and Hitchin had agreed that their FA Cup second tie should take place on Thursday 14th December 1871 at a neutral ground, the Kennington Oval. The Oval was equidistant from the two clubs' bases in Kent **and** Hertfordshire. However, with the gravity of the news coming through concerning His Royal Highness' health, the match was postponed. The sporting press made the following announcements:

ROYAL ENGINEERS v. HITCHIN POSTPONED

Several matches have been postponed in consequence of the critical condition of His Royal Highness Prince of Wales, and amongst others that were fixed for to-morrow between St. Bartholomew's and University Hospitals, the Prince being president of the former. The decision of the tie between the Royal Engineers and the Hitchin Club, for the Association Challenge Cup, which was fixed for yesterday, at The Oval, has likewise been put off. There are a great many matches on paper for to-morrow, but the majority of them, I imagine, will not be played. It would be a most painful contradiction to affect to share the public grief and at the same time to seek the pleasures afforded by football.
(Sportsman 16th December 1871.)

***

The spirit of Loyalty to the Throne which, despite all the ranting of Odgerses and Dilkes really prevails throughout the whole of the Queen's dominions was never more demonstratively shown than during the severe illness of the Prince of Wales. Closed theatres, meetings of the utmost importance abandoned for the time, and last, but not least, football matches postponed, marked the absorbing interest the people took in their Sovereign's health.

The Royal Engineers were to have played their tie for the Association Cup with the Barnes (newspaper error: Hitchin) Club on Thursday last, but in the face of the then alarming accounts from Sandringham was put off until a later date. (Sporting Life 20th December 1871.)

It was a shame that the match could not have been brought forward by two days to Saturday 16th when the other two second ties took place as there had obviously been a subsequent improvement in the Prince's health to allow these matches to go ahead. The Wanderers were preoccupied with their match against Clapham Rover on Clapham Common, so presumably the Kennington Oval would still have been free. Maybe there were other issues at play here, not least the ability to communicate between Chatham in Kent and Hitchin in Hertfordshire and maybe a hasty rearrangement of the fixture was not possible. Whatever the reason the match was put off until the New Year and a new date agreed for Wednesday 10th January 1872.

Quite why the members of Hitchin Club agreed to a midweek fixture is uncertain. They normally played on Saturdays and a midweek fixture would mean taking time off work for most of them whereas the Royal Engineers would be able to sanction leave for the whole team of soldiers from Brompton Barracks. Maybe the Hitchinites were in awe of the almighty Sappers, (i) as they were famously known, and bowed to their superiority in the world of Association football.

The Royal Engineers looked impressive as they marched away from their barracks, along Military Road and down Railway Street, to Chatham train station. The soldiers were dressed fully in their red tunics with gold braid and buttons, blue trousers with red stripes and blue caps. As well as the team, a number of senior officers connected with the team were making the journey down to the Kennington Oval to offer their support. They were going to catch the 11.40 a.m. train into Waterloo on the London, Chatham and Dover Railway. (LCDR).

The Royal Engineers side circa 1871-72

The LCDR was built in 1859 and its completion allowed the Corps of the Royal Engineers to move from their base at the Royal Arsenal in Woolwich out to the Brompton Barracks, the strategic location for the protection of the historic dockyard at Chatham. The railway had a chequered history and from its inception it was competing along parallel lines with the South Eastern Railway. The company was formed by Samuel Morton Peto and Edward Ladd Betts in partnership with a Thomas Crampton. It was a partnership made in blood as well as Edward Betts had married Morton Peto's sister, Ann. In August 1847, the couple gave birth to a third child, a son, to be named Morton Peto Betts, in honour of the wife's family. Morton was to be educated at Harrow School and was in the Headmaster's House.

It was around this time during the 1860s the Peto Betts company overstretched itself whilst extending the LCDR from London Bridge into Victoria. This led to a refinancing of its activities and the company issued some questionable shares and debentures that were designed to get round the finance laws of the time. Unfortunately, the hindrance of the company's overseas activities by war and a subsequent rush on its bank lead to its insolvency in 1866 and the partners' reputations were ruined. Luckily, the eighteen-year-old Morton Peto had finished his education and he left Harrow school in the summer of 1865 and went onto college at Cambridge. His father, unfortunately, soon fell into ill-health and in 1871 he was sent to Egypt where he subsequently died in Aswan on Sunday 21st January 1872, the day after his son was due to play for the Wanderers in a Third Round FA Cup tie against Crystal Palace.

The Royal Engineers were well aware of the Peto Betts family as the company had built the Grand Crimean Central Railway which had been instrumental in enabling the Sappers to get supplies and equipment to the siege of Sebastopol in the Crimean War. In fact, that very morning the Sappers had left Brompton Barracks under the shadow of the Crimean War memorial arch and gates. The memorial arch had been built outside the barracks to commemorate every officer and soldier of the Royal Engineers who had fallen in the war with Russia between 1854-56. This wouldn't be the last time that the Sappers would come across the Peto Betts family!

Meanwhile in Hitchin there had been a frantic effort to get a side together. As suspected, it being a weekday, most of the team which had performed admirably against Crystal Palace were unavailable

198

for a midweek match. Only two of the original line-up, William Hill (who would have bet on that?) and Ernest Woodgate, would play in today's game. The fabulous Baker brothers, George and Henry, were obviously tied up with military duties, given their roles as second lieutenants in the Hertfordshire militia. The two Reverends, William Hazlerigg and Charles Baker, must have been occupied with affairs of the cloth. Even the stalwarts of the club, William Tindall Lucas and Francis Shillitoe, were conspicuous by their absence. Somehow the Hitchinites managed to scratch around and get a list of eleven players to send into the Football Association. The new side consisted of relatives and players with some connection with the club. Thomas Mainwaring conscripted his brother Harry (ii) into the side and William Tindall Lucas asked his seventeen-year-old younger brother Francis (iii) to step in and take his place. Two players with connections to the local side, St. Albans Pilgrims, Henry Crow and T. Mackenzie (iv) were also included in the starting eleven. Finally, an Alfred Bailey and an Arthur Dawson, seemed to have been recruited from the street corners of the Hertfordshire town.

And so, the makeshift team headed to London on a grey and miserable January morning. They caught the Great Northern Railway train from Hitchin station into Kings Cross and then took the Metropolitan Line down to Vauxhall. As they headed into the depths of the steamy and eerie Underground, the darkness of the platform stations engulfed them. A few of the players had heard of the recently published book 'A Journey to the Centre of the Earth' by Jules Verne (1871) and were expecting to bump into a few prehistoric dinosaurs and reptiles. Mind you they did come across a few ape-like men as they got on the arriving train to The Oval. Something needed to be done to brighten up the whole of the Underground. As usual , Stella 'The Woman About Town' had her own views on how this could be accomplished.

'A brilliant idea struck me as I was travelling by Underground from King's Cross to Portland Road the other day, doing my 'sixpenny worth of sewer', as someone has called it. I thought, quite suddenly, as we were rattling along through the seemingly interminable tunnel all along the Euston Road, what a waste of space it was to leave those miles of walls passed unused. Why shouldn't they be turned to advertising account? Because they are dark and black, you say perhaps, and all the art of Willing and Co. would be thrown away. But my idea was brilliant in the fullest meaning of the word. Let the advertisements

As the players exited the Vauxhall Underground station the weather seemed to have got worse and a thick fog had descended on the capital. As they made the short walk up to the Kennington Oval the youngster, Francis Lucas, piped up:

"I've never been to London, and when I finally get an opportunity, I can't see any of its supposed wonders!"

It was true. As they walked down Harleyford Street and approached the impressive Kennington Oval ground, they could just make out the flag of the Surrey County Cricket Club fluttering on top the flagstaff outside the main entrance. Behind it stood two grey oblong shapes, one being the magnificent Oval pavilion and the other, the Racket Court shrouded in the fog. The players entered the pavilion and looked out onto the extensive cricket ground. The two famous gas-holders at the far end of the ground were nowhere to be seen. In fact, you could just about make out the flags and the two posts and the tape of the goal at the Harleyford Street end and that was it. To make matters worse, the Hitchinites soon realised they numbered only eight in total. Cecil Frederick Reid, the captain, hadn't made it along with William Foster and W. Hickes.

"We're in for a right thrashing today," grumbled Ernie Woodgate. "Whoever agreed to this midweek fixture needs to pay a visit to Doctor Palmer. (v) How are we going to take on the might of the Royal Engineers, one of the best teams in the land, with only eight players and no captain to boot?"
"Well, we can't back down now, can we? Have you seen the crowd that's paying to come into the ground? We have the honour of Hitchin and our football club to uphold and we must play our

best. Who knows, maybe they'll be confused in all this fog and think we have eleven players!"

William Hill was forever an optimist but even with the best will in the world, nobody could foresee anything but a convincing win for the Royal Engineers.

"So, who's going to be captain? We need somebody to go up for the coin toss and choose ends or kick-off. At least that's something we might win!"

"Let me do it, William., piped up the young Francis Lucas. "It would be an honour for me to lead out the side and something I can tell the family when we get back to Hitchin."

Nobody called William Hill, 'Bill Hill', it just didn't sit well with the young farmer and maltster. The Hill family lived next door to the Lucas's on Tilehouse Street in Hitchin and William had known Francis since he was a very young lad and he'd watched him grow up to be a very confident young man.

"Alright Francis, if the others are in agreement, you can have the honour of leading us out."

To be fair, the Royal Engineers were slightly inconvenienced as well today as they would be playing without their back pairing of Alfie Goodwyn and George Addison. Both of these experienced players had been instructed to remain at Brompton Barracks because of military duties. Their places were taken by two young Sappers, Henry Clarke and Charles Sherrard, both of whom would be making their debuts for the Sappers team.

The two sides looked resplendent as they walked out onto The Oval pitch to a warm smattering of applause from the crowd. The eight Hitchin players looked elegant in their black and magenta shirts and the Royal Engineers looked imperious, as an army regiment should do, in their blue and red hooped shirts and matching nightcaps. (vi)

The young Francis Henry Lucas met the 33-year-old Captain William Merriman out in the centre of the pitch. The difference in age and experience between the two men was clearly evident to the onlooking crowd as the two captains shook hands. The choice of ends fell to the young Francis and he was under instruction to play

201

with the slight wind behind them. The Hitchinites needed all the help they could get and they kicked off from the Pavilion End towards the two gasometers which they could now make out in the gloom beyond them.

It wasn't long before the quality of the Royal Engineers team began to shine through. Apart from their superiority in numbers, the Sappers outweighed the Hertfordshire side in terms of their strength, weight and style of play. The men from Chatham had developed a style of play based on their strengths of working as a team when out on manoeuvres with the Army. As well as the dribbling and rushing techniques used by most Association sides, the Sappers passed the ball between themselves in a style that would become to be known as 'combination' play. The inexperienced, makeshift Hitchin side had not come across this before and with only eight men in the field, the Royal Engineers ran rings around them.

Within minutes Henry Renny-Tailyour had scored a goal for the Engineers. Renny-Tailyour was an experienced player and as well as being an excellent dribbler of the ball, he also possessed a fierce accurate shot. Although he was born in India, he came from a Scottish background and his footballing talents had not gone unnoticed. He had made an appearance in the fourth unofficial international between England and Scotland on the 18th November 1871, outpacing the English defence and scoring the only goal for the Scots, in a narrow 2-1 defeat.

In accordance with the rules, the teams changed ends and the Hitchinites were now playing into the breeze. As soon as they received the ball, the eight men found themselves surrounded by opposition players. This unnerved the Hitchin team and under pressure a misplaced back pass was seized upon by Henry Renny-Tailyour and he coolly slotted the ball past the advancing Hitchin goalkeeper. Two-nil to The Sappers.

Ends were changed again and although the eight men of Hitchin now had the assistance of the wind, this was not of much use if you didn't have the ball. The young army side was well drilled in the differing skills needed to play sport and they had all participated in playing cricket, rugby and football at the Royal Military Academy in Woolwich. Hence, they all had an eye for the ball and could throw and catch well. Suddenly a desperate clearance from the Hitchin lines went out of play. The ball was quickly recovered and the resultant 'long throw' from Francis Marindin sailed over the

Hitchin 'backs' and landed at the feet of Henry Rich. Henry was one of the fastest forwards on the pitch and within seconds he whizzed past the Hitchin backs and the ball flew under the tape. It was now 3-0 to the Royal Engineers and this was turning into a rout.

Half-time offered no respite for the Hertfordshire men as they were exhausted already and were not looking forward to the next forty-five minutes. Shortly after the restart a fourth goal was scored and with the thick fog and overcast conditions the light was awful. A fifth goal came for the Royal Engineers with a change of tactics. George Barker, who was playing at the back, saw an opportunity to get the ball forward quickly and behind the tiring Hitchin defence. His long punt forward found Adam Bogle who took the ball forward and collided with the Hitchin goalkeeper. The ball spilled out from between them and it fell to none other than Henry Renny-Tailyour, who steadied himself in readiness for his shot. Two of Hitchin's backs, sensing the danger, dashed to protect their goal line but it was too late. Henry Renny-Tailyour wasn't going to miss a golden opportunity like this and his accurate shot passed between the posts and the flailing Hitchin defenders. By now an hour's play had passed and it was almost pitch black as darkness engulfed the Kennington Oval ground. The two captains conferred and it was agreed that a halt should be called to proceedings. The Hitchin side had battled admirably, in particular the young Francis Lucas and his neighbour William Hill.

Would this have been the result if Hitchin had been able to field a full-strength team against the Sappers? We will never know. What we do know is that the Hitchin side had surprised the mighty Crystal Palace team and who knows if the Prince of Wales had not taken ill, maybe John Pardoe's Hitchin team could have progressed to the final.

ROYAL ENGINEERS v. HITCHIN
FOOTBALL ASSOCIATION CHALLENGE CUP
SECOND TIE
Wednesday 10th January 1872
Kennington Oval, London
Attendance: ? (Kick-Off : 3.00 p.m.)

ROYAL ENGINEERS (5)	HITCHIN FC (0)
Jersey, nightcap and stockings, blue & red hooped shirts	Black and magenta hooped shirts and socks, white shorts.
Capt. William Merriman (c.)	Francis H. Lucas (c.)
Capt. Francis A. Marindin	William Hill
Lt. Adam Bogle	H. Mainwaring
Lt. George Barker	H. O. Crow
Lt. Henry Clarke.	Ernest Woodgate
Lt. William St. George Ord	T. McKenzie
Lt. Hugh Mitchell	Alfred Bailey
Lt. Henry B. Rich	Arthur W. Dawson.
Lt. Charles W. Sherrard	Cecil F. Reid **ABSENT**
Lt. Henry Renny-Tailyour	W. Hickes **ABSENT**
Lt. Charles T. Carter	William Foster **ABSENT**

Goalscorers: Royal Engineers
Henry Renny-Tailyour   (3)
Henry Rich   (1)
???   (1)

Author's Notes:

(i) The definition of a Sapper is a soldier who is responsible for military engineering duties such as building and repairing roads, bridges and airfields. Also, the laying and clearing of mines and the preparation of military defences in the field.

(ii) The match report indicated that a H. Mainwaring played in this match rather than Thomas Charles Mainwaring who played in the first tie. Thomas did have a brother named Harry Edward Mainwaring and it is assumed he took his brother's place.

(iii) The match reports of the day are confusing with regard to the Lucas family. The Field newspaper for the 13th January 1872 shows incorrectly that a W. F. Lucas played (not W. T. Lucas), whilst in The Sportsman on the same day reported a F. H. Lucas 'played well'. Match reports notoriously got players' names wrong and in particular their initials. Given the makeshift nature of the Hitchin side and the fact that Charles W. Alcock's newspaper 'The Sportsman' tended to be more accurate, I have assumed that William Tindall Lucas' young brother, Francis Henry, did step up and captain the Hitchin side that day.

(iv) Two new recruits for the Hitchin team were H. O. Crow and T. Mckenzie. This can only have been the Reverend Henry Oswald Crow of St. Alban Pilgrims who actually would play against Hitchin in a future game. Henry had a Pilgrims team mate, an H. McKenzie, and maybe T. McKenzie was one and the same person or a close relation.

(v) Doctor William Palmer was a notorious Victorian doctor who was found guilty of killing members of his family and a close friend to gain access to their life assurance pay-outs. He was known as the Rugeley Poisoner or the Prince of Poisoners for his dastardly deeds.

(vi) A number of teams still wore caps while playing football in the Victorian era. It was a legacy of the need to identify players, prior to the manufacture of football jerseys. Receiving a 'cap' to play for your side is still in existence in the game today and 'caps' are awarded to players who take to the field for their national side.

Draw for the Third Ties

THE ASSOCIATION CHALLENGE CUP
(Tuesday 9th January 1872)

THIRD TIES

Wanderers play Crystal Palace Club

Royal Engineers play Hampstead Heathens.

Queen's Park Club, Glasgow

According to the provisions made for provincial clubs, Queen's Park is exempted from competition until the next drawing.

The Sportsman – Saturday 13th January 1872

The initial draw for the third ties made on or just before the 9th January 1872 still showed Hitchin or the Royal Engineers to play Hampstead Heathens as their match was to be played on the following day, Wednesday 10th January 1872. By Saturday 13th January the teams in the third ties, as above, were known.

Chapter 21: 'Cuthbert John Ottaway, I Presume?'

Match 10: Wanderers versus Crystal Palace
FA Cup Third Ties
Saturday 20th January 1872
(Kick-Off 3.15 p.m.)

Doctor David Livingstone was a Scottish physician and a renowned explorer of deepest Africa. He was obsessed with trying to solve the age-old mystery of the source of the Nile. It's discovery, he believed, would bring him fame and the necessary power to abolish the East African slave trade. In 1866 Livingstone went missing and eventually in 1869 the New York Herald sent Henry Morton Stanley out to Africa to find him. He found Livingstone in the town of Ujiji on the shores of Lake Tanganyika on 10th November 1871, greeting him with the now famous words "Doctor Livingstone, I Presume?" Livingstone responded, "Yes, I feel thankful that I am here to welcome you."

The same quote could have been used when Cuthbert John Ottaway appeared on Clapham Common, two months later, sporting the blue and white hooped kit of Crystal Palace. Surely Charles William Alcock and Douglas Allport knew that Cuthbert had already played in the competition for Marlow in their first tie against Maidenhead. Charles' newspaper, The Sportsman, had reported on the match so it could easily have been checked. Also, both of these gentlemen, along with Charles W. Stephenson and Morton Peto Betts, were at the FA Committee meeting that had approved the rules for the Challenge Cup and Rule 4 was quite specific:

Rule 4: No individual shall be allowed to play for more than one competing Club, but the members of each representative team may be changed during the series of matches, if thought necessary.

So, why would these influential figures in the world of Association football allow their own rule to be blatantly broken by permitting a cup-tied player to take part in today's match? Was there some kind of collusion going on? After all, today's Wanderers team was to feature no fewer than five players from the scratched Harrow Chequers team in Morton Peto Betts, William Parry Crake, Gilbert George Kennedy, Edward Elliott and Alfred Horace Thornton.

Crystal Palace were also fielding their strongest side to date, as along with Cuthbert Ottaway, (i) they had drafted in Frederick Chappell and Philip Rouquette. Frederick Chappell (ii) was at Oxford University with Cuthbert and had already played for Scotland in the third unofficial match, a 1-1 draw on the 25th February 1871, under the pseudonym of Frederick Maclean. Philip Rouquette came from the Forest Club and had been instrumental in their reincarnation in 1868. Charles Alcock would also have known that these three players weren't regulars in the Crystal Palace side. Charles had already played for the Palace team three times this season and against them once, as recently as the 25th November 1871, in a game at The Oval which featured none other than a 22-year-old W. G. Grace playing for the Wanderers.

A young Cuthbert Ottaway at Oxford showing off his rackets trophies.

So, was there some collusion between the FA Officials to relax the rules for this game, given the crowd reported at Clapham Common that day numbered 2,000 and the Football Association would want to showcase this match with the most skilful players available? Surely not! Heaven forbid!

As it was, the two captains had agreed on the neutral ground of Clapham Common for this important match. Douglas Allport would not have wanted the Wanderers to have had the advantage of a home crowd at The Oval and besides, all future games in the FA Cup would have to be played here according to the rules of the competition. Charles Alcock may well have learned of the small pitch that the Maidenhead Club had encountered when visiting Crystal Palace and may have wished to avoid any similar upset. Clapham Common was the perfect location and equidistant between the homes of the two sets of players, involving just a short train ride for both.

The clash of these two titans, both founding members of the Football Association, had generated great interest all over the Capital and the crowd of 2,000 had greatly exceeded expectations. Upon arriving on the Common, the players had found the upper end of the ground festooned with horses and carriages of all types. Given the time of year, people were arriving in covered Hansom cabs or on horse-drawn omnibuses. It seemed that all of London society wanted to witness this historic competitive match and they were all dressed in their finest winter attire. The ladies wore their finest wool and velvet cloaks, complete with a pair of hand muffs, which were sure to contain a ceramic hand warmer to keep their fingers warm during the match. The gentlemen wore their long Ulster coats, top hats and knee-length boots. Not everyone found the fashions of the day practical. On this very day, Stella 'The Woman About Town' wrote in this morning's Sporting Times:

'Some very sensible man has been writing once more to ask why he and his fellows dress in a way that involves torture to every part of his body. Talk about women's fashions, indeed, women never choose things so ugly and inconvenient as you men. Look at the chimney-pot hat, that torments the head it does not keep warm, and the face it protects from neither sun nor rain. Look at the terrible boots you squeeze your poor feet into; just think of the torture your tight collars and starched shirt-fronts involve. Why do you do it? Is there no man brave enough to dress comfortably; to defy paltry public opinion; and cease to be the slaves of senseless fashion? Let you men do this, and you will be in a much better position to rate us women on our folly and extravagance. Jump upon your chimney pots, throw away your starch-stiffened linen; burn your ugly, heavy boots; cut up your hideous 'Ulsters' into blankets; abandon for ever the utterly useless waistcoat; and relegate the perky 'cutaway' coats of the period to the limbs of leather stocks and trouser straps; and then talk to women about our bodices

and Grecian bends, and high-heeled boots, and chignons. But while your own eyes are full of big beams, you had better not try to extract the scaffolding-poles out of ours.' Sporting Times (20th January 1872)

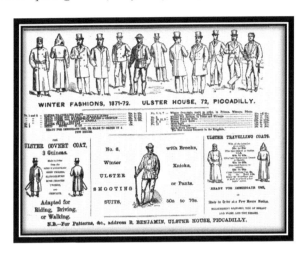

Winter fashions 1871-2 – Men's Ulster overcoats.

Given the size of the crowd, people were stood five deep, all around the pitch, and jostling to get a decent view of the action. It took some time to get them all settled and it was no surprise that the game didn't kick-off until 3.15 p.m. It would now be dark when 'time' was called and there would be no possibility of any extra time should it be needed. This game would show the tactics which were now being developed in the game as Crystal Palace deployed two backs (as opposed to one) and a half-back to protect their goalkeeper from the marauding Wanderers forwards. It also showed that the position of goalkeeper was still pretty fluid as Charles W. Stephenson, the Wanderers goalkeeper, had the honour of having the first disallowed FA Cup goal. Guess what? The goal was disallowed for handling!

THE ASSOCIATION CHALLENGE CUP.
WANDERERS V. CRYSTAL PALACE CLUB

On Saturday last this match, one of the third ties in the competition for the above cup, was played on Clapham Common, the ground having been kindly lent for the use of the contending clubs by the Clapham Rovers. The Wanderers were hardly so well represented as they might have been, while the Crystal Palace captain had collected an exceptionally strong team, and, by adhering throughout to defensive tactics, succeeded in averting the defeat that was generally anticipated for his side. At quarter past three o'clock, the ball was kicked off on behalf of the Crystal Palace, who had lost the toss, and were reduced to occupy the lower portion of the ground, although to compensate for this disadvantage, they had the assistance of a slight breeze.

The backs on either side were Douglas Allport (half-back), Alfred J. Heath and Philip G. Rouquette (back), and Alexander Morten (goalkeeper), for the Crystal Palace; A. C. Thompson (half-back), E. Lubbock (back), and C. W. Stephenson (goal keeper) for the Wanderers.

For the first quarter-of-an-hour the Wanderers closely besieged their opponents and Charles W. Alcock and Alexander G. Bonsor each made an excellent try at goal, that by the former just passing over instead of under the tape. In this way the game continued until shortly before half time, when the Crystal Palace forwards, conspicuous among whom were Armitage, Chenery, and Lloyd, made several well executed rushes, but the backs of the Wanderers were fully equal to the attack and the call of time arrived without the achievement of a goal by either side. Consequently, ends were changed but there was little alteration in the aspect of affairs, as despite the well-concerted play of the Palace forwards, they were unable to keep their adversaries away from the neighbourhood of their goal.

Shortly before the end of the game, Charles W. Stephenson, after having just previously threatened the goal, absolutely succeeded in landing the ball between the Crystal Palace posts; but the umpires decided that the handling rule had been infringed, and the claim of the Wanderers was not admitted. After this the Wanderers worked with redoubled vigour, but their efforts were unsuccessful, and time was called at a quarter to five o'clock, leaving the match drawn, without any score to either club. With the exception of their backs, who were in irreproachable form throughout, the Wanderers showed the disinclination to help each other, that is the only weak point in their play, and this should certainly be remedied. The Crystal Palace forwards were one and all most energetic from first to last; but they hardly showed the pace of their opponents and individually their play was much inferior. The Field (27th January 1872)

And so, with the match ending in a scoreless draw and with no opportunity of any extra time, it was up to the FA Committee to determine whether the game would need to be replayed.

WANDERERS v. CRYSTAL PALACE
FOOTBALL ASSOCIATION CHALLENGE CUP
THIRD TIE

Saturday 20th January 1872
Clapham Common,
Attendance: 2,000 (Kick-Off : 3.15 p.m.)

WANDERERS (0)	CRYSTAL PALACE (0)
Orange, violet and black shirt and stockings, white shorts	Blue & white hooped shirts and socks, blue serge shorts
Charles W. Alcock (capt)	Douglas Allport (captain)
Charles W. Stephenson (gk)	Alexander Morten (gk)
Edgar Lubbock	Alfred J. Heath
Morton Peto Betts	William Bouch
Alexander G. Bonsor	Charles E. Smith
William P. Crake	Charles C. Armitage
Thomas C. Hooman	Alfred H. Lloyd
Albert C. Thompson	Charles J. Chenery
Alfred H. Thornton	Cuthbert J. Ottaway
Gilbert G. Kennedy	Frederick P. Chappell
Edward H. M. Elliott	Philip H. G. Rouquette

Goalscorers:

Author's Notes:

(i) As we know, the twenty-two-year-old Cuthbert John Ottaway excelled at sports. He would go on to achieve a level of athletic performance at 'Blue' level in five sports at Oxford University; cricket, rackets, real tennis, athletics and Association football. Moreover, he would become the first recognised captain of the England football team in the first official international against Scotland played at Hamilton Crescent, Partick in Glasgow on the 30th November 1872. Cuthbert was educated at Eton School and excelled at sports at an early age. He would have played the Eton 'Wall Game' in the courtyards of the school and developed his eye for the ball. He would also have played the 'Field Game' which was more akin to Association football, where passing was forbidden and dribbling was the key. He also excelled at cricket and at the age of nineteen he was chosen to play for the Kent County Cricket Club against the M.C.C. in August 1869. He scored a promising 51 in the first innings but was out for a duck in the second. On both occasions he was bowled by one W. G. Grace.

(ii) Frederick Chappell was educated at Marlborough before going up to Oxford University, where he was a member of Brasenose College. Although he went on to represent the university, he did not win a 'blue'. Frederick also took to the field alongside Cuthbert in the first official international against Scotland.

Frederick Chappell – drafted into the Crystal Palace FA Cup side

Chapter 22: 'Heathens Sapped of Strength'

Match 11: Royal Engineers v. Hampstead Heathens
FA Cup Third Ties
Saturday 27th January 1872
(Kick-Off 3.00 p.m.)

The Crimean War Memorial and Gates – Brompton Barracks, Chatham

I stood in front of the imposing Crimean War Memorial Arch and Gates at the entrance to the Brompton Barracks. On the very top parapet of the central arch, I could make out the inscription:

THE CORPS OF ROYAL ENGINEERS
TO THEIR COMRADES WHO FELL
IN THE WAR WITH RUSSIA MDCCCLIV

Beneath this inscription is a banner, supported by two angels joined together by intricate laurel work, bearing the mottos of the Royal Engineers:

QUO FAS ET GLORIA DUCUNT
(Where Right and Glory Lead)

UBIQUE
(Everywhere)

On each column of the central arch and the two supporting side gates are transcribed the names of the battles fought in Russia between 1853-56 and the names of the 274 soldiers who fell during the conflict:

KERTCH, TCHERNAIA, SEBASTOPOL, BALACLAVA, ALMA, INKERMAN

Today I had an appointment with Major Glen Lishman. As well as being a Major in the Royal Engineers, Glen is currently the Head of Football for the army side and has been involved in the team for the past 15 years. It was my honour to visit the Brompton Barracks and to try and locate the site of today's match, played 150 years ago, on the area of ground which is known as Chatham Lines.

I tried to imagine the Hampstead Heathens team walking up to the gates of the barracks rather in awe of their surroundings. Approaching the Memorial Arch they would have been greeted by two Royal Engineers sentries, immaculately dressed in their red & black uniforms and armed with rifles. I wondered what their response would have been to:

"Halt! Who goes there? Friend or foe?"

"Erm, we've come to play a game of football. Can you let us in, please?"

Today's third tie was to be played on Chatham Lines which had been constructed in 1755 as a defensive fortification to protect the landward side of Chatham Dockyard against any potential attacks from the French in the Seven Years War fought between 1756-

1763. The Lines were laid out high on a hill overlooking the dockyard and comprised of earth ramparts and ditches enhanced by intermittent bastions to enable defensive fire on the enemy. Given its elevated position the football pitch was notorious for being 'one of the blowiest grounds in all of England.'. (i)

The Hampstead Heathens would need all the wind assistance they could get today and they might need to employ some defensive tactics themselves as again they had turned up short and today they had only nine men. Two of the Heathens must have got lost on their way down from London. The remaining nine probably turned to that famous Hampstead Heathen, the romantic poet John Keats for inspiration:

"I must choose between despair and energy – I choose the latter." - the letters of John Keats.

The Heathens may have to choose both today!

Francis Arthur Marindin looked around at the faces of his young army lieutenants. He would captain the side today as Captain William Merriman was unavailable, as he was making preparations for his wedding to Emily Jane Anna Elizabeth Somerset, in two week's time. Emily, was the daughter of none other than Colonel FitzRoy Molyneux Henry Somerset, also of the Royal Engineers. Francis often stood in as captain and so he was well drilled in his task.

"Right, I want no slacking today just because the opposition are two short. The Hampstead Heathens must be a decent side to have got this far in the competition. They came through after a replay against the Barnes Club, playing with ten men and I want no complacency to seep into our game. We are without Captain William Merriman and Lieutenant Adam Bogle today and I will not tolerate a defeat on my watch. Understood?"

"Yes, sir." they replied in unison.

Secretly, they were quietly confident today as despite losing Merriman and Bogle, they welcomed a few of their stars back into the side who had been missing for the game against Hitchin. Into the side came the two attacking players, Edmund Creswell, the youngest Sapper, nineteen year old Edmond Cotter and at the back the player they could rely on, the dependable Alfie Goodwyn.

ROYAL ENGINEERS V HAMPSTEAD HEATHENS

The above match was played at Chatham on Saturday, January 27th, and resulted in a victory for the Royal Engineers by three goals to none. This was one of the third ties for the Association Challenge Cup. The Heathens at first had to face the Sappers with nine men, and were reinforced halfway through the game by the arrival of one of their two missing members. The ball had not been started any great length of time when, after some spirited play on the part of Lieuts. Rich and Renny-Tailyour, it was taken close in front of the Heathens' goals, and after an exciting scrimmage driven between the posts. The game throughout was hardly fought, but the superior numbers of the sappers told heavily, and before the end of the game they had added two more goals to their score, this winning by three goals to none. For the Heathens, Messrs Barker and S.R. Tatham played up well throughout; whilst for the Royal Engineers, Lieuts. Mitchell and Rich were conspicuous.
(Sportsman – Wednesday 31st January 1872.)

On Saturday, likewise the Hampstead Heathens—the title, I need scarcely say, is reference to locality and not to irreligion—journeyed down by the L. C. and D. to Chatham, where they got well beaten by the Royal Engineers. It was one of the games of the third tie for the Association Challenge Cup, and the victory was gained by three goals. Renny-Tailyour being, as usual, conspicuous for his fine play. He will form one of the Scotch Twenty at Oval on Monday, but more of this presently.(Sportsman Saturday 3rd February 1872)

And so, the Sappers came through unscathed with a comfortable 3-0 victory. Furthermore, Henry Renny-Tailyour, the scorer of five goals so far in the competition and well in the running for the Golden Boot, had also been picked to represent Scotland at rugby! (ii)

ROYAL ENGINEERS v. HAMPSTEAD HEATHENS
FOOTBALL ASSOCIATION CHALLENGE CUP
THIRD TIE

Saturday 27th January 1872
Chatham Lines, Brompton Barracks
Attendance: ?, (Kick-Off : 3.00 p.m.)

ROYAL ENGINEERS (3)	HAMPSTEAD HEATHENS (0)
Jersey, nightcap and stockings, blue & red in horizontal stripes	White with blue binding, blue cap
Ct. Francis Marindin (Capt.)	J. Percival Tatham (capt.)
Lt. George Barker.	Sherman R. Tatham
Lt. William St. George Ord	R. Barker
Lt. Hugh Mitchell	A. Bird
Lt. Henry B. Rich	Charles B Dimond
Lt. Charles W. Sherrard	Alling M.S. Erskine
Lt. Henry Renny-Tailyour	George P. Leach
Lt. Charles T. Carter	H. P. Leach
Lt. Edmund Creswell	H. Latham
Lt. Edmond Cotter	R. B. Michell
Lt. Alfred Goodwyn	

Goalscorers: Royal Engineers
  Henry Renny-Tailyour   (2)
  Hugh Mitchell   (1)

Author's Notes:

(i) Henry Waugh Renny-Tailyour, became the first and only player to represent his country (Scotland) in games played under both Association football and Rugby rules.

- England 2 v. Scotland 1 – Football – Saturday 18th November 1871 (Unofficial international 4)

- England 4 v. Scotland 2 – Football – Saturday 8th March 1873 (Official international 2) Henry Renny-Tailyour scored Scotland's first official international goal in the above match.

- England v. Scotland – Rugby – Monday 5th February 1872

Henry Waugh Renny-Tailyour (c.1890)

(ii)   Possible location of the Outer Lines 'PITCH' next to Brompton Barracks (1) and near the R.E.'s current Number One football pitch. (2)

Draw for the Fourth Ties

THE ASSOCIATION CHALLENGE CUP
(Wednesday 7th February 1872)

FOURTH TIES

The fourth ties in this competition were drawn yesterday (Wednesday), with the following result:

Wanderers v. Queen's Park, Glasgow.

Royal Engineers v. Crystal Palace Club.

According to the rule regulating the final ties, both of these matches will have to be played in London.

Sportsman – Thursday 8th February 1872

On Wednesday 7th February 1872, the FA Committee met to discuss the draw for the fourth ties (semi-finals). The third tie between Crystal Palace and the Wanderers, which had finished scoreless, had still not been replayed so a decision must have been made to allow both teams to progress to the fourth ties. (i) With the inclusion of Queen's Park and the victorious Royal Engineers the draw would now neatly consist of four teams.

The methodology used for the draw will never be known (i) but it does seem a coincidence that the Wanderers and the Queen's Park Club had been trying to organise a match between themselves, at a venue in the north of England such as Carlisle or Newcastle upon Tyne, for the last six months. The match was to be played for a trophy with a value of eleven guineas, or for eleven medals valued at one guinea each. However, Charles Alcock changed his mind and preferred playing two international matches between the countries, one to be held in Edinburgh, the other in London. The Queen's Park Club favoured a club competition (not surprising really as the Scottish team would have been made up of predominantly Queen's Park players anyway) and stuck to their guns. It seemed no side wanted to back down and therefore an amicable solution was that the two sides met in the FA Cup competition. Coincidence or not? You decide.

At the same meeting an FA Sub-Committee was formed to 'select and purchase the new Challenge Cup'. It seems incredulous that the competition was three months old and the design and manufacture of the trophy had still not been finalised four weeks before the final. The Sub-Committee was comprised of three committee members, Charles W. Alcock (Wanderers), Douglas Allport (Crystal Palace) and Alfred Stair (Upton Park).

A week later on 13th February 1872 the Sub-Committee met again. Two designs were submitted for consideration. One from Benson & Co. and the other from Martin, Hall & Co. of Sheffield.

The winning design by the silversmiths Martin, Hall & Co. was 18 inches high, stood on an ebony plinth, held a quart and cost £20. This was the trophy that would be given to the winning team and it was known as the 'Little Tin Idol', as the design featured the small figure of a football player standing proudly on the top of the Cup.

Author's Notes:

(i) The minutes of the FA meeting of the 7th February 1872 stated;

'Letters concerning the drawn match between the Wanderers and Crystal Palace were read from Capt. Marindin, C. W. Stephenson, R. W. Willis, and D. Allport. A discussion took place as to whether this match should be played out, or the Clubs drawn again in the fourth ties. Ultimately, it was decided that the names of the four remaining clubs should be drawn in the usual manner.

Chapter 23: 'A Day for Thanksgiving'
Match 12: Royal Engineers v. Crystal Palace
FA Cup Fourth Ties
Saturday 17th February 1872
(Kick-Off 2.55 p.m.)

Active preparations are being made for the approaching Thanksgiving Service. Within the Cathedral, which is now closed to the public, a large number of workmen are busy erecting the seats, the number of which has been altered from 7,000 to 12,000 even this latter number is trifling in comparison with the applications made for them but, of course, everybody cannot be present. The Houses of Parliament will be strongly represented, and the clergy, both Established and Dissenting, will have tickets distributed amongst them. All along the route which the procession is to take, there is an evident desire to give the Royal party a hearty welcome. Temple Bar is to be decorated from a design by the City architect, and a triumphal arch erected at the bottom of Ludgate Hill. The houses on either side of the Strand, Fleet Street, and Ludgate Hill, will be gay with flags and banners some of them are being repainted expressly for the occasion, and even the Chatham and Dover Company are putting a clean face upon their ugly bridge. Many of the householders, ever mindful of the 'main chance, are already advertising seats in their windows, 'from garret to basement', to view the procession and one enterprising contractor has engaged all the vacant spaces, and is rapidly putting up seats, which will be let at two guineas each. It is now definitively settled that Her Majesty will return by way of the Embankment an arrangement which naturally causes much dissatisfaction. It is not often that her loyal subjects get a glimpse of their loved sovereign, and the journey up Oxford Street would be at least as pleasant as that along the river side. The Committee of the Stock Exchange have ordered the day to be kept us a special holiday and the Banks will be closed by an Order in Council.

The Graphic (Saturday 17th February 1872)

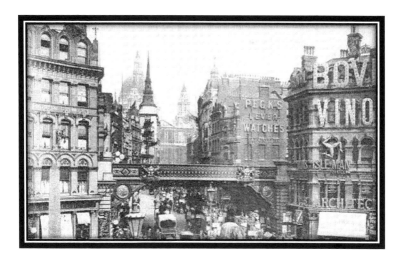

The ugly bridge of the London, Chatham and Dover Railway, at Ludgate Hill where the Royal procession passed on the 27th February 1872.

At the beginning of the month of February 1872 it was announced that His Royal Highness the Prince of Wales had fully recovered from his bout of typhoid fever. Obviously, the three Burton ales had done the trick and a day of Thanksgiving was set for Saturday 27th February 1872, with a procession through London by the Royal Family and a special Thanksgiving Service to be held at St. Paul's Cathedral. All anybody could talk about was the chance to see their sovereign Queen Victoria in person and to give thanks for the return to health of her son, Albert. Football was again relegated to small paragraphs in the Victorian press. Even Stella, our 'Woman About Town', was getting excited about the approaching events.

DETERMINED as I have been not to get excited about the National Thanksgiving, I find that as the day approaches, I am warming up to a high pitch of interest, spite my endeavours to be philosophically calm and careless. You cannot walk from Charing Cross to St. Paul's, as I did today, without getting imbued more or less with the all-pervading topic of the times. Sitting down now calmly I have something very like seats on the brain. Irresistible impulses urge me to rush out with a pocketful of guineas and book places at all the principal points of interest on the route. I want to be at Temple Bar to see the Lord Mayor fall off his horse, and the Sheriffs clinging to the cruppers (i) of

223

their saddles; I feel I must be present at the ceremony inside St Paul's, that I may tell my grandchildren, if I ever have any, about the historical scene; I particularly desire to see the Bible presented to Alexandra in Fleet Street; and come what may, I have taken a vow that I will hear the 30,000 children sing the National Anthem in the Green Park. And yet a week ago I protested I should spend the 27th at the British Museum or in the country. But what with the outward and visible signs of the coming gala, and the glowing accounts that appear every day in the newspaper, I am now concerned I was callous. I am watching the revival of battered old Temple Bar with as much interest as a lady of fashion watches the enamelling of her own face; I have stood by the five minutes together and watched the men picking out the Fleet-street lamp-posts with blue and gold; I exercise quite maternal solicitude over the colossal arch at the bottom of Ludgate Hill; I delight to see Paterfamilias (ii) go stealthily into Messrs; 'Willing's little office and book seats, and then come out blushing as if he had done something he was ashamed of; I feel disgusted when I see how the trumpery 'Echo' has disfigured the railings round the Church of St. Clement Danes by covering them with vulgar show boards; I rejoice in the general washing down and cleaning up that is going on; I try and fancy who are the people that buy the penny daubs (iii) announced to be panoramas of the royal procession which are already on sale; I wonder why the Lord Chamberlain's tickets are bigger than a 'c'rect, card.' I rejoice —in short, I am gone half mad, like all the rest of London, about the great event to come off on the 27th. Sporting Times – (Saturday 24th February 1872.)

The great stand on the site of the Law Courts – Thanksgiving Day

Perhaps, knowing the Thanksgiving Day was on the horizon, the Royal Engineers and the Crystal Palace Club, had arranged their fixture within ten days of the draw for the fourth ties being announced. This match was to played in London, in accordance with Rule 16 of the competition which stated that:

'The ties in the final two drawings for the season 1871-72 shall be decided in London upon a ground which shall be hereafter chosen by the Committee.'

Amazingly, the Committee had chosen the home of Charles Alcock's Wanderers, the Kennington Oval, to host the Fourth Ties and the Final Tie.

***

This was the second occasion that the Royal Engineers had travelled down to the Kennington Oval for an FA Cup game. The first match against Hitchin had been affectd by the illness of the HRH Prince of Wales. This match was engulfed by news of his recovery.

Again the Royal Engineers were to be without Lieutenant Adam Bogle and Captain William Merriman who had a reasonable excuse as he was on his honeymoon. However, the Sappers welcomed back Lieutenants George Addison and Herbert Muirhead. George Addison was the son of a spinner and a Yorkshireman from Bradford. Alongside his team mate, Alfie Goodwyn, they made up one of the best defensive partnerships in the land. One thing was for certain Crystal Palace were going to have to work hard if they were going to penetrate the Sappers defence.

Cystal Palace also fielded a strong side showing their intent. The cup tied Cuthbert Ottaway was playing again, alongisde his fellow student from Oxford University, Fred Chappell. Unfortunately, Douglas Allport and Charles Armitage were playing but carrying injuries received in their last match against Clapham Rovers the previous Saturday. However, this was still going to be a very close game.

Once again the Kennington Oval was packed and another large crowd of around 2,000 swarmed around The Oval pitch vying to see the action. The teams took their positions on the pitch and Douglas Allport and Captain Francis Marindin headed up to the centre circle to make the toss.

Captain Marindin was successful and, as it was a bright and sunny day, he chose to play from the upper end of the ground. This meant the Sappers had a slight breeze behind them but more importantly the oppositon would have the low winter's sun in their faces. This tactic seemed to work and for most of the first 45 minutes the Royal Engineers set siege to the Crystal Palace goal. They in turn were denied by the admirable play of the 'Palatials' backs and the forty-year-old goalkeeper, Alex Morten, was 'toujours prêt' again and made several very fine saves. On the odd occasion that Palace did manage to get the ball forward, some hefty clearances from Philip Rouquette managed to find their way to Cuthbert Ottaway and William Bouch. Both of these fine dribblers each went on a run but they were to find their way blocked by the either Alfie Goodwyn or George Addison. There was no way through. At one point a shot from the Sappers' forwards went just over the Crystal Palace tape but at half-time the match was scoreless and so ends were changed.

Unfortunately, Crystal Palace were not to receive the same assistance from the sun and the wind as the Sappers. It was now 3.40 p.m. and the intensity of the sun was beginning to fade and the wind had dropped. The second-half was a much more even contest with the two Oxford students, Cuthbert Ottaway and Freddie Chappell, making most of the forward moves for Crystal Palace. Again, the Sappers' backs were called upon to do their work and the military men's goal was never really threatened. As the clock ticked down the Palace team tired and given the injuries to two of their key players, it was no surprise that the Sappers made one 'good rush forward and it seemed as though success would at last crown their great efforts.' (iv) But it was to no avail and when time was called the match remained scoreless. The Royal Engineers offered Crystal Palace the chance to play an extra half-an-hour to get a result but the Palatials declined, probably conscious of their players injuries and so the game would have to be replayed.

The reporter from the Field newspaper summed up the Crystal Palace effort by claiming:

'there was too much dribbling and not sufficient 'dash' among the Sydenham players.'

Whatever, the men from Sydenham would be having their own 'Thanksgiving' service today and they were overjoyed that the game had been drawn and they would survive to fight another day.

226

ROYAL ENGINEERS v. CRYSTAL PALACE
FOOTBALL ASSOCIATION CHALLENGE CUP
FOURTH TIE

Saturday 17th February 1872
Kennington Oval, London
Attendance: 2,000 (Kick-Off : 2.55 p.m.)

ROYAL ENGINEERS (0)	CRYSTAL PALACE (0)
Jersey, nightcap and stockings, blue & red hooped shirts	Blue & white hooped shirts and socks, blue serge shorts
Ct. Francis Marindin (Capt.)	Douglas Allport (captain)
Lt. William St. George Ord	Alexander Morten
Lt. Hugh Mitchell	William Bouch
Lt. Henry B. Rich	Charles C. Armitage
Lt. Henry Renny-Tailyour	Alfred H. Lloyd
Lt. Charles T. Carter	Charles J. Chenery
Lt. Edmund W. Creswell	Cuthbert J. Ottaway
Lt. Edmond W. Cotter	Frederick Chappell *
Lt. Alfred G. Goodwyn	Philip G. Rouquette
Lt. George W. Addison	Charles J. Farquhar
Lt. Herbert H. Muirhead	Lawrence H. Neame

The Field newspaper (24th February 1872) still had Frederick Chappell down under the pseudonym used in the England v. Scotland match, Frederick Maclean.

Author's Notes:

(i) A crupper is a piece of tack attached to the back of a saddle and is used on horses to keep a saddle, harness or other equipment from sliding forward.

(ii) Paterfamilias - the male head of a family or household.

(iii) daubs - paintings executed without much skill

(iv) quoted in the match report in 'Bell's Life – Saturday 24th February 1872.'

Chapter 24: 'Enter John Brown and the Scots'

Match 13: Wanderers versus Queen's Park
FA Cup Fourth Ties
Monday 4th March 1872
(Kick-Off 3.40 p.m.)

On the 29th February 1872 an attempt was made on Queen Victoria's life as she returned to Buckingham Palace. Luckily for her the renowned Scot, John Brown her faithful servant, was at her side.

ATTEMPT OR THREAT TO KILL THE QUEEN.

The Queen had taken her usual drive, and was enthusiastically received. On returning to the Palace, when the carriage entered the gates, a youth followed it, and when it drew up at the door, he presented himself first on one side and then on the other, and held a pistol pointed at the Queen. The Queen was not alarmed but screened herself behind the frame of the carriage. The attendants dismounted and secured the youth. The pistol had not been fired, it was possibly not even loaded; it was an old-fashioned flint-lock instrument, and had a piece of red cloth projecting from its muzzle. The fellow had with him a document for the Queen to sign for releasing the Fenian prisoners now in confinement. He was about eighteen or nineteen years of age.

(Illustrated London News - Saturday 2nd March 1872)

The first witness called was John Brown, her Majesty's personal attendant. Nobody but a blind man could have any doubt as to Mr. Brown's nationality long before he opened his mouth,' and the moment he did so the blind would, figuratively speaking, have his eyes opened. His accent is genuine "Aberdeen-waw" Scotch of the most undiluted character; residence among the Southrons has not impaired the breadth of a single vowel, or the fine bickering rattle of a single "r." As he stood in the witness-box in his kilt, one involuntarily thought of Rob Roy among the trousered "bodies" of Glasgow. The national caution was developed in Mr. Brown's replies to some of the questions. He never committed himself to a deliberate "Yes;", it was always "That's quite right." He called the prisoner uniformly 'the boy'. "I gied him a bit of a shove back," said Mr. Brown, before he ran round to the other side of the carriage," and there the Scot laid hold of him again. "I took hold o' him," Mr. Brown proceeded, "with one o' my hauns, and I grippit him with the other by the scruff o the neck."' ' This hold he never relaxed "till half a dizzen had a grip o' him, - grooms, equerries, I kenna how mony there was-so then I thocht it time to gie up." Here Mr. Brown chuckled with a grim jocularity.

(London Daily News - Saturday 2nd March 1872.)

THE ATTACK ON QUEEN VICTORIA IN THE PRIVATE GROUNDS OF BUCKINGHAM PALACE

John Brown 'grippit' Arthur O'Connor by the scruff o' the neck.

***

The following Saturday 2nd March 1872, a group of nine footballers met on platform two of the Queen Street station in Glasgow. They'd probably read about John Brown's exploits in that morning's papers and rightly they would have been proud of their fellow countryman's actions in protecting the Queen. Appropriately, the team were the Queen's Park Football Club and they were about to catch the 8.55 p.m. overnight train on the East Coast Mainline, down to London in order to play their first match in the Football Association Challenge Cup. Ironically the Scottish side had been the first to pay their one guinea subscription to play in the Football Association Challenge Cup and now they would be the last team to take part. Their difficulties in arranging their first and second round ties against Donington School and then a subsequent bye in the third tie (after Donington withdrew from the competition) meant that the men from Glasgow had reached the semi-finals without playing a single game, whereas their opposition today, the Wanderers, had already played two matches. As the reporter in The Sportsman (presumably not Charles Alcock) commented:

'I can hardly understand this arrangement which seems very much like a man entering himself for a billiard handicap, looking on during the majority of heats, and then playing in the final one with a man who has perhaps had to win four of five games with sheer hard work.'
(The Sportsman – 17th February 1872)

The team arrived in London at 9.40 a.m. on the Sunday morning, so at the least the Scots had time to recover from their long train journey. Their Secretary, Mr. David N. Wotherspoon, had sensibly telegraphed Charles Alcock to agree that the date for the match should be fixed for Monday 4th March 1872, kick-off at half past three o'clock in the afternoon. (i) It was very noble for Charles Alcock to agree to play the fixture on the Monday as both himself and Tom Hooman would be playing in an important London v Sheffield game on the Saturday 2nd March and presumably both would be tired from their exertions. Tom Hooman wouldn't make the side for this game against the Scots but the ever-present Charles couldn't miss this opportunity to captain his side in this historic game. Also, it being a Monday, a few other FA Cup regulars would have to miss out because of commitments elsewhere. Two key players that would miss this game were the civil engineer, Morton

231

Peto Betts and Edgar Lubbock, the solicitor, both of whom presumably had work commitments. However, Charles and the Wanderers were never short of players and into the side came Charles Wollaston, an Oxford undergraduate who had only started playing for them in February; Henry Emanuel, who had played one previous game and Henry Stewart who was making his debut.

The other two players who would make up the Queen's Park side were the brothers, Robert and James Smith. Both were already living in London, having played for Queen's Park before moving south in 1868 and 1870 respectively. The two brothers had been instrumental in flying the flag for Scottish Football in London. (ii)

Robert Smith — First Captain and Treasurer of Queen's Park Football Club and his younger brother James.

The Scots weren't without injury problems of their own as their half-back, James J. Thomson, had been injured in a game just a few days before the trip to London and his place was to be taken by William Gibb. William was a forward player rather than a back and therefore the Scots had to reshuffle their side at the last minute. Also, it must be noted that given the lack of teams playing Association football in Scotland at that time, Queen's Park had only played one competitive match that season and that had been five months ago in October 1871. It was a match at home against another Glasgow team called Granville which ended in a one-nil victory to Queen's Park. All other games would have been practice games between the members on a pitch that was hardly deemed

232

suitable for playing sport as the area known as 'Queen's Park' was deemed uneven to walk on, contained hillocks and was overgrown in places and restricted in size. (iii) The one advantage the Scots did have was that they had developed their footballing style of play without any of the prejudices of the public-school game that was prevalent south of the border and their players' skills with the ball would have been developed naturally.

***

In the mid 1860's a group of young men from northern Scotland would gather on Saturday afternoons to socialise and keep fit by playing numerous athletic sports. One of these was the practice of knocking a leather football around one of the spacious parks in Glasgow. The Park they chose was the Queen's Park Recreation Ground to the south of the city and the River Clyde. There were no particular rules and no boundaries to the area of play. It was basic football with 'jumpers for goalposts' played for the love of the game. It is believed the young men joined in a 'kickabout' with some members of the local Y.M.C.A. and soon two-sided games were taking place on the area of the park in front of the imposing Deaf and Dumb Institution on Prospect Hill Road on the east side of Queen's Park (known as the South Side Park).

The Glasgow Deaf and Dumb Institution – circa 1868

233

Gradually their numbers increased and soon plans were afoot to create a football club and, on Tuesday 9th July 1867, a number of gentlemen met at No. 3 Eglington Terrace, Victoria Road, a stone's throw from the main gates leading into Queen's Park and the football club bearing its name was formed. A committee of thirteen members was created with Mr. Mungo Ritchie elected as President, Lewis Black as captain and Robert Smith (our cashier now in London) as Treasurer. The appointed Secretary, William Klingner, was asked to source a set of rules for the club to play football and a copy of the Association Rules duly arrived from the famous cricketer James Lillywhite's shop in London. These were adapted to form the Queen's Park's 'Rules of the Field'.

The Smith brothers (Robert and James) were given the task of procuring balls, posts and flags and these were to be stored next to the chosen pitch in the lodge of the Deaf and Dumb Institution. Next, they had to decide on a kit (uniform) to play in and a reversible red and blue cowl or nightcap was supplied to each member to identify which side they were playing for. The club's first jersey was to be blue in colour and all members were to be in possession of an individual club badge to be worn on the arm to distinguish the colour of their side whilst playing. (iv)

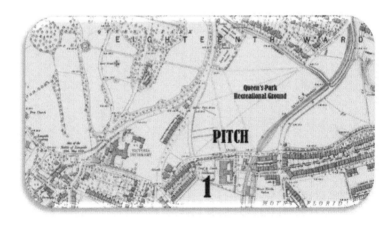

Map showing the location of the Glasgow Deaf and Dumb Institution (1) on the east side of Queen's Park and the place where Scottish Association football started in the mid 1860's.

The Club's first difficulties were finding opponents to play football against. Rugby had taken off in Scotland and there were a few clubs playing to the rugby code. There were two or three in Edinburgh along with the Glasgow Academicals, formed in 1865 and the West of Scotland Club formed a year or so later. As for football clubs these were very scarce in Scotland. After adopting their 'Rules of the Field' the Queen's Park Club received two challenges to play; one from Ayr Football Club and the other from the Thistle Club which had its headquarters on Glasgow Green. Given the cost and difficulties of travel to Ayr, the challenge from the local Thistle club was accepted by the Queen's Park Club and, on the 1st August 1868, they played their first match on the South Side Park, running out two-nil victors.

Other matches in the early days were against provincial sides such as Hamilton Gymnasium and Airdrie. There was another side that played on Glasgow Green and that was Drummond Football Club. Drummond was a team made up of young men from Perthshire who had moved to Glasgow to seek their fortunes. They played in the magnificent colours of Drummond Castle and wore distinctive pale red and green tartan caps.

Coming into the 1871-72 season, Queen's Park had played just eight matches, scored twenty goals and 13 touch downs and had the proud record of not conceding a single goal. Unfortunately, in 1871 they had only been able to arrange that single game against Granville. Charles Alcock's Wanderers team had already played nearly thirty games this season including the two FA Cup matches. It was hardly adequate preparation for the Scots. What Queen's Park did have in their favour was a secret weapon called 'passing'. Richard Robinson, who detailed the club's history on its 50th anniversary, explained the means by which the passing game was developed:

The club... never neglected practice, and this practice was indulged in systematically. Sides were arranged— North v. South of Eglinton Toll, Reds v. Blues, Light v. Heavy Weights, President's Team v. J. Smith's Team (a series of six games), and Clerks v. The Field, etc. In these games the dribbling and passing, which raised the Scottish game to the level of a fine art, were developed. Dribbling was a characteristic of English play, and it was not until very much later that the Southerners came to see that the principles laid down in the Queen's Park method of transference of the ball, accompanied by strong backing up, were those which got the most out of a team. Combination was the chief characteristic of the Queen's Park play.

Charles Alcock would have been well aware of the advantages of 'combination' play as he would have come across it many times in the London versus Sheffield matches and, of course, in the England versus Scotland games where he would no doubt discussed its merits with the Scot, Robert Smith, who was now a FA Committee member representing Queen's Park and Scottish Football. (v) The Royal Engineers also adopted a form of passing in their play and the Wanderers had played them numerous times over the last few seasons. However, the relative success of his teams in these matches probably led him to hold onto the belief that the traditional dribbling game played in the south of England and developed over the years in the public schools was football in its purest sense.

***

It was a bright spring day when Charles stepped out of the front door of Grassendale House on Rosendale Road and made the short walk to the West Dulwich station to catch a train up to the Kennington Oval. He was deep in thought as he sat in the carriage looking out of the window at the open countryside as they sped past Brockwell Hall Park. He'd been thinking all night as to how his team could conquer the Scots. Both a place in the final of his Cup competition and the honour of England was at stake and he could afford no slip ups. He felt his side was strong enough to win, despite the absence of Morton Peto Betts and Edgar Lubbock, and he felt his new recruits would be up to the task ahead. What he didn't know was the individual strengths of the Queen's Park team. He had only ever seen the two Smith brothers play and had no knowledge of the others. They appeared to be quite a young and inexperienced side so surely his wealth of knowledge accumulated over many years of playing against the best sides in England would see them through. Not only that, he had drafted in the debutant, Henry Holmes Stewart, a native Scot born in Kirkcudbrightshire who could act as the translator of the tactics being shouted out by the Queen's Park captain. Surely, he had everything covered?

As the train passed through Herne Hill, he could see the city of London stretching out in front of him. It was not long before he would arrive at his stop at the Camberwell New Road (vi) station.

236

It was then just a short ride in a Hansom cab up to The Oval. Charles had asked his team to arrive early so they could discuss the game ahead. Approaching the ground, he was surprised to see the crowds already entering through the Kennington Oval gates. This game had generated a lot of interest in the Capital and the fact that admission was free had meant a lot of the crowd were arriving early to secure the best viewpoints in the ground. In fact, a lot of the ladies who were entering the stands would be hoping for a repeat of the action seen at the recent England versus Scotland rugby match held just a couple of weeks earlier when a Scotsman lost his troosers!

'TAKING THE BREEKS AFF A HIELANMAN'

It would seem that an Englishman has achieved the proverbially difficult feat of taking the breeks aff a Hielanman at the recent football contest at The Oval. A Scot had got possession of the ball, and was making off with it, when one of the English players caught him by the waist of his knickerbockers and literally bereft him totally of that indispensable garment, which was of the lightest material. This happened exactly in front of a stand in which there were some thirty or forty ladies watching the game with the deepest interest. The victim threw himself flat on his face, and called for an Ulster coat : friends and foes crowded round and formed a ring, within which he managed to put on that extraordinary vestment; and he then was able to retreat into the tent, one English player leaving the game at the same time with him. —Court Journal. (The Days' Doings - Saturday 17th February 1872)

The Scottish team arrived at the Kennington Oval at around 3.00 p.m. in readiness for the 3.30 p.m. kick-off. After a rest on Sunday they had done a bit of sightseeing before catching an omnibus to the ground. When they arrived ouside The Oval ground, they were stunned by the size of the crowd that had gathered. They had never witnessed anything like this. They managed to fight their way through the throng surrounding the pavilion and enter the back door and through to the changing rooms. Some of the younger players such as Billy Ker and Billy McKinnon were looking a bit over-awed by the occassion and so their captain and goalkeeper tried to calm their nerves. Robert Gardner, a grain salesman from Glasgow, was quite a cool customer himself. Although he was only twenty-four, he wasn't going to let the responsibility of being captain or the historic nature of the occasion get the better of him.

He looked upon football as healthy exercise and learning about sportsmanship was as important as the result. He was a prime example of the Queen's Park motto, 'Ludere Causa Ludendi' - To Play for the Sake of Playing.

As a goalkeeper he was one of the best in the land and one of the first to master the technique of 'narrowing the angle'. He wanted to win the match against the English Wanderers, of course, but he didn't want his team fretting about the result. His calm nature soon permeated through to his two young team-mates and they calmly got changed into their blue and white kits.

Robert Gardner, captain and goalkeeper – Queen's Park FC

Although still only 19, Billy Ker was a reliable back. He was quick and accurate with his interceptions and clearances. Today he would be playing alongside 20-year-old Joe Taylor, a drapery clerk, who was keen to smother the attacks of the English forwards with his woven Scottish fabric. Drapery seemed to be a theme within the Queen's Park side with the forwards, Donald Edmonston owning his own draper's shop and Alex Rhind, who would soon be a travelling salesman for a drapery firm. Robert Leckie and Billy McKinnon were both commercial clerks although the latter was quite a character. Billy McKinnon was an accomplished tenor and was often prone to breaking out into song in the changing rooms. He was also a free-spirit with regard to football and he would go on to shock the English when he did an 'overhead kick' in the first official international in November 1872.

The two Smith brothers were already changed, having arrived early from their new residence in South London. Although they were brothers, they couldn't be more different in character when they got on to a football field.

Robert, the elder brother, was in the same mould as his captain. He was by no means implusive and dealt with situations calmly. He couldn't be considered a brilliant forward by any means but by working hard in the field for the team he warranted his place.

James was the exact opposite. He was an impetuous player who made things happen. Mr. Archibald Rae, a fellow team mate who hadn't been able to make the trip to London, would often tell an amusing anecdote of James. Apparently, whilst playing against the Hamilton Gymnasium Club, he had leapt on the top of a hedge to win a touch-down for his side. In those days a touch-down counted as a point in the game. James gave everything for the cause. This was a team to be reckoned with.

**

Both teams ran down the steps of the pavilion to great applause from The Oval crowd. A rope had been strung along both sides of the pitch, about ten yards from the field of play, to ensure the crowd couldn't unintentionally spill onto the field and interrupt the game. The pitch looked 'exceptionally fine' despite the 5th unofficial England v. Scotland having been played there just ten days earlier.

Charles William Alcock won the toss and chose to play from the east end of the ground in front of the gasworks. This meant the Wanderers would be playing into a slight breeze and would have the sun in their faces. This was probably a tactic knowing the Scots may have to face the sun, as it set in the west, later in the game. This meant the kick-off fell to the Scots side and at 3.40 p.m. David Wotherspoon kicked off on behalf of the Queen's Park team.

In the first fifteen minutes it was all Queen's Park. The Scots surprised the English with the 'superior, dash and energy' of their play and their style of following up the ball so quickly confused the English backs. Both David Wotherspoon and Robert Smith had made some 'plucky runs' into the English half. If only their dribbling had been better on occassions then surely they would have breached the English goal. Unfortunately, during these early Scottish attacks Donald Edmonston twisted his knee. As there were no substitutes allowed he carried on bravely, not wishing to let his team down.

The constant Scottish attacks spurred the English into action and Charles Alcock rallied his troops. The Wanderers started to impose their style of play on the game and their superior weight started to have an impact. Charles Wollaston, William Parry Crake, Tom Pelham and Alex Bonsor, all threatened the Scottish goal but unfortunately to no avail. There were two further chances for the English before half-time. Charles Alcock made a good run down the side and crossed to Tom Pelham but the chance eluded him. Then there was a 'bully' (similar to a scrum) right in front of the Scottish posts but again the chance went begging. Despite the pressure, the Queen's Park backs, Billy Ker and Joe Taylor, had been up to the task and kept the English forwards at bay. With no score at half-time ends were changed and the Scots now found themselves playing into the setting sun.

The Wanderers kicked off and tried to apply more pressure to the Queen's Park goal but the cool play of Robert Gardner in goal and the skill of the young backs in front of him turned the game in the Scots' favour and their forwards were playing well together despite the injury to Edmonston. Another surprise for the English was the habit of the Scots to propel the ball forwards with their heads. This was greeted by some amusement from The Oval crowd but after witnessing the positive effect this had on the game, the laughter quickly turned to hearty applause.

With ten minutes to go Charles Alcock took a shot on goal and believed he'd scored. He appealed to the two umpires, Alfred Stair and James Kirkpatrick, who immediately came together to discuss the incident. After a short discussion, they both agreed that the ball had passed just over the tape and therefore 'no goal' was the decision. The match restarted and the Scots played energetically right until the end when 'time' was called at 5.10 p.m. After one and a half hours of play the verdict of The Sportsman newspaper was that 'the Caledonians were far the lighter team but like the 'Blades of Sheffield' they made up for weight by activity'. (vii)

The Wanderers offered to play on for an extra 30 minutes but this was graciously declined by the Queen's Park side. This was not a surprising response given the injury that had been sustained by Donald Edmonston. What was surprising was that the declaration of a drawn match meant that the match would have to be replayed. However, the cost of returning to Glasgow and travelling back down to London for a replay, and then staying on for a potential final, after the other semi-final between the Royal Engineers and Crystal Palace had been decided, was financially prohibitive for the Scots and so, there and then, they scratched from the competition. The feeling was that the honour of a drawn match against a very strong Wanderers side, chosen from the cream of English football, was satisfaction enough for the Caledonians. Mind you, had the Scots originally been lead to believe otherwise? (viii)

The strength of Scottish football was there for all to see and this result was a fitting answer to the defeats suffered in the 'unofficial' internationals. This FA Cup match had been followed with great interest by Scottish clubs and was it any coincidence that a new club called Glasgow Rangers were formed by a group of rowing enthusiasts in the very same month of March 1872?

After the game, the players returned to the pavilion, where after showering and recovering from the play, they took cabs to the Freemasons Tavern to dine together. Glasses were raised and toasts made to the success of the first football match played between men south and north of the border and also to the future of the Football Association. It would be fitting to think that after a few more glasses of claret, Billy McKinnon got up on to the floor and sang a few Scottish ballads in his exquisite tenor voice.

Billy McKinnon – a brilliant dribbler and one of the first exponents of the 'overhead kick'. Billy also had a talent for singing and was a tenor in the Glasgow Male Voice Choir.

WANDERERS v. QUEEN'S PARK
FOOTBALL ASSOCIATION CHALLENGE CUP
FOURTH TIE

Monday 4th March 1872
Kennington Oval, London
Attendance: 2,000+, (Kick-Off : 3.40 p.m.)

WANDERERS (0)	QUEEN'S PARK (0)
Orange, violet and black shirt and stockings, white shorts	Blue jerseys & reversible blue & red cowls, white shorts
Charles W. Alcock (capt)	Robert Gardner (capt)
Reginald C. Welch	Joseph Taylor
William P. Crake	William Ker
Albert C. Thompson	Robert Leckie
Edward H. M. Elliott	James Smith
Robert E. W. Crawford	Robert Smith
Thomas H. Pelham	Donald Edmonston +
Alexander G. Bonsor	David Wotherspoon
Charles F. Wollaston	Alexander Rhind *
Henry Emanuel	William Gibb *
Henry H. Stewart	William McKinnon *

* These three players were not reported as having played in the game by the London press. (ix)

+ Also has been spelt Edmiston and Edminston.

242

Author's Notes:

(i) THE VISIT OF A GLASGOW CLUB TO LONDON.

The match between the English Wanderers and the Queen's Park club of this city will be played in London at Kennington Oval this afternoon from half-past-three to five o'clock. The Scotchmen left Glasgow by the 8.55 train by the East Coast line on Saturday night, and arrived in London at 20 minutes to 10 o'clock yesterday morning. (North British Daily Mail - Monday 4th March 1872)

(ii) Robert Smith would go on to represent Scotland and Queen's Park in the 2nd, 3rd and 4th unofficial internationals. Both Robert and James would sign up to play for the South Norwood Football Club, just over a mile south of Crystal Palace Park. They would also both play in the first official England versus Scotland game on 30th November 1872, making them the first brothers to play international football.

(iii) *Sir,—Permit' me to draw the attention of the Parks' Committee of our Town Council to the recreation part of the Queen's Park. It is ostensibly set apart for games, such as cricket, golf, football, etc., but at present it is very ill adapted for any of these, or indeed for any games at all. True it is, that all these are practised within it, but the space adapted for them might, with very little outlay, be doubled. Allow me also to offer my opinion as to how that might be done. At present anyone walking over the park may observe how uneven it is. For instance, there is a space of three or four acres behind the bowling green which is never occupied at all, because it is not anything like level. Again, at the south corner and stretching along towards the east, there is another large strip which it is impossible to play or even walk on, on account of nettles and other weeds. There might also be a good slice taken off the west corner of the little hillock in the centre, and put to fill up some of the holes round about it. If these and a few other things, which in themselves seem trivial, were done, they would double the available space and triple the enjoyment of those who frequent this (notwithstanding its drawbacks) most excellent park. Trusting those who have the power may also have the will to do something towards improvement, now that it is nearly deserted of players for six months to come, and that when spring comes round the recreation part may look (to put it mild) half as well as the other part of the park, (North British Daily Mail - Wednesday 25th October 1871)*

(iv) The original Queen's Park blue jerseys, white shorts and blue and white hooped socks were worn by the Scotland team in the first official international against England on 30th November 1872. Nearly all the players were from Queen's Park anyway, although the Smith brothers were recorded as playing for their new London club, South Norwood, and William Ker was credited as now playing for Granville.

In the week leading up to the match, David Wotherspoon's sister, Marion, wanted the team to look their best and so she embroidered a red lion rampant onto their shirts. Scotland went on to adopt the badge and the Queen's Park blue jersey as the national team's colours and so in 1873, David Wotherspoon suggested changing the Queen's Park jersey to the now famous black and white hoops.

SEASON 1873-74.
Standing—Angus M'Kinnon, J. Dickson, Thomas Lawrie, Charles Campbell, R. W. Neill.
Sitting—R. Leckie, Jos. Taylor, H. M'Neil, J. J. Thomson, J. B. Weir, Wm. M'Kinnon.

The earliest photo of the Queen's Park side 1873-74, now in their black and white hooped shirts, showing five of the players that were in the original squad for the FA Cup semi-final;
(Robert Leckie, Joseph Taylor, James Thomson, James Weir and William McKinnon are all sat in the front row)

244

(v) Queen's Park are credited with introducing a collective and 'scientific' form of team-based passing which would become known as 'combination' football. This changed the nature of the Association game as the culture in London at this time was largely one of dribbling and 'backing up'.

(vi) Camberwell New Road is a closed railway station in Camberwell, South London. It opened in 1862 but was closed to passengers in 1916 and closed to all traffic in 1964. The possibility of the station's re-opening has been raised in recent years.

(vii) The details of the match between the Wanderers and Queen's Park have been condensed from the match reports in the following newspapers:

The Globe – Monday 4th March 1872
Glasgow Daily Herald - Tuesday 5th March 1872
The Scotsman – Tuesday 5th March 1872
The Sportsman – Tuesday 5th March 1872
Morning Post – Tuesday 5th March 1872
The Field – Saturday 9th March 1872 (see below)
The Sportsman – Saturday 9th March 1872
The Scotsman – Monday 18th March 1872
North British Daily Mail - Monday 18th March 1872

ASSOCIATION CHALLENGE CUP.
WANDERERS V QUEEN'S PARK

On Monday last, the above match took place at The Oval forming one of the fourth ties for the above cup. Before proceeding to the details of the contest itself, we may remark that the Glasgow eleven, by their visit, have earned for themselves the distinction of being the first Scotch club, that has ever journeyed so far southward as London, and that their enterprise in venturing so long a distance to contend against such powerful foemen is the most remarkable event in the annals of modern football. At twenty to four o'clock in most propitious weather—though exception might be taken even here on the ground that it was too warm for football and on a ground in perfect condition, the ball was kicked off by Wotherspoon on behalf of Queen's Park, the captain of the Wanderers, electing to play for the first half of the game in opposition to both wind and sun. Any impressions that the Wanderers would have an easy victory were soon dispelled as the Scotchmen played in such energetic style and followed the ball up

245

so quickly after the Sheffield fashion, that for the first quarter of an hour they rather surprised their English opponents. After the first burst, the play settled down into a more even groove, but still the Glasgow eleven caused the Wanderers no little anxiety, and on two occasions, had they only been able to dribble, without doubt the goal of the Wanderers, would inevitably have fallen, the ball being entirely in their possession. As it was, in each case the danger was averted, and the play proceeded, Wollaston. Stewart, Emanuel. and Parry all showing good form for the one, and Wotherspoon, Weir, Taylor and Ker for the other side. The next event was a good run down the side of the ground by C. W. Alcock, at the end of which the ball was well middled to Pelham, but the chance was allowed to escape, and so was another from a 'bully' right in front of the posts, just before half time was called. After change of positions the fight still raged as keenly with hardly any preponderance to either side, despite good runs by Emanuel and Bonsor. During the last ten minutes the Wanderers worked with the greatest resolution, but although they once drove the ball just over the tape of the Scotch goal, and at the end had an easy chance, which their captain failed to utilise, their efforts came too late, and at ten minutes past five o'clock the game was declared drawn. Thus, in the impossibility of remaining for a second trial, the Glasgow eleven withdrew from further competition, leaving the Wanderers to contend in the Final tie. The play of the Scotchmen was most creditable throughout as their forwards worked with unwearyingly energy and their backs Ker and Taylor, both showed great pluck and precision of kicking. Their style of play is very much after the fashion of Sheffield, as they dribble little, and usually convey the ball with a series of long kicks, combined with a judicious plan of passing on, while their method of driving the ball with the head is precisely the same as that adopted in Sheffield. We may state, with the exception of two of their members who are resident in Surrey, that the Scotch players all travelled from Scotland for this one match, and that their appearance in London, may fairly be termed the most interesting incident of the present season. The umpires were Messrs A. Stair (Upton Park) for the Wanderers, J. Kirkpatrick (Civil Service) for Queen's Park club; Mr. T. Lloyd, jun. (Crystal Palace) being referee.*
(THE FIELD – SATURDAY 9TH MARCH 1872)

* William Parry Crake.

(viii) According to Richard Robinson, in his book 'History of Queen's Park Football Club 1867 – 1917', it had been agreed that Queen's Park would travel to London *'in the faith that arrangements had been made with the two other contending clubs that their tie should be played off before ours with the Wanderers, so that in the event of the Wanderers*

246

suffering a defeat from us we should be able to play the final tie on the following day.'

Why the replay between the Royal Engineers and Crystal Palace couldn't have been played in the two weeks before the Scots arrived is unknown but it did deny them the possibility of playing in the final. However, when they realised this was not the case, they seemed more than satisfied with the end result.

'did not the brilliant fight of the Queen's Park in London serve to restore the somewhat tarnished fame of Scotland?'

Although the team could not remain in London for a further game, two players did stay behind and in fact, Robert Gardner and David Wotherspoon both guested for the Wanderers in a 0-0 draw against Clapham Rovers on Saturday 9th March 1872. They may have been interested to discover their team also included a bearded fellow called William Gilbert Grace!

(ix) The Queen's Park team reported in the English national press was as follows;

Robert Gardner (capt.)
Donald Edmonston
William Ker
Robert Leckie
James Smith
Robert Smith
Joseph Taylor
David Wotherspoon
James Hepburn *
James Weir *
J. E. A. Walker *

I have chosen to go with the team quoted by Richard Robinson in his book 'History of Queen's Park Football Club 1867 – 1917', as it is likley that the English newspapers of the time simply recorded the players on the initial team sheets that had been sent to them. According to Robinson the three players marked with a * did not take to the field.

Chapter 25: 'Who'd be a Goalkeeper?'
Match 14: Royal Engineers v. Crystal Palace
FA Cup Fourth Ties REPLAY
Saturday 9th March 1872
(Kick-Off 3.00+ p.m.)

I was keen to investigate whether I could find a reason why this match could not have been replayed prior to the 4th March 1872. If it had been, there would have been a proper conclusion to the Wanderers versus Queen's Park match and then the first FA Cup Challenge Final would have been between the two true victors of the semi-finals. It wasn't as though either of the teams weren't able to play football prior to this date. In fact, both sides had played matches before the 4th March. Crystal Palace had played the Forest School on Tuesday the 20th February 1872 at Walthamstow followed by an interclub match between the Captain's Eleven and The Rest on Saturday 24th February 1872. They even played a match against the Civil Service at the Kennington Oval on Saturday 2nd March 1872, the very day that Queen's Park set off from Glasgow. The Royal Engineers were also active during this time playing a match against Clapham Rovers on Saturday 24th February 1872. So why couldn't these friendlies have been cancelled and the match played before the Scots arrived in the Capital?

The answer lies in the two other key FA matches that were played during this time. The first was that the last unofficial international match between England and Scotland was played at The Oval on the 24th February 1872. This game featured two key players from both sides, Charles Chenery of Crystal Palace and Hugh Mitchell of the Royal Engineers. Henry Renny-Tailyour was selected to play for Scotland but withdrew from the game citing an accident he had been involved in at the Brompton Barracks.

The second concerned the third of a recent series of matches played between the London and Sheffield Football Associations. The series was currently being drawn with one win a piece when each was playing according to their own Association rules. The third and deciding match was to be played on Saturday 2nd March 1872 at Brammall Lane in Sheffield according to the Sheffield rules in the first hour of the game and the London rules in the second hour. The Northerners ran out 2-1 victors whilst playing to their rules in the first hour and with no further score in the second hour 'The Blades of Sheffield' were declared victors. There were six players with links to Crystal Palace playing in the London side that day, Douglas Allport, Alex Morten, Frederick Soden and Alfred Lloyd who were Palace regulars and Charles Chenery and Percy Currey, who were listed as Wanderers' players but who had already turned out for Palace a few times this season. Given the importance of these two matches you can see why the replay was pushed back to the following weekend. The Royal Engineers were particularly happy as it meant that they could welcome their captain, William Merriman, and Adam Bogle back into the side. It also gave Henry Renny-Tailyour a little more time to recover from the injury he had sustained in the Quarter-Final against the Hampstead Heathens and which had dogged him in the original semi-final match.

Although Crystal Palace were relieved that they could rest the players who had played for London in the two-day trip to Sheffield, they were going to be missing their star, Cuthbert Ottaway, who couldn't take part in this semi-final replay. Maybe he had other sporting engagements to meet at Cambridge University although his fellow student, Frederick Chappell, was able to play. Or, could it be that the ever-efficient Royal Engineers personnel had spotted that Cuthbert had already played in the first tie for Marlow and after the first semi-final match had raised the point with the FA that Cuthbert shouldn't be allowed to play again as he was cup-tied?

Whatever, the teams returned once again to The Oval. The kick-off was due to take place at 2.45 p.m. but given that another large crowd was gathering around the pitch, it was just after 3.00 p.m. when the match actually started. The first few minutes of the game were pretty even and Crystal Palace seemed as though they were going to be as difficult to break down as they had been in the first match. However, as the Royal Engineers began to turn up the heat, both in terms of the physicality of the match and their quick style of 'combination' play, the Palatials seemed to tire and the Royal Engineers took full advantage. They ended up scoring three goals and conceding none and if it hadn't been for the Palace goalkeeper, 40-year-old Alec Morten, the advantage could have been a lot greater. His ability to clear his lines whilst under pressure (Toujours prêt, encore) could not be faulted and he took a few cuts and bruises to bed with him that night. The reporter from the Bell's Life newspaper describes the action:

ROYAL ENGINEERS v CRYSTAL PALACE.

On Saturday afternoon these teams met at The Oval to play off the last ties of the Association Cup. The Engineers had the best of it soon after commencing and finally won the match by three goals to nothing. Play began soon after three o'clock, and the contest was pretty equal for some time, the territories of both being in turn invested; but this state of things did not exist for any great length of time, the Crystal Palace team, who were clearly overweighted soon began to show signs of weakness, and a short time only had elapsed when their goal was invested, and Lieut. Mitchell sent the ball under the line. Ends were reversed and operations were repeatedly carried on in the quarters of the Palace, and their goal-keeper had a very narrow escape of being carried through, being severely mauled just in front of the goal post. After this the ball was again set in motion, and in a very short time Renny-Tailyour brought it from the centre of the ground, and kicked a splendid goal. Once more the goal-keepers changed ends, and again the Engineers carried the ball down the ground towards their opponents' line, where the battle was renewed with increased vigour. Very little time elapsed ere the goal-keeper again got mauled, and the post where the melee took place swayed about in the most astonishing way, and it certainly looked as if the fragile erection would come to grief. The overthrow of the goal, however, was frustrated for a time, but before the hour for discontinuing play Renny-Tailyour was once more successful in reducing the Palace goal. Very little dribbling was displayed in the match, and those who took a most prominent part on the side of the Engineers were Rich, Mitchell, and Renny-Tailyour. For the Crystal Palace Chenery was, perhaps, the most prominent, but the greatest praise is due to A. Morten, the duties of goal-keeper in this match being most onerous.

(Bell's Life in London and Sporting Chronicle - Saturday 16th March 1872)

Meanwhile there was a silent osbserver sat at the back of the long room in the Surrey Cricket Club pavilion, who was watching the game with special interest. It was none other than Charles William Alcock, the Wanderers captain and creator of the FA Cup. He now knew who his Wanderers' opponents would be in the first-ever FA Cup Final and he needed a plan to stop the Royal Engineers. He made a few notes and then headed out of the Kennington Oval to catch his train home. He had seven days to come up with a way of negating the power and style of play of the Sappers as he knew they would be favourites to win. The Royal Engineers were now being called 'The Invincibles' as they had not yet lost a match this season.

ROYAL ENGINEERS v. CRYSTAL PALACE
FOOTBALL ASSOCIATION CHALLENGE CUP
FOURTH TIE - REPLAY

Saturday 9th March 1872
Kennington Oval, London
Attendance: ?, (Kick-Off : 3.00 + p.m.)

ROYAL ENGINEERS (3)	CRYSTAL PALACE (0)
Jersey, nightcap and stockings, blue & red in horizontal stripes	Blue & white hooped shirts and socks, blue serge shorts
Capt. Francis Marindin (c)	Douglas Allport (capt.)
Capt. William Merriman	William M. Allport
Lt. Hugh Mitchell	Alexander Morten
Lt. Henry B. Rich	William Bouch
Lt. Henry Renny-Tailyour	Alfred Bouch
Lt. Edmund W. Cresswell	Charles E. Smith
Lt. Edmond W. Cotter	Charles C. Armitage
Lt. Alfred G. Goodwyn	Alfred H. Lloyd
Lt. George W. Addison	Charles J. Chenery
Lt. Herbert H. Muirhead	Frederick Chappell
Lt. Adam Bogle	Philip G. Rouquette

Goalscorers: Royal Engineers:
Hugh Mitchell (1)
Renny-Tailyour (2)

THE

FA CUP

FINAL

(SATURDAY 16ᵀᴴ MARCH 1872)

Chapter 26: Please Do Not Strain the Ropes!
Match 15: Wanderers v. Royal Engineers
FA Cup FINAL TIE
Saturday 16th March 1872
(Kick-Off 3.05 p.m.)

Saturday 16th March 1872. The end of the football season. Most of the Football Association clubs had played their last match of the season and were winding down for the summer. The clubs that shared grounds with their local cricket sides were putting their football equipment into storage and the groundsmen were starting to prepare the cricket squares in readiness for the summer ahead. A lot of the football clubs ended their season with an annual athletics tournament which was a good fundraiser and seemed to attract a large number of spectators, the majority of whom were of the fairer sex.

In the newspapers all the talk was about the 29th Oxford and Cambridge Boat Race that was due to take place the following weekend. This very Saturday (16th) was the time for boat race trials and the Oxford and Cambridge crews were out early to practice on the River Thames. They both had intended to go out on the Saturday afternoon but were swamped by the crowds that had arrived on special train excursions run by the South Western Railway Company and also by the passenger steamboats commandeered by the Iron Steamworks Co. Ltd. It seemed as though nobody would be attending the FA Cup Final further back up the river at the Kennington Oval.

The crowd was so large it extended all along the towpath from Hammersmith to Putney and it was clear that the Thames police would have their work cut out to clear the way for the crews. The Cambridge crew tried to row as far as Chiswick but got stuck in amongst the tiny craft that were spread out along the Thames, trying to watch the action. In the end they got to Craven Point and had to turn back.

The Oxford crew decided to forgo the practice and instead preferred a walk across Putney Common to where the Barnes Football Club were holding their annual athletics event in J. Johnstone Esq.'s Limes Field, next to the White Hart Inn. Their arrival caused considerable excitement amongst the crowd and in particular amongst the ladies but unfortunately the hopes of the fairer sex were dashed as the young oarsmen were shepherded into the central enclosure. The athletics events featured a number of footballers. The Highton brothers of Barnes were both running in the one mile steeplechase with Edward Highton also taking part in the three quarter of a mile handicap and the two miles flat race. Their fellow team-mate, Charles Ommaney, was to feature in the vaulting whilst Frederick Soden, of Crystal Palace, ran for the Amateur Athletics Club (A.A.C.) and Thomas Kitson of Upton Park's preferred event was the 350 yard hurdles.

Surprisingly, the umpire of the walking events was none other than Mr. Ebenezer Cobb Morley who, as President of the FA, you would have thought would have been at the Kennington Oval for the first-ever Football Association Challenge Cup Final.

'The Little Tin Idol.'

255

THE TEAMS – 16ᵀᴴ MARCH 1872

THE WANDERERS		ROYAL ENGINEERS	
GK	Reginald C. Welch	GK	Capt. William Merriman
FB	Edgar Lubbock	FB	Capt. Francis Marindin
HB	Albert Thompson	FB	Lt. George W. Addison
FW	Charles W. Alcock	HB	Lt. Alfred G. Goodwyn
FW	Edward E. Bowen	FW	Lt. Hugh Mitchell
FW	Alexander Bonsor	FW	Lt. Edmund Cresswell
FW	Morton Peto Betts	FW	Lt.Henry Renny-Tailyour
FW	William P. Crake	FW	Lt. Henry B. Rich
FW	Thomas Hooman	FW	Lt. Herbert H. Muirhead
FW	Robert W.S. Vidal	FW	Lt. Edmond W. Cotter
FW	Charles Wollaston	FW	Lt. Adam Bogle

Saturday 16ᵗʰ March 1872

Kick-Off: 3:05 p.m.

Venue: Kennington Oval, London

Attendance: 2,000

Referee:

Alfred Stair (Upton Park)

Assistant referees:

John H. Giffard (Civil Service)

James Kirkpatrick (Civil Service)

Match rules:

90 minutes normal time.

WANDERERS : PLAYER PORTRAITS

GOALKEEPER: REGINALD COURTENAY WELCH

Age: 20 (17TH October 1851)
Born: Paddington, London
Education: Harrow School
Future Profession: Army Tutor

Reginald (de) Courtenay Welch is, as his lengthy name suggests, a man you can rely on. A player who has played both in goal and at full-back. The defence of his goal is paramount. He has been described as a 'good and safe keeper who works hard and kicks accurately.'

An accomplished cricketer, a member of the MCC and a pioneer skier in Switzerland, Reginald will be hoping the Wanderers will be having a celebratory après-ski after today's Final.

FULL-BACK: EDGAR LUBBOCK

Age: 25 (22 February 1847)
Born: Westminster
Education: Eton College
Future Profession: Director of the Bank of England

Edgar is the tenth of eleven children, the offspring of Sir John Lubbock, the former head of the Lubbock & Co. Bank. Having made the final eleven of the Lubbock team, Edgar will be hoping he makes the final eleven of the Wanderers team today. He is an outstanding defender who can play at full-back and half-back. He has the 'finest kick anywhere and his aptitude for kicking the ball in the most difficult position is unequalled. He is the bane of all forwards.'

Another great defender of his goal and known as the 'King of the Backs' because of his reliability. 'The ease with which he kicks the ball in the most difficult positions suggests the belief that at one time in his life he must have gone into training with a view to an acrobatic career.'

Although he's training to be a barrister, Albert is not a 'law unto himself' and he'll be doing his utmost to stop those Royal Engineers forwards.

Age: 23 (13th July 1848)
Born: Kirby Hall, Yorkshire
Education: Eton College
Future Profession: Barrister

Charles William Alcock needs no introduction because of his unique involvement in the development of the game of football and his idea for the introduction of this FA Challenge Cup.

The Founder of the Forest Club and the Wanderers, Charles often found himself playing football three times a week.

He is said to be 'a hard-working forward' with 'a good shot in the neighbourhood of the goal' and is 'second to none in every department.' He is a powerful and robust player who often finds himself on the scoresheet.

Age: 29 (2nd December 1842)
Born: Bishopwearmouth, Sunderland
Education: Harrow School
Current Profession: Sports Journalism
'CAPTAIN

Age: 35 (30th March 1836)
Born: Glenmore, County Wicklow, Ireland
Education: Blackheath Proprietary
Current Profession: Harrow Schoolmaster

In two weeks', time Edward Ernest Bowen will be 36 and he is the oldest player on the pitch. Despite his age Edward hasn't married yet. They say he still has his inner child inside him. He is proficient at rowing, athletics, shooting, skating, cycling and mountaineering. Edward also played one English County Cricket match for Hampshire in 1864 but was dismissed for a duck in both innings. He is also the composer of the Harrow School song 'Forty Years On'.

How on earth did he find the time to play football?

Age: 20 (7th October 1851)
Born: Polesden Lacey, Surrey
Education: Eton College
Future Profession: Brewer

Despite his tender age, Alex is a strong bustling forward and he uses his weight to his advantage. Added to this he is an excellent dribbler and plays a straight game making him a valuable forward and a threat around the goal area.

Alex is a brewer by trade with the firm Combe and Delafield which would later be incorporated into Watney's in 1898. Alexander is a hefty lad and maybe he was the instigator of the slogan 'Watney's Red Barrel'

Age: 24 (30th August 1847)
Born: St. Pancras, London
Education: Harrow School
Future Profession: Civil Engineer

The term 'all-rounder' has to be applied to Morton Peto Betts. Not only can he play in every position on the football pitch, he is also currently a valuable member of the FA Committee. He can play in goal and he can play as full-back as he has a good strong charge to ward off any opposition forwards. Not only this, he is also a neat and effective dribbler and so he will be looking to push up front today to try and put pressure on the Sappers' goal. Morton is also an accomplished cricketer and is currently on Middlesex C.C.C. books.

Age: 20 (11th February 1852)
Born: Madras, India
Education: Harrow School
Future Profession:
Merchant

One of the finest forwards of the 1870s, William is said to be one of 'the neatest dribblers of the day, slow but very sure' and 'very useful on the side'. He made his debut for the Wanderers on 5th January 1870 at Crystal Palace, having been introduced by his team-mate Edward Bowen. He has also played for the Barnes and Harrow Chequers Football Clubs and in 1871 he was invited to play in some unofficial England v Scotland Internationals. One match report said that Crake 'deserved no little praise for the energy of [his] following-up throughout the game.'

260

Thomas Hooman is another young 'all-rounder' who is good at all sports including cricket, rowing, boxing, shooting and golf. He will also run in a sprint race for England in 1872. His speed and ability to dribble makes him an accomplished player who is perfect for the big occasion.

The son of a carpet manufacturer, Thomas will be hoping they will be rolling out the 'red carpet' for him at the end of today's game.

Age: 21 (28 December 1850)
Born: Kidderminster, Worcs.
Education: Charterhouse School
Future Profession: Merchant Ship Broker and manufacturer of Portland Cement.

Despite being the youngest player in the Wanderers team and the only player still at school, Robert has the confidence to play in the position of centre forward. As well as being fast, he is known as the 'prince of dribblers' and is well known for his marvellous side shots at goal. He is so admired that he got to play in an early pre-official international last year at the tender age of 16 years 183 days. Not only is he good at football but Robert also excels at rugby, cricket, rowing and golf.

Age: 18 (3rd September 1853)
Born: Abbotsham, Devon
Education: Westminster School
Future Profession: Currently a student but soon to become a vicar.

Age: 22 (31st July 1849)
Born: Felpham, Sussex
Education: Lancing College
Future Profession: Solicitor

Charles, who plays at inside-right and also on the wing, has excellent dribbling and shooting skills. Although he is slight of build, Charles has the ability to play well against the best of men. A bit of a poacher around the goal, Charles guides the leather with consummate skill, and is unerring with his shots on goal.

Definitely a player for the Royal Engineers' backs to watch out for.

ROYAL ENGINEERS : PLAYER PORTRAITS

GOALKEEPER: CAPTAIN WILLIAM MERRIMAN

Age: 33 (2nd April 1838)
Born: Kensington, London
Education: Addiscombe College
Profession: Soldier

Captain William Merriman is known as one of the best goalkeepers of the day. Plucky, cool and difficult to get past, William always does the right thing at the right time.

Always keen to be outdoors on a sports field William takes part in athletics, cricket, golf, rowing, hunting and shooting. Whilst stationed in Bombay, India he became the vice-commodore of the Royal Bombay Yacht Club and Steward of the Bombay Turf Club. He really was a Merry Man!

FULL-BACK: CAPT. FRANCIS ARTHIR MARINDIN

Age: 33 (1ST May 1838)
Born: Weymouth, Dorset
Education: Eton College
Profession: Soldier

'CAPTAIN

Francis Marindin is a renowned goalkeeper and full-back, very experienced in both of these positions. He was influential in the founding of the Royal Engineers football team in 1863. He was also interested in applying a 'scientific' approach to the game – advancing by means of measured inter-passing rather than simple kick and rush.

A member of the FA Committee and a colleague of the Wanderers' Charles Alcock, he will be looking to stop his good friend from scoring today.

263

Age: 22 (18TH September 1849)
Born: Bradford, Yorkshire
Education: Cheltenham College
Profession: Soldier

The son of a Yorkshire spinner, George is made of true northern grit and along with his team-mate and half-back, Alfred G. Goodwyn, they make up one of the best defensive partnerships around.

George is described as being 'a very sound back' and as 'playing beautifully at (the) back.'

He is also a useful cricketer and a member of the M.C.C.

Age: 22 (13th March 1850)
Born: Bengal, India
Education: RMA, Woolwich
Profession: Soldier

The other half of the great defensive partnership with George Addison, Alfred can play at either full-back or half-back. He has proved himself to be a most fine defender, kicking with great skill and rarely allowing himself to be passed.

George and Alfred have been the reason that the 'Sappers' have got through to today's final, having played three matches without conceding a goal.

Alfred is still celebrating his 22nd birthday which was on Wednesday last and he will be hoping to continue the celebrations around 4.35 p.m. today.

Age: 22 (3rd December 1849)
Born: Marylebone, London.
Education: Harrow School
Profession: Soldier

Although born in England, Hugh Mitchell is of Scottish descent and qualifies to play against England in the forthcoming Internationals.

Hugh plays as a forward who is described as 'a good charger and a useful forward who sticks to the ball well.'

He's a good friend of his fellow team-mate Edmund Cresswell. Hugh may have had an ulterior motive for his friendship with Edmund as later, he is to marry his sister 'Katie' and they go on to have seven children

.

Age: 22 (7th November 1849)
Born: Gibraltar
Education: Bruce Castle School, Tottenham
Profession: Soldier

The son of Gibraltar's Chief Postmaster, Edmund is currently the Secretary of the Royal Engineers Committee and on the FA Committee. His secretarial skills extend into his army career where he mainly works in administrative roles. He graduated from the Royal Military Academy of Woolwich on the same day as his team-mates, Hugh Mitchell and Henry Rich. He currently has a 15-year-old sister, Mary Catherine 'Katie' Creswell, who we know his fellow forward and college mate, Hugh Mitchell, currently has his eyes on.

Age: 22 (9th October 1849)
Born: North-West Province, India
Education: Cheltenham College
Profession: Soldier

Although he was born in Mussoorie in India, Henry's father was Scottish and so he was another of the Royal Engineers' ranks who qualified to play for Scotland in the recent unofficial International against England at The Oval.

Probably one of the most important members in the side, it is Henry's goals that have got the Royal Engineers into today's Final. Henry has also played rugby for Scotland and is currently the only player to have represented his country playing both codes of the game.

Age: 22 (14th June 1849)
Born: Berbice, British Guiana
Education: Marlborough College
Profession: Soldier

The son of a Colonel of the Royal Engineers, Henry comes from a 'rich' military background.

He is generally played as a forward and is 'ranked as one of the best football players of his day' who 'strives hard to pass the backs'

As well as being a footballer, Rich is also an athlete who is reputed to be 'one of the fastest runners on the athletics track,' so the Wanderers backs will have to be aware of his speed.

Age: 21 (10th December 1850)
Born: Brighton, Sussex
Education: Eton then
Wellington College
Profession: Soldier

Herbert Muirhead plays as a forward for the Royal Engineers and he is 'noted for his excellent and fine runs.'

His father is the biographer of James Watt, the Scottish engineer and inventor of the Watt Steam Engine. His mother was the granddaughter of Watt's partner, Matthew Boulton, who installed these revolutionary machines in the factories and mills all over England.

Herbert will be hoping to build up a 'full head of steam' on the pitch today and steamroll the Wanderers' defence.

Age: 20 (13th February 1852)
Born: Valletta, Malta.
Education: RMA, Woolwich
Profession: Soldier

The youngest 'Sapper' on the pitch, Edmond is a forward who 'revels in rushes and scrimmages.'

He also has a rich military background and his father, John, was a sergeant in the army and heavily involved in the Crimean War. Edmond was born in Malta and then went to St. Munchin's College in Limerick, Ireland.

Edmond is also a good cricketer and in later life he will go onto to make an appearance for Warwickshire in the County Championship in 1877.

Adam Bogle is another Scot in the side born north of the border in Glasgow.

Bogle plays as a forward who 'displays the vigour and robust play typical of the Royal Engineers' attackers, with their combined rushes on opposing defences.'

The Wanderers' backs, Edgar Lubbock and Albert Thompson, will be out to bamboozle Bogle.

Age: 23 (21st June 1848)
Born: Glasgow.
Education: Harrow School
Profession: Soldier

THE

MATCH

WANDERERS
VERSUS
ROYAL ENGINEERS

(SATURDAY 16TH MARCH 1872)

A great event in the football world will come off today at the Kennington-Oval. The 'Association Cup' is to be contested for. This may now, perhaps, be considered as the Blue Riband of Football. The Cup was only established this year, and during the whole of the present season the various clubs belonging to the Association have been playing against each other, until now there are only three clubs left in that have not been beaten. These clubs are the celebrated Wanderers, the Royal Engineers, and the Queen's Park Club, Glasgow. The Scotchmen not long ago played the Wanderers, but the game was drawn; and as this northern club could not arrange to come so far south again, they have retired from the contest, and thus have left the final tie between the Wanderers and the Royal Engineers. The Wanderers Club comprises nearly all the best football talent in the country. The great players, who have represented the universities and public schools, are mostly to be found enrolled in this, the leading club of the Association. The Wanderers, in fact, are the 'crème de la crème' of the Association players. At any time, as has been proved, the Wanderers would be most difficult to beat; but on this occasion they will, no doubt, be especially formidable, for now they will be enabled to muster in their greatest strength. In their other ties they have been liable to lose for the occasion the services of some of their best men, whose first allegiance may have been due to their local club; whereas now that all but the Royal Engineers have been disposed of, they will all be free to play as required. It will be seen, therefore, that the scientific soldiers will have a task before them that might well cause them to feel doubtful of

success. The habit of working together and understanding each other's play will materially help the Engineers. The Wanderers will probably bring into the field more players of admitted excellence than will their opponents, with their much more limited area of choice. The leading club will doubtless show more exceptionally brilliant individual form than the Engineers can be expected to show. But, if we mistake not, there will be an amount of cohesion, co-operation, and almost of discipline among the soldiers that will at all events go far to place them on a par with their, so to speak, more loosely organised but highly skilled rivals. Anyhow, the game cannot but be unusually exciting. Greek is about to meet Greek, and the tug of the mimic war must be severe. The victors will until next year claim to be at the head of the Association clubs. But the vanquished will still be able to say that they have proved themselves superior to all others save the winners of to-day. It should be remarked that in one respect this match will be unsatisfactory. The Association does not represent half of the Football Clubs in the country, and therefore the contest between the Association Clubs can only determine which among those clubs is the strongest, and not which is the strongest club in the whole country.

The love for and the practice of football has so greatly increased of late years that already it may be looked on as one of the great national pastimes. Formerly the game was confined almost, if not quite, exclusively to schools and colleges. Now the game has spread so much that nearly every district, town and village has its club or clubs. It is needless and beside the mark to moralise on this. It is a fact significant, according to the views of the onlooker. Athleticism is clearly in the ascendant. Never was there more excitement about the great boat races. Cricket is more than ever the rage, almost the madness, of the people of England. Athletic sports at school and university are established institutions. Foot- ball has grown from a mere school game into a general winter amusement. It would seem as if, while the wear and tear of brain augments, that, as a corrective, muscular exertion is felt insensibly to be almost a necessity. Be this as it may, however, the fact is undeniable; athletic exercises of various kinds gain ground in the country. The great (boat) race of next Saturday and the great football match of today will, by the crowds of excited spectators assembled to witness them, testify to this phase, this characteristic of the stirring times we live in.

Morning Post - Saturday 16th March 1872

271

THE FINAL
VENUE: KENNINGTON OVAL,
SURREY CRICKET GROUND.

EIGHTEEN FORTY FIVE
——————— SURREY CCC ———————

A match between the Montpelier and Upper Clapton Clubs was played on this ground on Thursday last : the excellent play of these two clubs, and the high condition of this noble piece of ground met with general applause from a numerous and respectable company. The following was the result; Clapton, first innings, 143; Montpelier, first innings, 79 and 4 wickets down. (The Era - Sunday 20th July 1845)

The first-ever cricket match played at the Kennington Oval was a one-day game between a Mr. Houghton's Montpelier side and a team from Clapton, played on 17th July 1845. It took a lot of hard work to get the game on as the pitch had previously been a cabbage patch before it became a market garden. The ground had been in an awful condition and was a health hazard stinking of decaying vegetables.

We have received a letter from Mr. Houghton, the gentleman who has recently converted Kennington Oval into a cricket ground, denying the allegations contained in letter which appeared in our paper last week, to the effect that the change he had made was calculated to bring low company into the neighbourhood. He says he has fenced in and covered with green turf a plot of ground which was before a mere depository for decayed vegetable matter, emitting the most noxious effluvia, and converted a place which before was a public

272

nuisance to the purpose of one of the most manly and healthful sports of England. (Globe - Monday 19th May 1845)

The idea for a Surrey County Cricket Club had first been discussed in 1844 and the first match was then played at The Oval on August 21st and 22nd 1845, between the Gentlemen of Surrey and the Players of Surrey. In 1847, the original market garden dwelling on the site had been converted into a Club House and by 1855 the Kennington Oval could boast of its own Members' Pavilion and pub, the Surrey Tavern. Mr. Houghton lost interest in the Montpelier Club and as he became more engrossed in solving his debts, the grounds were subsequently taken over by the Surrey County Cricket Club.

Surrey Tavern, Kennington Oval, SE11 - circa 1880

Charles William Alcock arrived at The Oval early on the Saturday morning. He had instructed his Wanderers team to meet him in the Surrey Tavern to discuss their tactics over a light lunch. Ever since he had scored the winning goal in the Harrow Cock House Cup Final, back in 1859, he had dreamt of this day. This was the culmination of many years of hard work and now his Football Association Challenge Cup was going to propel his Wanderers side and the game he loved into the hearts of the British public. Of course, there was one other thing left to do and that was to beat the Royal Engineers and become the first winners of the Challenge Cup.

The layout of the Kennington Oval main buildings, showing the entrance through the Surrey Tavern with the Racket Court to the side and the Pavilion to the rear. (Circa 1871)

Charles had picked his strongest eleven from the cream of the public schools of England. In his side were five Old Harrovians, three Old Etonians, a Carthusian and an ex-scholar of Lancing College in Sussex. The final player, Robert Walpole Sealy Vidal, was still studying at Westminster School. Everyone of today's players had made an appearance for England in at least one of the unofficial internationals against Scotland. Robert Vidal had played in all five making his first appearance in March 1870 at the tender age of 16 years 183 days. It was the youngster whom Charles turned to when discussing his tactics for the day.

Robert Walpole Sealey Vidal of the Wanderers: Did he have a plan to outwit the mighty Royal Engineers?

"Listen up lads. Robert, here, has something very exciting to tell you about today's opponents. We may think that the Sappers are unbeatable but he knows a way of stopping them."

The more senior players stopped what they were doing and listened to the young man intently. Each and every one of them had the utmost respect for the 'prince of dribblers' and knew his experience in the game matched theirs already, despite his tender years. As it happened, Robert had captained his Westminster School side against the Royal Engineers on the 10th February and the school had managed to secure a 0-0 draw against the mighty Sappers. Charles Wollaston looked up from his seat at the long wooden dinner table and smirked:

"How did you manage to do that? We thrashed you 3-0 just a few days later and, as it was a mid-week match, we weren't even playing our strongest eleven."

"Listen up, Charles," was Charles Alcock's retort. "What Robert has to say might just work for us and win us the Cup."

"That's correct," said Robert. "The Engineers will be expecting us to play our usual formation with just one half-back and a full-back protecting our goalkeeper. What I did to nullify the noted rushes of the Sappers forwards was to ask my brother to come back and help out in defence. We know the main goal threat will come from Henry Renny-Tailyour and Hugh Mitchell and if we stop them from scoring, they can't win." (i)

"Exactly," said Charles rubbing his hands with glee, "and if we adopt the tactics used by the Scots when they surprised us in that match the other day, then I think we may have the key to our success in the field today. If you remember, Queen's Park attacked us from the off and caught us off our guard. They were relentless for the first fifteen minutes and we could have easily conceded a goal or two. Imagine if we can unsettle the mighty Engineers who are used to winning and haven't conceded a goal as yet. If we can score just one goal it could unnerve them and then, if we adopt Robert's defensive tactics against their goal threats, the usually well organised Sappers could be in disarray."

"Sounds like a plan," chirped up Morton Peto Betts who often played at the back and in goal. "I'm an engineer and I always like to have a plan."

***

The Royal Engineers had plans of their own. They too had witnessed the Wanderers' semi-final game against Queen's Park and had been surprised that the Scots had played an even more expansive passing game than their own brand of 'combination' football. Captains Marindin and Merriman had got the soldiers well drilled into their style of play, which didn't rely on the skills of one individual, but rather the strength of the collective force. They also knew that they had to watch out for the young Robert Vidal who had surprised them by his speed and excellent dribbling skills for one so young. He'd played for the Wanderers in the 1-1 draw against the Royal Engineers back on the 11th November 1871 when the First Round FA Cup ties were being played. Also, Morton Peto Betts captained the Wanderers' side that day as Charles Alcock was captaining and playing in goal for a scratch Wanderers' side in a 13-a-side game at Cambridge University on Monday 13th November 1871. This Wanderers' side featured none other than Hitchin Football Club's star player, William Tindall Lucas, who had played in the FA Cup First Tie goalless draw against Crystal Palace.

"Can someone explain to me why Morton Peto Betts has put his name down on today's team sheet as A.H. Chequer? Does he think we're daft or something? We know he will be playing today and we also know he is A Harrow Chequer. I don't think any of the Harrow Chequers should have been allowed to play in this competition. After all, they entered a side originally and then they scratched as soon as they realised they would be playing their sister team, The Wanderers."

Lieutenant Adam Bogle was a dour Scot born in Glasgow. He'd been muttering to himself since getting into the carriage with his team-mates at Chatham railway station. The Sappers were going to be well-supported today as a trainload of soldiers from the Brompton Barracks were making their way down to London on the next train along with the wives of Captain Marindin and the newly wed wife of Captain Merriman. William Merriman tried to console his young Lieutenant and dropped into the seat beside him.

"Look Adam, we know The Wanderers have a lot of unfair advantages over us. They have the pick of the public-schools of England and also they draft in good players from the other sides they meet on their travels. I know that this season alone they have used over 60 different players. Our advantage is our togetherness. We play and train together regularly. We know each other's game. As our motto says we are everywhere (Ubique) and, thanks to our combination game, we remain undefeated. Let's make sure our football does the talking and let's bring the Cup back to Chatham."

Adam Bogle knew his superior officer was talking sense and he was personally fired up to teach these public-school boys a lesson. As the soldiers exited Vauxhall station, they looked resplendent in their red and black military uniforms as they marched up the Harleyford Road. The weather had been cloudy when they left Kent but it was now turning out to be a glorious, sunny spring day.

The crowd was already arriving for the big event as the well-to-do London gentry alighted from their horse-drawn carriages onto the circular pull-in in front of the Surrey Tavern. The gatemen manning the entrances to The Oval to the side of the tavern charged the crowd the one shilling admission fee. One shilling was quite a sum in these Victorian times and the crowd was therefore expected to be somewhat less than the massive turnout for the Wanderers versus Queen's Park Semi-Final when entrance had been free. However, looking at the top hats of the gentlemen and the brightly coloured dresses of the ladies, the crowd were not short of money and some of them were paying extra to allow their horse drawn landaus into the ground. The low-slung carriages acted as a grandstand for the occupants to be able to see the football action over the top hats and bonnets of the tightly packed crowd in front of them. Some of the ladies had even had the foresight to bring their opera glasses with them to ensure they got a close-up view of these athletic young men showing off their newly developed footballing skills. Not wanting to miss a trick a couple of bookmakers had set up a stall just outside the ground and were offering odds of 7/4 on the Sappers to win.

"There you go, Adam, if the bookmakers think we are going to win then it must be so. They're never wrong."

"That's true, William, maybe the omens are in our favour."

A Victorian landau, ideal for seeing over the heads of the crowd at a football match.

Charles and his Wanderers' team could hear all the commotion going on outside the open windows of the Surrey Tavern. A few of them looked impressed by the sight of the Royal Engineers marching in full uniform up to the ground. Charles turned and calmed his men.

"Remember our plan lads and let's stick to our tactics and I'm sure that come half past four we can emerge victorious."

Both teams emerged from The Oval Pavilion to bright sunshine and warm applause from the crowd. The Wanderers looked resplendent in their orange, violet and black striped shirts and stockings, complete with white knickerbockers and caps. They looked quite the butterflies they were meant to be. The Royal Engineers looked no less magnificent in their famous red and blue striped shirts with matching nightcaps and cowls.

The pitch itself sparkled iridescent green under the bright spring sunlight and the colourful corner flags fluttered gently in the breeze. The edges of the pitch were now marked with whitened lines and then at ten yards from the touchlines, a very long rope was staked along all four sides of the pitch to keep the gathering crowd at bay. At one end of the ground the Surrey Cricket Club tents were erected for the convenience of the ladies. Here they could seek shelter during inclement weather or seek shade when the sun shone brightly. (ii)

The two captains, Alcock and Merriman, jogged up to the centre of the pitch for the all-important toss of the shilling coin. It was estimated that a crowd of around 2,000 were present to witness the kick-off of the first-ever FA Cup Final. As the excited mass of people pressed forward to see the start, a shout went out:

'PLEASE DO NOT STRAIN THE ROPES!'

Alfred Stair of Upton Park had been nominated as the match referee and along with the two umpires, James Kirkpatrick and John Giffard, both of the Civil Service, they tossed the silver coin into the air. (iii) Charles Alcock called successfully for the Wanderers and chose to play from the Harleyford Road end, forcing the Sappers to play with the sun in their faces and into a gentle breeze.

The Sappers took up their positions at the north-east end of the ground with the two gasometers of the Phoenix Gas Company behind them. Captain William Merriman looked down the ground towards the Wanderers goal in front of the pavilion. In the distance he could make out the distinctive tower of St. Mark's Church just below the setting sun. Having lost the toss, it was the Royal Engineers' prerogative to kick-off and at 3.05 p.m. it was time for the first-ever FA Cup Final to get under way.

Within seconds the Royal Engineers were swamped by the Wanderers forwards and it took them completely by surprise. Whenever they got the ball there were at least two Wanderers' players immediately on them, barging or charging them down. The inability of the Sappers forwards to make their normal rushes on the opposition goal put more pressure on the backs and Captain Francis Marindin, George Addison and Alfie Goodwyn were having difficulty in keeping the young Robert Vidal and Thomas Hooman at bay. Both were making mazy dribbles down the touchlines and threatening to breach the Sappers goal.

Charles Alcock looked at his schoolboy forward in admiration and the youngster caught his eye and winked. The tactics were working and the Sappers didn't know how to respond.

After ten minutes Lieutenant Edmund Cresswell managed to recover the ball from a clearance from one of the backs. He tried to set off on a run towards the Wanderers goal but was immediately brought to the ground with a thump. As he fell, he landed awkwardly on his shoulder and quite quickly realised something was wrong. He was attended briefly by one of the military medics who couldn't ascertain if the shoulder was dislocated. His manipulations caused Edmund some pain so eventually Edmund pushed him away and, as there were no substitutes allowed, he decided he would carry on.

This knocked the wind out of the Sappers' sails and on 15 minutes Robert Vidal broke away from a scrimmage and went on another run down the wing. This time he looked up and before the Engineers' full-back could get into position, he middled the ball to none other than Morton Peto Betts, who side footed it past Captain Merriman in the Sappers' goal. It was one-nil to the Wanderers and annoyingly 'A. H. Chequer' had scored the first-ever FA Cup Final goal.

As per the rules the sides changed ends and the Royal Engineers now had the breeze behind them and it was the Wanderers who had the sun in their eyes. The expectant crowd now looked forward to the Sappers taking control of the game and to them producing the rushes and 'combination' play they were famous for. But it didn't happen. On the contrary, the Wanderers started to produce some of best football the public had ever witnessed and on twenty minutes they had scored again and this time it was none other than Charles William Alcock that had struck the ball under the Sappers tape. All those memories of his winning goal in the Cock House Cup came flooding back and Charles was sixteen again and celebrating wildly like that young schoolboy on the playing fields of Harrow.

Suddenly, there was a shout from one of the umpires who ran over to confer with his opposite number. After much discussion it was adjudged that the Wanderer, Charles Wollaston, had handled the ball during the build-up of the move and consequently the umpires concurred that the goal could not stand. Charles was deflated. However, he had now the dubious honour of scoring the first disallowed goal in FA Cup history.

At last, the Sappers were spurred into action. Herbert Muirhead went on a fine run and got the ball within a few yards of the centre of the Wanderers posts. He was about to shoot when the ball was intercepted expertly by Albert Thompson, the Wanderers half-back, who was having an excellent game. Also, Reginald Welch who hadn't had much to do all game, pulled off a fine save from Henry Renny-Tailyour, just before half-time.

Again, the crowd expected the favourites, the Royal Engineers, to come storming back into the game but the injury to Edmund Cresswell and the fact that their talisman, Henry Renny-Tailyour was carrying a knock to his knee from an earlier round, seemed to 'sap' the energy out of the Sappers.

The Wanderers continued from where they had left off in the first half and dominated the game and again, they came close to scoring. They hit the post after a prolonged 'bully' in front of the military goal and if it hadn't been for the efficient goalkeeping of Captain William Merriman, they would have increased their lead. Any chance of the Sappers getting back into the game were dispelled by the brilliant back play of Edgar Lubbock and Albert Thompson, the reliability of which allowed the Wanderers forwards to attack without fear.

'Time' was called just after 4.30 p.m. and the two sides marched off the field to rapturous applause. The first FA Cup had been a resounding success and although Charles William Alcock hadn't managed to score the winning goal, it would be his Wanderers team that would be awarded the Football Association Challenge Cup and as a consequence, they would proceed directly to the Final next year. (iv)

The Wanderers had to wait nearly a month to finally get their hands on the FA Cup trophy. It would be presented to them at their annual dinner to be held in the Pall Mall restaurant in Charing Cross on Thursday 11th April 1872. This was no cheap affair and members of the FA could purchase tickets from Mr. Charles William Alcock for the princely price of seven shillings and sixpence.

Despite the entrance fee, the Pall Mall restaurant was packed and at 7.00 p.m. the evening's festivities commenced. As Charles Alcock was to be presented with the trophy, the most senior Wanderer Ernest Edward Bowen, the 35-year-old classics master from Harrow School, took the chair. An enjoyable meal was had by all and at the end, Douglas Allport of the Crystal Palace Club raised his glass to toast 'The Football Association.' It then fell to the President of the FA, Ebenezer Cobb Morley, to present the Cup to the captain of the Wanderers side. As Charles held the trophy in his hands for the first time, a broad grin spread across his face. This would be the first Wanderers' Cup win of many he felt. This tournament, his tournament, was here to stay. The other members of the Wanderers' side proceeded to collect their silk badges provided by the Football Association. They also collected a gold medal, suitably inscribed, with a value of about 50 shillings, from the Wanderers' Committee.

An original FA Cup winners medal from 1872
- National Football Museum

Further toasts were made to the 'Wanderers' and to 'The Unsuccessful Competitors for the Cup', to 'Captain Marindin and the Royal Engineers,' and finally to 'William Burrup and Surrey Cricket Club' without whom the Wanderers would not have had a home and a venue to stage the Final.

The overall winner was of course 'Association football' which could now be considered as one of Britain's great national pastimes.

Was it any coincidence that the footballers had chosen to host their celebratory meal in the very room that their arch rivals, the 'Rugby Men', had formed the Rugby Football Union on the 26th January 1871?

By introducing the Challenge Cup, it had stolen a march on its arch rival, rugby, and soon it would be challenging cricket for the top spot in the nation's sporting hearts.

Yes, our national game was born on that spring day, Saturday the 16th March 1872, at the Kennington Oval and we can all thank

'CHARLES ALCOCK AND THE LITTLE TIN IDOL!'

Author's Notes:

(i) WESTMINSTER SCHOOL V. ROYAL ENGINEERS

The Royal Engineers and the Westminster School resumed on Saturday their old acquaintance in the football arena—venue Vincent-square—when an exciting contest was the result. Aware of the strength of his opponents, the school captain, R. W. S. Vidal, took the precaution to add to his inner defences by detaching his brother to cooperate with W.S. Rawson and H. S. Jackson in the rear. These, by their well-judged kicking, aided by the excellent goal-keeping of R. Murphy, were enabled to check the rushes of the Royal Engineer forwards, though on one or two occasions Lieuts. Renny-Tailyour, Rich, and Barker carried the ball into close proximity with the school goal. Presently the tide of battle was carried in the opposite direction, and R.W.S. Vidal missed the goalposts of the Military by a couple of feet only. At half-time no advantage had been obtained on either side, and to the end the match was carried vigorously, though without any decisive result for either party. This was decidedly one of the best matches of the season. (Sportsman 17th February 1872)

(ii) the description of The Oval pitch is taken from the report of the England versus Scotland rugby match that appeared in The Field newspaper just a couple of weeks earlier. It seems logical to think that The Oval groundsmen would have laid out the pitch in the same fashion with regards to the colourful flags, whitened lines and the rope staked along the edges of the pitch.

(iii) it is believed that the FA Cup Semi-Finals and Final saw the addition of a referee to adjudicate if the two umpires didn't agree. Another adoption from the rules of the Sheffield Football Association.

(iv) The Football Association Challenge Cup meant exactly that. The following season all entrants would play off against each other, with the winner earning the right to challenge the Wanderers for the right to hold the cup for another season. And so, in 1872-73 Oxford University won through the prior ties and earned the right to play the Wanderers in the Final. Unfortunately, they lost by two goals to nil and therefore the Wanderers held the Cup for another year. This was the only year that this happened and the following season the Wanderers were expected to take part in the knockout competition.

Chapter 27: Where Are They Now?
150 Years Later (2021-22)

Barnes FC

Barnes FC got to the Second Round of the first FA Cup tournament. The Club continued playing football until 1894 when they then switched to Rugby Union. Their last FA Cup appearance was in October 1885 when they lost 7-1 to Lancing Old Boys.

A new football club 'Barnes Albion' was founded in 1926 by Robert Sears and Leslie Kilsby. They subsequently reverted to their original name, Barnes FC in 1935-36 and continued playing until around 1989-90.

Football is still being played in Barnes today and Barnes Eagles (maybe that should be Beagles!) were formed in 1971 to offer junior football to 5 to 16-year-olds. They also have an adult team called 'Barnes Eagles Senior' who play in the Premier Division of the Leatherhead and District Sunday Football League.

There is a project underway, led by Chairman Ranko Davidov, to form a new club under the original name of Barnes FC. The intention is to create a community club that will compete in the Kingston & District Football League in the Season 2022-23 and eventually play in the FA Cup once again. The new club badge (pictured here) represents the knight's emblem of the Borough.

Civil Service FC

Whilst they lost to Barnes in the very First Round of the first FA Cup tournament, the Civil Service FC were playing a long game. Having celebrated their 150th birthday in 2013, they're the only surviving club considered a founder member of the Football Association.

Their long history means they've helped to spread the word about Association football across the world playing sides like Slavia Prague in the old Czechoslovakia and Germania in Berlin. For almost a century they've played home games at their ground in Chiswick. Their first team currently play in the Southern Amateur League.

Clapham Rovers FC

Clapham Rovers FC got to the Second Round of the First FA Cup losing narrowly to the eventual winners, The Wanderers. The team then went on to win the trophy in 1880 beating Oxford University 1-0 at the Kennington Oval. They had also reached the FA Cup Final the previous year losing narrowly 1-0 to the Old Etonians and these achievements proved that Clapham Rovers Football Club were one of the leading teams of the Victorian era.

In 1879, Clapham Rovers' James Prinsep set a record for being the youngest player in an FA Cup Final, at 17 years and 245 days, a record that held until 1964 when it was broken by Everton's Howard Kendall. The Club continued playing in the FA Cup up until the end of the 1886-87 season.

Clapham Rovers have survived much longer than most of the early FA Cup entrants lasting until the outbreak of the First World War. The Club was resurrected in the mid-1990s and now play in the Southern Sunday Football League on the Clapham Common Extension pitches.

Crystal Palace Club

Crystal Palace Club were thrashed 3-0 by the Royal Engineers in the semi-final replay of the first FA Cup when they were without their star player, Cuthbert Ottaway. This proved to be the original Crystal Palace's best performance in the FA Cup and they entered each year up until the season 1875-76 when they were coincidentally beaten 3-0 again in the Second Round by the Wanderers. By this time Crystal Palace were no longer playing at home on the Park's cricket ground. A list of their fixtures for 1875-76 showed that all their matches were to be played on the opposition's grounds. (Ironically they had become football's new 'wanderers' and in fact, in a fixture to be played against South Norwood on 29th December 1875, they were listed as Crystal Palace Wanderers.)

It appears as though the increase in the popularity of football was to prove to be its undoing. As more matches were being played, this meant more potential damage to cricket pitches and football clubs were being asked to look elsewhere to play the sport. The season of 1875-76 would prove to be the last for the Crystal Palace Club which was struggling to field a side and with no home ground they stopped playing football altogether.

Some 20 years later, in May 1894, the cricket ground in the Crystal Palace Park was rebuilt into arena complete with grandstands capable of hosting, horse shows, football, cricket and polo matches. Surrey County Cricket Club had also put a stop to football being played on their hallowed cricket ground at the Kennington Oval, so the FA were looking for somewhere to host the FA Cup Final. The new arena at Crystal Palace Park fitted the bill perfectly and it went on to host all the FA Cup Finals between 1895 and the outbreak of the First World War in 1914. During this time a new team called Crystal Palace played three 'exhibition' matches in 1895, 1896 and 1897. However, the players involved mainly had strong links with the renowned 'Corinthians' side of the day.

With the advent of professionalism in 1885, the formation of the Football League in 1888 (covering the North and the Midlands) and the formation of the Southern League in 1894, the prospect of forming a new football club suddenly had financial appeal to the Directors of the Crystal Palace Company. They had seen how successful Woolwich Arsenal had been in drawing in large crowds to their matches and so in 1905 a new team and company was formed called 'The Crystal Palace Football and Athletic Club Co. Ltd.' and they would play in the Southern League Division 2.

The newly formed Club immediately took part in the FA Cup in 1905-06 and despite getting to the Quarter Finals in 1906-07, never got to play in an FA Cup Final on their own ground. Crystal Palace FC have reached the FA Cup Final on two occasions since and each time they have been beaten by Manchester United. In the season 1989-90 the match went to a replay after a 3-3 draw. The replay being won 1-0 by United. Then in 2015-16, Jason Puncheon scored first to give Crystal Palace FC the lead over Sir Alex Ferguson's Manchester side. Unfortunately, this led to the excruciating sight of Alan Pardew, Palace's manager, doing some kind of 'dad' dance on the touchline. Luckily, for the sake of English football fans all over the world, Palace's lead only lasted three minutes when United equalised and then went on to be victorious by two goals to one.

Crystal Palace FC have been in the Premier League since 2013-14 with a best finish of tenth place in the Season 2014-15. The Club now play at Selhurst Park in the London Borough of Croydon, their home since 1924.

Donington School

Perhaps the quirkiest entrants in the first-ever FA Cup tournament were Donington School from a small village near Boston in Lincolnshire. After their misfortune in drawing the most distant club, Queen's Park in Glasgow, they inevitably had to withdraw from the competition. The school did not enter the FA Cup again and in 1949 it was renamed the Thomas Cowley School and remains in existence today.

A team of ex-pupils did play an exhibition match in Glasgow against Queen's Park in May 1972 as part of the Football Association's Centenary celebrations. The match was won 6–0 by Queen's Park.

Great Marlow (Marlow) Football Club

"Hi Terry, it's Ian Chester here. Is everything still OK for our meeting this afternoon?"

"Erm, well there's been a bit of a problem. We've just had a cloudburst and the torrential rain has washed away all the white lines around the pitch. I need to organise for it all to be marked out again. There's a chance the referee won't allow the game to go ahead so I'll catch up with you later!"

Such is the lot of a non-league Chairman in the modern era of football. My meeting with Terry Staines, the current Chairman of Marlow Football Club, was to be held during the Club's historic FA Cup Preliminary Round game against Slimbridge FC. It was 150 years since Great Marlow's first foray into the FA Cup and the 2-0 away defeat against local rivals Maidenhead. As we know the club has entered the competition every year since it was created only missing out once when their entrance application had been late.

Finally, I caught up with Terry outside the quaint 'Alfred Davis' main stand built in 1928 in memory of their long serving Club Secretary. The pitch had been remarked, the player's socks had all been found, a suitable shirt had been found for the goalkeeper and the game was going ahead. I'm sure Ed Woodward never has these sort of issues to deal with before a Manchester United match!

Terry was kind enough to show me around the clubhouse and boardroom. At the entrance the noticeboard proudly displays some of the letters and minutes from the Club's initial meetings in November 1870. Also, around the walls and behind glass cabinets are numerous mementoes from Marlow's rich 150-year FA Cup history.

The Alfred Davis Memorial Stand (1928), Marlow FC

In 1992, for the first time in 100 years, Marlow FC played in the First Round Proper against West Bromwich Albion at the Hawthorns unfortunately losing 6-0. This was followed by a Third Round tie against Tottenham Hotspur in January 1993. This match was switched to White Hart Lane and played in front of 21,000 people with Spurs running out 5-1 winners. Then the following season the club actually drew Peter Shilton's Plymouth Argyle side at home in what was dubbed as:

'THE BIGGEST GAME TO EVER BE PLAYED AT THE ALFRED DAVIS MEMORIAL GROUND IN MARLOW.'

A crowd of around 3,000 people witnessed Argyle escape a potential banana skin eventually running out 2-0 winners. Other displays show the certificate presented to the club in 1980 in the 100th FA Cup competition and there is a poster on display announcing the 'Cuthbert Ottaway Memorial Cup' played in 2013 on the 150th Anniversary of the formation of the FA in 1863. If you ever want to feel the true spirit that the FA Challenge Cup competition generates then visit Marlow. It oozes out of the terraces and the clubhouse walls.

Around 1879-80 Great Marlow Football Club became Marlow FC. The club's best FA Cup performance to date was reaching the semi-finals in 1881-82 when they lost 5-0 to Old Etonians. Could they go one better today?

MARLOW FC v. SLIMBRIDGE FC
FOOTBALL ASSOCIATION CHALLENGE CUP
PRELIMINARY ROUND
Saturday 21st August 2021
Alfred Davis Memorial Ground, Marlow: Kick-Off: 3.00 p.m.

A crowd of 208 watched in anticipation as the match against Slimbridge FC unfolded. For the first 30 minutes the game was pretty even with nothing much to choose between the sides until Marlow's striker, Nnamdi Nwachuku, received the ball on the edge of the Slimbridge penalty box, turned and drove a sweet shot into the bottom left corner of the goal. Then just before half-time came the sucker punch as Nwachuku turned provider as he headed a well-directed free kick into the path of Junaid Bell who duly converted.

In the second half it was all Marlow and they had several opportunities to increase their lead. A third goal eventually came in the 71st minute when Isaac Olorunfemi controlled a cross and then slotted the ball nicely into the bottom right-hand corner of the Slimbridge goal. The final score was 3-0 to Marlow and the 'Blues' 150th Anniversary FA Cup dream was still very much alive.

Marlow's FC's digital programme for their FA Cup Preliminary Round tie against Slimbridge FC on 21st August 2021 featuring Chairman, Terry Staines, and the 1st Team Manager, Mark Bartley, holding the current FA Cup trophy.

Marlow FC followed this up with further FA Cup victories against Sheppey United (1Q) and Abbey Rangers (2Q) before finally being knocked out by Harrow Borough FC 2-1 (3Q), ironically just two miles down the road from Harrow School, where Charles Alcock scored that so important goal to win the Cock

House Cup, 162 years previously. Marlow FC currently play in the Isthmian League Central South Division (Season 2021-22).

Hampstead Heathens

The Hampstead Heathens' unceremonious departure from the first FA Cup at the hands of the Royal Engineers was the last match they ever played. Their brief rise and fall was typical of the fleeting nature of early Victorian football clubs. Some of their players are believed to have renounced football for 'respectable' careers such as becoming 'men of the cloth.'

Harrow Chequers

The Harrow Chequers failed to even get a team together for their FA Cup First Round match against the Wanderers in 1871. However, as we know, one of their players, Morton Peto Betts, did go on to score the first-ever FA Cup Final goal playing for the Wanderers under the pseudonym A.H. Chequer. The Chequers were never destined to play an FA Cup match scratching from the competition on three occasions. Subsequently, they became the Old Harrovians who were successful in reaching the FA Cup semi-final in 1887-78 going out to a 2-1 defeat to the Royal Engineers.

Hitchin (Hitchin Town) Football Club

The original Hitchin Football Club suffered a 5-0 defeat to the Royal Engineers in the Second Round of the first FA Cup after a credible First Round 0-0 draw against the mighty Crystal Palace. Amazingly they then scratched from the competition twice in the following years when drawn each time against Clapham Rovers (1872-73 & 1874-75). What was it about the Rovers that Hitchin FC didn't like?

They did take to the field again in the FA Cup in the 1873-74 season when they drew Maidenhead FC in the First Round. It was agreed the game would be played in London, at the Lillie Bridge ground, as it was equidistant from both clubs and easier to get to by train. It was a close game but Maidenhead FC came out on top with a 1-0 victory and progressed to the next round.

Sometime around the turn of the 19th Century, and after the advent of professionalism in 1888, Hitchin FC became known as Hitchin Town FC. Unfortunately, the renamed club folded in 1911 after getting into financial difficulties. Football did, however, survive in the town with teams such as the Hitchin Blue Cross Temperance Brigade which featured a few of the ex-Hitchin Town players, Hitchin Athletic FC and the wonderfully named 'Hitchin Union Jack'. Hitchin Town FC resurfaced 17 years later in the spring of 1928.

'Hitchin Town Football Club is to be revived and the new Club has entered the Spartan League Division II. The team will wear all white and with a badge or monogram, to be decided on later.' (Biggleswade Chronicle - Friday 11th May 1928)

Hitchin Town FC currently play in the Southern League Premier Division Central and have a proud record in the FA Cup reaching the Second Round Proper on a couple of occasions.

BIGGLESWADE TOWN v. HITCHIN TOWN
FOOTBALL ASSOCIATION CHALLENGE CUP
1ST QUALIFYING ROUND
Saturday 4th September 2021
Langford Road, Biggleswade
Attendance 408: Kick-Off : 3.00 p.m.

It was on a bright September's day that Chris Gedge and I pulled into the car park of Biggleswade Town FC or 'The Waders' as they like to be known. There was a decent crowd filing through the turnstiles and it was clear that quite a few had made the short trip from Hitchin to see this historic 150th Anniversary FA Cup match. Today Hitchin Town would be playing in magenta and black rather than their usual yellow and green shirts. The club has created a special edition shirt, stamped with the motif 'FA CUP ORIGINALS 150 YEARS 1871 – 2021' to commemorate the 150th Anniversary of their appearance in the first FA Cup and this was a fitting tribute to their original colours.

The Hitchin crowd were also wearing a mixture of the current yellow & green home shirt and this new commemorative shirt. There were also a few sporting a beautiful magenta polo shirt emblazoned with a badge shouting '150 YEARS (1865-2015) Football in Hitchin' The fans certainly understood their football history and were rightly proud of their historic roots.

Hitchin fans sporting their commemorative shirts, rightly proud of the town's rich football heritage.

Hitchin Town had never lost to Biggleswade Town in their previous six Cup encounters so would the FA Cup Gods be on their side today? It certainly seemed so when, with twelve minutes on the clock, they were awarded a penalty as the ball rose sharply and struck a Biggleswade defender on the hand. It seemed a bit harsh on 'The Waders' but a confident Alex Brown stepped up and planted his kick beyond the reach of the Biggleswade keeper, much to the delight of the 'Canaries' fans.

1-0 was still the score at half-time and at the restart Alex Brown's brother, Luke, netted for the Canaries again with a beautiful strike that sailed into the top right-hand corner of The Waders goal. It was a good time to score and Biggleswade now had to throw caution to the wind to try and get back into the game. However, despite some sustained Waders' pressure, it was Hitchin who scored again and Callum Stead's 78th minute goal was enough to propel the Canaries through to the 2nd Qualifying round of the FA Cup with a convincing 3-0 victory. A fitting result for this historic club and I'm sure the fans drank a few pints of their specially brewed 'Hop Field 1871' ale when they got back to Hitchin. I'm sure the Reverend John Pardoe would have approved!

'Hop Field 1871' is a specially brewed commemorative ale, which can be found on sale at Hitchin's Top Field ground.

Unfortunately, Hitchin Town were to go out of the FA Cup 2021-22 in the 2nd Qualifying round losing 3-0 away at Cheshunt.

Maidenhead (United) FC

After being undone by a reportedly small pitch in their Second Round tie against Crystal Palace, Maidenhead Football Club were determined to prove their footballing prowess. They did this by reaching the FA Cup Quarter Finals in each of the three following seasons.

Unfortunately, in 1872-73, they lost heavily 4-0 to Oxford University on the college grounds. The following season, 1873-74, they fared no better being thrashed 7-0 on their home ground by the Royal Engineers. This time they were without the services of some of their key players, whilst the Sappers had amassed their strongest eleven with one Henry Renny-Tailyour outstanding again. Their third Quarter Final, in 1874-75, was a much closer affair as they went down narrowly to the Old Etonians by a disputed 'handled' goal at the Kennington Oval. Maidenhead, again felt hard done by and lodged an appeal with the FA, which ultimately was unsuccessful and the Old Etonians progressed to the Semi-Finals.

Maidenhead have entered the FA Cup every year except for the season 1876-77 when, as we know, they decided not to enter for financial reasons.

After the First World War, Maidenhead FC merged with another team in the town called Maidenhead Norfolkians and eventually became known as Maidenhead United around 1920.

Maidenhead United currently play in the Vanarama National League and will enter the 2021-22 FA Cup in the 4th Qualifying Round. They will pay Hastings United at home at York Road on Saturday 16th October 2021 and Magpies fans will be hoping they can progress past the First Round Proper for the first time in their long history.

Queen's Park FC

After their appearance against the Wanderers in the 1871-72 FA Cup semi-final, Queen's Park didn't appear in the FA Cup again until the 1883-84 season due to financial constraints. However, when they applied to enter again, they made an immediate impact and reached the Final in 1884 losing 2-1 to Blackburn Rovers.

It was the same again in 1885 when they again lost out to the Rovers, this time going down 2-0. Queen's Park continued to compete in the FA Cup until 1887 when the Scottish Football Association banned its member clubs from entering the English competition.

Another contribution of the Scottish Club to English Football was the introduction of the solid crossbar. Although it first appeared in the Sheffield Rules code, Queen's Park were responsible for its use in Association football when the club successfully put forward a motion for its introduction at a meeting of the Football Association in 1875.

The Queen's Park Club has remained true to its amateur roots since its foundation in 1867. However, in 2019 a major change was made to the club's constitution when its members decided they wished to end amateur status and allow the club to hire professional players. Part of the motivation for the proposal was that several good players had been lost without the club receiving any compensation due to its status.

The Club are currently in the process of moving to their own ground next to Hampden Park (Lesser Hampden) with the ownership of the national stadium having now passed on to the Scottish FA. The side are currently playing in the SPFL 1 at the Firhill Stadium, the home of Partick Thistle, as they await the move into their new 1,800-seater stadium.

Reigate Priory FC

Reigate Priory's entry into the first-ever FA Cup was their only foray into FA Cup football. Even then they didn't play an FA Cup tie as they scratched from the competition after being drawn against the Royal Engineers. However, the club is one of the oldest football clubs in the world still playing on its original ground to be found at Park Lane in Reigate, Surrey. Reigate Priory FC currently play in the Mid Sussex Football League – Championship. (2021-22).

Royal Engineers AFC

In the 1871-72 season, the Royal Engineers played twenty matches. They won fifteen, drew four and lost only one, the FA Cup Final against Wanderers. They scored fifty-four goals and conceded just three. The Royal Engineers have a very proud FA Cup history and have reached four finals (1872, 1874, 1875 and 1878). They won the Cup in 1875 beating Old Etonians 2-0 in a replay after a 1-1 draw. Both matches were refereed by one Charles Alcock. The scorer of all three goals in the two Final matches was, of course, Henry Renny-Tailyour.

When the Football League was formed in 1888 for professional Association football clubs, the Royal Engineers remained strictly amateur and consequently the Army formed its own Football Association in the same year. Their teams were organised by battalion and later by regiment. The Royal Engineers Depot Battalion won the FA Amateur Cup in 1908.

A commemorative Cup presented to the Royal Engineers in 1972 to mark the centenary of the Challenge Cup competition.

In recent decades the Royal Engineers have remained at the forefront of football in the Army, regularly winning competitions at both unit and Corps level and continue to play the game in the spirit of their illustrious forebears. In the 2012-13 season the Royal Engineers AFC commemorated their 150th Anniversary with a celebratory dinner and some high-profile fixtures. They played Gillingham FC at their Priestfield Stadium and also took part in a pre-season tournament involving Chatham Town, West Bromwich Albion and Nottingham Forest. The Sappers now play on what is known as the Number One pitch next to the original R.E. cricket ground in Chatham and they also run Ladies and Veterans teams.

Currently there is a project under way to raise funds to restore Captain Francis Marindin's family grave which has been found in the Crombie Old Parish Churchyard in Torryburn near Dunfermline. Francis Marindin was President of the FA from 1874 to 1890 and also refereed nine FA Cup Finals; the first in 1880 and then every Final between 1883 and 1890.

Major Glen Lishman proudly shows off the Sappers Number One pitch located on the Great Lines, Chatham.

Upton Park FC

Despite their early exit from the first FA Cup in 1871-72, Upton Park did reach the quarter-finals on four separate occasions in 1876-77, 1877-78, 1881-82 and 1883-84.

Upton Park were a proud amateur club and they sparked the legalisation of professionalism in the game after complaining about Preston North End's payments to players after the two met in the FA Cup in 1884. Preston were disqualified but the incident made the FA confront the issue and, under threat of a breakaway, they allowed payments to players the following year. The club were wound up in 1887 but were resurrected four years later in 1891. Their commitment to their amateur status led them to be chosen to represent Great Britain at the inaugural Olympics in Paris in 1900. They went on to win the tournament beating a side representing France 4-0 in the Final. Although a gold medal was not awarded to the side at the time, the IOC have since retrospectively awarded one. Upton Park continued to play football until around 1911 when the club was dissolved.

Upton Park playing against France in the 1900 Olympics in Paris.

In 2016, coinciding with West Ham United's move to the London Stadium, Upton Park were 'reformed' as an amateur club and staged the final game at the Boleyn Ground, against Royal Engineers winning the match 2-0.

For the winners of the First FA Cup, it was the start of a golden, if brief, era of success. Because the FA Cup is a Challenge Cup the Wanderers had a bye to the Final the following year, 1873. They retained the trophy by beating Oxford University 2-0 and then added three more FA Cup victories before the end of the decade, beating Old Etonians 3-0 (1876), Oxford University 2-1 (1877) and the Royal Engineers 3-1 (1878). Their haul of five FA Cups still leaves the Wanderers 10th equal in the list of Clubs with the most victories. The Club was dissolved at the end of 1883 with their last game appropriately being played against Harrow School at the Oval on the 18th December. Charles Alcock was present, of course, acting as an umpire in HIS club's last ever match, a 6-1 victory.

The Wanderers' Club was reformed in 2009 with the aim of playing exhibition matches in the aid of charitable causes. The Club now play in the Surrey South Eastern Combination League.

A re-enactment of the 1872 FA Cup Final took place at the Oval to celebrate the 140th anniversary of the tournament. The result was reversed this time with the Royal Engineers coming out on top by seven goals to one.

Match programme: Wanderers versus Royal Engineers 7th November 2012.

Chapter 28: Charles Alcock & The Little Tin Idol.

After the resounding success of the FA Challenge Cup tournament, both football and Charles William Alcock went from strength to strength. From a personal perspective, his family was growing and both he and his wife Eliza went on to have 8 children on almost an annual basis:

William Edward Forster Alcock (1865-1887)
Elizabeth Maud Alcock (1869-1937)
Florence Caroline Alcock (1870-1938)
Charlotte Mabel Alcock (1872-1903)
Charles Ernest Alcock (1873-1874)
Helen Mary Alcock (1874-1946)
Marion Frances Alcock (1875-1922)
Violet May Alcock (1878-1952)

To accommodate their expanding family, the Alcocks moved from Grassendale House in West Dulwich to more substantial premises in and around London, moving six times over the next 26 years. Charles' career as a sports writer and journalist also blossomed. Apart from his Football Annual launched in 1868, he became the editor of the James Lillywhite's Cricketers' Annual from 1872 to 1900. With the growing popularity of football, Victorian society were hungry for more publications on the new national pastime and in 1874 he wrote a small book entitled 'Football, Our Winter Game'

Illustration: Football, Our Winter Game – Charles W. Alcock (1874)

With all these responsibilities, you would think that football and journalism would be enough to keep Charles busy but, on the contrary, Charles had only started. In 1872, shortly after captaining the Wanderers to FA Cup success, he became the first paid Secretary of Surrey County Cricket Club.

Then in October of that year he persuaded the FA Committee to take part in an international match between England and Scotland at the West of Scotland Cricket Ground in Partick, Glasgow. Despite opposition to his idea, because of the cost of travel, Charles got his way and on the 30th November the first recognised international Association football match in the world took place between England and Scotland ending in a 0-0 draw.

This was the match where the Scots surprised the English with their technique of heading the ball and it also showcased Billy MacKinnon's famous overhead kick. Unfortunately, Charles sustained a thigh injury two weeks before the game in a friendly (?) match between Eton & Harrow and therefore couldn't lead his team out against Scotland. Instead, he represented his country as umpire with the England captaincy awarded to one Cuthbert Ottaway.

The year of 1875 proved to be a watershed year for Charles and, as he approached his 33rd birthday, his lifetime of playing sports was catching up with him. He did, however, get to play in his first full international, a 2-2 draw against Scotland, at the Oval on 6th March 1875, but after a match between the Wanderers and Queen's Park played at Hampden on 9th October 1875, he retired.

Football programme of Charles W. Alcock's last match played at Hampden against Queen's Park on 9th October 1875.

Charles was not finished yet though and he turned to officiating football matches. He was referee at both the FA Cup Final and the replay between the Royal Engineers and the Old Etonians in March 1875. He then went on to referee the 1879 Final between the Old Etonians and Clapham Rovers. Also, now that Charles had relinquished his football career he had more time to devote to his administrative duties. In cricket, he used his experience in organising international matches to convince a Lord Harris to get together an England cricket team to play against the touring Australians at the Oval in 1880. This became the first cricket Test Match to be played in the world. A subsequent defeat to the Australians in 1882 and a mock obituary in the 'Sporting Times' led to the legendary burning of the cricket bails and the creation of the oldest cricket tournament in the world, 'The Ashes'.

Charles, in later life, sat at his desk pondering over his next revolutionary idea for world sport.

Charles Alcock held the post as Secretary of the FA up until 1895. He also served as Secretary of Surrey Cricket Club right up until his death on 26th February 1907.

In his life he ensured the success of football, as he pointed out:

"What was ten or fifteen years ago the recreation of a few has now become the pursuit of thousands. An athletic exercise carried on under a strict system and in many cases by an enforced term of training, almost magnified into a profession."

Charles is buried in the West Norwood Cemetery in London.

The Little Tin Idol

'The Little Tin Idol' was awarded to the winning FA Cup finalists each year between 1872 and 1895. However, in August 1895 a football outfitter in Birmingham asked the current holders, Aston Villa, if he could display the trophy in his shop window. William Shillcock was a friend of the Chariman, William McGregor (creator of the Football League in 1888) and supplier to the Villa and the England national team and so the club agreed.

The vicrtorious Aston Villa side pictured with 'The Little Tin Idol' after their 1-0 FA Cup victory over neighbours, West Bromwich Albion, in 1895.

On the morning of 12th September 1895, William Shillcock entered his shop and saw his till's cash drawer lying empty on the counter. There was some broken plaster on the floor and a small hole in the roof but the shop's two safes and other valuables were untouched. Shillcock thought it was a curious burglary until he checked the display window and discovered that the FA Cup was gone.

A £10 reward was offered for its return but no infornation was forthcoming and Aston Villa were fined £25 for losing the Cup whilst in their posssession. Various rumours abounded about the fate of 'The Little Tin Idol' and an uncorroborated confession from a Harry Burge suggests the silver cup may have been melted down and used in the production of half-crown coins.

A second FA Cup was produced and used up until 1910 when it was presented to Lord Arthur Kinnaird, the FA's long serving President. He died in 1923 and the Cup has recently been auctioned in 2020 by the West Ham Chairman, David Gold, for a hammer price of £620,000. This is the Cup depicted in the photos of this book and it is currently on display in the National Football Museum.

And so, if you are sitting comfortably in your lounge watching England play Scotland in Euro 2020 or standing on a windy and rainy terrace in the North of England watching Atherton Colleries versus Marine in this season's FA Cup, or indeed watching England play Australia in The Ashes then look to the sky and raise the glass you're holding and announce a toast to;

'CHARLES ALCOCK & THE LITTLE TIN IDOL'

APPENDICES

Appendix 1: Rules of Harrow Football (1858)

Harrow Game

1.   The Choice of Bases is determined, in House Matches by tossing; but in the ordinary School Games that Side has the Choice, on which the Head of the School (or in his absence the Highest in the School present) is playing.

2.   The Bases are 12 ft. in width, and the distance between them, in House Matches, must not be greater than 150 yds. The width of the ground must not be more than 100 yds.

3.   The Ball must be kicked off from the middle of the ground, halfway between the two Bases.

4.   If when the Ball is kicked, from Hand or otherwise, any one on the same side, but nearer the opposite Base, touches or kicks the Ball, he is said to be Behind, only if one of the opposite Side be between him and the party who kicked the Ball. Anyone who is thus Behind is considered as being virtually out of the Game, and must wait till the ball has been touched by one of the opposite side: nor must he interfere with any one of the opposite Side, or in any way prevent or obstruct his catching the Ball.

5.   The Ball may not be caught off any other part of the Body but the leg below the knee, or foot; but if after being kicked, it hits any other part of the Body, before falling to the ground, it may then be caught.

6.   Whoever catches the Ball is entitled to a free kick if he calls Three yards; but whoever catches the Ball, and does not call Three yards, is liable to have it knocked out of his hands.

7.   The Ball, when in Play, must never be touched by the hand, except in the case of the Catch, as above stated.

8.   All Charging is fair, but neither Holding nor Tripping is allowed.

9.   If the Ball is kicked beyond the prescribed limits of the Ground, it must be kicked straight in again; and then must not be touched by the Hands, or Arms below the Elbow.

10.   When the Ball goes behind the Line of either of the Bases, it must be kicked straight in (as by Rule 9), and then must not be touched by any one belonging to the Side, behind whose Base it was kicked, until it has been touched by one of the opposite Side.

11.   Bases can only be obtained by kicking; but when any one catches the Ball near the opposite Base, he may jump the Three yards and go back to get a free kick: or if he catches it at so short a distance from the Base that he can carry it through by jumping the Three yards, he may do so.

12.   All Shinning and Back shinning is strictly prohibited.

13.   After a Base has been obtained, the two Sides change their respective Bases.

14.   There must always be two Umpires in a House Match.

15.   The above Rules should be put up conspicuously in every House at the beginning of every Football Quarter, and new Boys should be required to make themselves thoroughly acquainted with them.

Author's Note: These rules have been taken from the following source. – Thesis submitted for the degree of Doctor of Philosophy at the University of Leicester by Graham Curry B.Ed (Hons.) (Nottingham), (M.A. Leicester) – May 2001. And I quote: 'I have recently been fortunate (December 1999) to have been in contact with the archivist at Harrow School, Mrs. Rita Gibbs, from whom I procured a set of Harrow School Football Rules which differ slightly from those quoted by Percy Young, History of British Football (1968: 68-70) the year 1858 was written by hand in the top right-hand corner and, although this might not be seen as proof of dating, I feel that there seems little reason to disbelieve its authenticity.'

Another source, Puddings, Bullies and Squashes: Early Public School Football Codes, by Malcolm Tozer identifies these rules as having been written by Mr. E. E. Bowen in 1865.

Appendix 2: Rules of the Forest Club (1861)

The rules of the Forest Football Club were largely based on those which had been drawn up at Cambridge University circa 1856, but with a few additional rules of their own:

Rules of the Forest Foot-ball Club.

At the commencement of the play, the ball shall be kicked off from the middle of the ground: after every goal there shall be a kick-off in the same way or manner.

After a goal, the losing side shall kick-off; the sides changing goals, unless a previous arrangement be made to the contrary.

The ball is out when it has passed the line of the flag-posts on either side of the ground, in which case it shall be thrown in straight.

The ball is behind when it has passed the goal on either side of it.

When the ball is behind it shall be brought forward at the place where it left the ground, not more than ten paces, and kicked off.

Goal is when the ball is kicked through the flag-posts and under the string.

When a player catches the ball directly from the foot, he may kick it as he can without running with it. In no other case may the ball be touched with the hands, except to stop it.

If the ball has passed a player, and has come from the direction of his own goal, he may not touch it till the other side have kicked it, unless there are more than three of the other side before him. No player is allowed to loiter between the ball and the adversaries' goal.

In no case is holding a player, pushing with the hands, or tripping up allowed. Any player may prevent another from getting to the ball by any means consistent with this rule.

Every match shall be decided by a majority of goals.

But Forest added a few of their own club rules:

That captains be chosen at the commencement of play, who shall have the direction of places, etc., etc., throughout the game.

That the length and breadth of ground be marked off with flags, and that the distance between the goal-posts do not exceed eight yards.

That in the event of the bursting of the ball, a new one is to be placed at the centre of the ground, and that the side commencing the game have the kick-ff.

That for any wilful infringement of the rules of the game, a fine of Two Shillings and Sixpence be inflicted.

Appendix 3: Rules and Regulations for the Government of the Sheffield Football Club (1857)

1. That this Club be called the Sheffield Football Club.

2. That the Club be managed by a Committee of five members (three to form a quorum) of which the officers of the Club shall be ex-officio members, to be elected at the annual general meetings.

3. That the annual general meeting of the Club shall be held on the second Monday in October in each year for the purpose of electing officers for the ensuing year and for other purposes.

4. That the Committee shall be empowered to call a special general meeting of the Club on giving seven days' notice by circular to each member, specifying the objects for which such meeting is called, and the discussion at such special meeting shall be confined to that object alone. The Committee shall also call a special meeting of the Club on the written request of six members.

5. That each member on his admission to the Club shall pay 2s. 6d. subscription for the current year and that the annual subscription shall be due on the first day of November in each year.

6. That it shall be necessary for members wishing to retire from the Club to give notice in writing to the Hon. Secretary on or before the first day in October.

7. That the Committee shall have power to make a further call, in addition to the annual subscription if they shall deem it necessary for the purpose of the Club, such further call not in any case to exceed 2s. 6d. per year.

8. That the Committee shall (during the season) meet once in every fortnight for the dispatch of business.

9. That the season shall commence on the first day in November and end on Easter Eve in each year.

10. That the play day of the Club be Saturday from two o'clock until dark.

11. That every candidate for admission to the Club shall be proposed by one member and seconded by another, his name and usual place of residency having been given to the Secretary, the Proposer and Seconder each subscribing his own name. The candidate will be balloted for by the Committee according to the priority of their nominations.

12. No ballot shall be valid unless three Committeemen vote, and two black balls shall exclude.

13. That all disputes during play shall be referred to the members of the Committee present at the ground, their decision to be final.

14. That the officers for the season be:
President: Frederick Ward;
Vice-Presidents: J.A. Sorby and I. Ellison;
Committee: Messrs. W. Prest, I. Pierson, W. Baker, J.K. Turner and J.E. Vickers;
Honorary Secretary and Treasurer: N. Creswick.

15. That each member shall have the privilege of introducing one or more friends in company with himself during each season if within six miles of Sheffield; such friends shall be introduced once only.

16. That the Committee shall take immediate cognizance of any infringement of these Rules, and it shall be their special duty in case any circumstances shall occur likely to endanger the stability or to interrupt the harmony and good order of the Club to call a general meeting in the mode above described. In the event of two thirds of the members present at such meetings deciding by ballot on the expulsion of any member such member shall cease to belong to the Club.

17. That the Rules, together with the Laws relating to the playing of the game, shall be forthwith printed and afterwards, as often as the Committee shall think fit, and one copy shall be delivered to any member on application to the Secretary. Any member may obtain additional copies at the rate of sixpence each copy on a like application.

Appendix 4: Sheffield Playing Rules (21st October 1858)

1. The kick-off from the middle must be a place kick.

2. Kick Out must not be from more than twenty-five yards out of goal.

3. Fair catch is a catch direct from the foot of the opposite side and entitles a free kick.

4. Charging is fair in case of a place kick (with the exception of a kick-off as soon as a player offers to kick) but he may always draw back unless he has actually touched the ball with his foot.

5. No pushing with the hands or hacking, or tripping up is fair under any circumstances whatsoever.

6. Knocking or pushing on the ball is altogether disallowed. The side breaking the rule forfeits a free kick to the opposite side.

7. No player may be held or pulled over.

8. It is not lawful to take the ball off the ground (except in touch) for any purpose whatever.

9. If the ball be bouncing it may be stopped by the hand, not pushed or hit, but if the ball is rolling it may not be stopped except by the foot.

10. No goal may be kicked from touch, nor by a free kick from a fair catch.

11. A ball in touch is dead, consequently the side that touches it down must bring it to the edge of the touch and throw it straight out from touch.

12. Each player must provide himself with a red and dark blue flannel cap, one colour to be worn by each side.

Appendix 5: The Laws of the Game (December 1863)

1. **Pitch measurements and size of goals**

   The maximum length of the ground shall be 200 yards, the maximum breadth shall be 100 yards, the length and breadth shall be marked off with flags; and the goals shall be defined by two upright posts, 8 yards apart, without any tape or bar across them.

2. **Kick-Off**

   The winner of the toss shall have the choice of goals. The game shall be commenced by a place kick from the centre of the ground by the side losing the toss, the other side shall not approach within 10 yards of the ball until it is kicked off.

3. **Changing ends**

   After a goal is won the losing side shall kick-off and goals shall be changed.

4. **Scoring a Goal, Ball in play**

   A goal shall be won when the ball passes between the goal posts or over the space between the goal posts (at whatever height), not being thrown, knocked on, or carried.

5. **Throw Ins**

   When the ball is in touch the first player who touches it shall throw it from the point on the boundary line where it left the ground, in a direction at right angles with the boundary line and it shall not be in play until it has touched the ground.

6. **Offside rule**

   When a player has kicked the ball any one of the same side who is nearer to the opponent's goal line is out of play and may not touch the ball himself nor in any way whatever prevent any other player from doing so until the ball has been played; but no player is out of play when the ball is kicked from behind the goal line.

7. **Goal Kicks and Corners**

   In case the ball goes behind the goal line, if a player on the side to whom the goal belongs first touches the ball, one of his side shall be entitled to a free kick from the goal line at the point opposite the place where the ball shall be touched. If a player of the opposite side first touches the ball, one of his side shall be entitled to a free kick (but at the goal only) from a point 15 yards from the goal line opposite the place where the ball is touched. The opposing side shall stand behind their goal line until he has had his kick.

8. **Handball rule**

   If a player makes a fair catch, he shall be entitled to a free kick, provided he claims it by making a mark with his heel at once; ad in order to take such kick he may go as far back as he pleases, and no player on the opposite side shall advance beyond his mark until he has kicked.

9. **Handling**

No player shall carry the ball.

10. **Fair Play**

Neither tripping nor hacking shall be allowed and no player shall use his hands to hold or push his adversary.

11. **A player shall not throw the ball nor pass it to another.**

12. **Picking up the ball.**

No player shall take the ball from the ground with his hands while it is in play under any pretence whatever.

13. **Boots**

No player shall wear projecting nails, iron plates, or gutta percha on the soles or heels of his boots.

Definition of Terms:

A **Place-Kick** is a kick at the ball while on the ground, in any position which the kicker may choose to place it.

Hacking is kicking an adversary intentionally.

Tripping is throwing an adversary by the use of the legs.

Knocking on is when a player strikes or propels the ball with his hands or arms.

Holding includes the obstruction of a player by the hand or any part of the arm below the elbow.

Touch is that part of the field, on either side of the ground, which is beyond the line of flags.

Mem. — Handling is understood to be playing the ball with the hand or arm.

Appendix 6: FOOTBALL IN BATTERSEA PARK, BY THE RULES OF THE LONDON ASSOCIATION.

(THE FIELD – SATURDAY 9TH JANUARY 1984)

We have already congratulated the gentlemen who have taken part in the many meetings held during the last ten or twelve weeks to discuss, the principles of football and the rules by which it ought to be played, upon the result of their deliberations. Our opinion respecting the rules which they ultimately agreed upon was formed by an extensive knowledge of all the existing games; and we did not hesitate to say that they appeared to be framed upon the true principles of the game, in accordance with modern opinions upon the character which our pastimes should ever maintain, and so as to meet all points in the game which have led to so many vexatious disputes. We went last Saturday to watch with great interest the game played by them in Battersea Park. hoping to find them in practice as satisfactory as they were in print. This hope, if it was not completely realised, was at least so far verified as to entitle us to repeat our congratulations, and say that no club need now languish for want of a well-digested code of laws, which admit of scientific play, exclude the features which lead to disputes, and those which are too violent, and at the same time ensure the game from any want of spirit or tameness.

Though the game played by the sides of the President (Mr Pember) and the Secretary (Mr Morley) was not absolutely the first attempted by the new rules, it was the inaugural one; and a better locality for it could not have been found than Battersea Park. If football should, as it promises at the present time to do, again become a popular and national pastime, the inhabitants of London will have ready provided for them in Battersea Park capital grounds for playing it; and great as is already the value of this resort for the summer pastimes, it will be doubled by furnishing a similar area for a scarcely less interesting one during the six months that cricket is impracticable. We throw out this hint for the begat of our readers who are in some measure prevented from becoming football players because they consider they had no ground. Both ground and rules are ready made for them.

We naturally and very generally associate football with the mild autumnal days, and those scarcely less pleasant ones of which our modern winters furnish so many examples, and which are like April rather than December or January days. It was, however, no such day last Saturday, as our readers will doubtless remember. The thermometer was, in the open air, several degrees below freezing point; there was a cold wind, ice three-quarters of an inch thick, hard ground, and people in the streets were buttoned up to their throats. The frost had but newly begun, or the game must have been abandoned; as it was, the turf was hard enough to make falls—falls were and always will be of common occurrence in football—far from pleasant. Even the hardy and dauntless students at the schools, who play in rain, or snow, or fog, have to forego their favourite pastime when the ground gets frostbitten and as hard as flagstones. The frost, however, was not considered sufficiently severe to prevent the game being played. The spectators, of whom there were a goodly number, felt themselves to be at a great disadvantage. With nothing to do beyond seeing, the cold made itself felt at fingers' ends and toes very keenly. But meanwhile, the gentlemen who were engaged in the game, with only their coloured jerseys to protect their shoulders, and many of them with " roofless heads," defied the cold and enjoyed the bracing air as skaters do, or as did the nudes of whom Barclay Wrote In his fifth eclogue :

> The sturdy plowman, lustie. strong, and bold.
> Overcometh the winter with driving the foote-ball,
> Forgetting labour and many a grievous fall.

The ground was at the Battersea end of the park, and the goals nearly due east and west, at a distance of about 100 yards, with a breadth of 80 yards. Law 1 of the Association provides for the maximum length at 200 yards, with a breadth of 100 yards. These proportions are larger than any we know. For all the purposes of the game, the size of ground used in Battersea is quite sufficient, though scarcely so great as the majority of grounds, which are about 150 yards long. With powerful kickers, such as some of the gentlemen who played in this game, the ball might with a favourable wind be kicked from the place kick, in the centre at the opening of the game, through the goal ; but this would very rarely be done.

The brilliant sunset, almost directly in the faces of the players from the eastern goal, gave the opposite side an obvious advantage. This was, however, reversed when the first goal was kicked. The wind, though not very high, made itself felt. It blew across the ground, and, being unequal, the players found it impossible to make due allowance for it ; consequently, many kicks which aimed at goal resulted in the ball falling many yards wide of the mark. The mention of the ball prompts us to offer a remark, which, though not applicable to the Association, is to very many clubs. It is a very common error to think it cannot be too large, and clubs that now use a No. 6 would find a No. 4 very much pleasanter to play with; easier to manage, less affected by the wind, and, in fact, generally very far superior. The Rugby ball, which is oval, is an exceptional case ; but we would strongly advise players to select a 4 size, in preference to any other. In ancient days the ball was a bladder, as the following will show :

> And now in the winter, when men kill the fat swine,
> They get the bladder and blow it great and thin,
> With many beans and peason put within:
> It rattleth, soundeth, clere and fayre,
> While It is throwen and caste up in ayre.
> Each one contendeth and hathe a great delite
> With foote and with hande the bladder for to smite;
> If it fall to grounde they lift It up agayne
> And this way to labour they count It no payne.

Whatever we have done with laws since then, no one will doubt the superiority of the balls which Mr Lillywhite supplied, to the ancient bladder. We have already pointed out the analogy between the rules and those of Cambridge. Having now seen them both in practice, we may say they accord even more closely than we anticipated. The Association have an advantage in the matter of distance-posts, which they erect at 15 yards distance from the corners; and on a line with these, opposite that spot of the goal-line over which the ball passed before being touched down, the kick at goal is made. At Cambridge these posts are 25 yards from the goal-line, a distance which makes kicking a goal too difficult to be very often accomplished; and, as we have before observed, the effect of all existing rules is to make goals too exceptional. There is one other point in which the Association rules have an advantage—they permit catching : the others do not. Both admit the use of the hands to stop the ball. It would be unnatural to forbid it; but in the play on Parker's Piece there was no running with, or holding the ball. Neither was any striking allowed. All these were frequently seen in the game on Saturday. They are very objectionable, and will, we hope, be excluded. A rule forbids carrying the ball, and probably when players become more familiar with the new code it will not be seen. Striking the ball is even a graver error ; and playing it with the hands, pushing it along when it might just as well have been played with the feet, is also very much to be deprecated, and ought to be entirely discontinued. The off - side rule will, like some others, work all the better for practice; but as it was, every player endeavoured to keep in his proper position, and refrained from play when he was not so. We shall not be considered hypercritical in making these remarks, even though this was the trial game of the new laws. It would be a great mistake not to mention what appear to be the only blemishes in so good a set of rules. The game was vigorously played, the ball flew about the ground with great rapidity, and there was some very fine kicking on both sides, though it was evident upon which the greater strength lay. Two goals were obtained, but was never an instance of a touch-down beyond the goal-line by the side besieging a goal. As a rule, the ball was kept well in the ground, and when it went out at the sides was promptly thrown in again. We have repeatedly said that a certain amount of shinning is unavoidable: this game proved the remark. With a law to forbid it, and with every care upon the part of the players to avoid it, kicks would of necessity reach the shins now and then. How can it be otherwise, when two players run at the ball, arrive at the same instant of time, and one hits and the other misses the ball, or kicks at the moment it leaves the toe of his opponent? Tripping and pushing are disallowed. Charging is of course permitted, and adds not a little to the interest which the game has, both for players and spectators. Waller has given us a capital description of this feature, which applies to-day just as forcibly as it did when he wrote :

> As when a sort of laity shepherds try,
> Their force at football; care of victory.
> Makes them salute so rudely breast to breast,
> That their encounter seems too rough for Jest.

The charge, though a player may throw his whole strength into it, and bring his shoulder with a very powerful butt against that of his opponent; is not dangerous unless a very little man charges a very big one, which is not often the case. It is simply a try who can stand firmest on his legs; and when one or both bowl over, they are soon up again, none the worse for it, and indeed repeating the figure again at the earliest opportunity. The game football, as we saw it played in Battersea Park, is one in which gentlemen and boys might engage together; at which all classes might play in common as they do at cricket, without any fear of results, but with general pleasure and mutual advantage. The clubs which compose the Association have hitherto been very energetic supporters of the game, playing matches, club against club, almost every week through the season. It was the difficulty occasioned by the variety, each club having its own especial code of laws—of the rules which, in conjunction with the general interest of the game, led to the formation of the Association. For the future these matches will be played upon the one set of rules, and an increased interest is felt in the game. This arrangement cannot fail, moreover, in proving, more satisfactorily than the old one did, the superiority of the best club., as they will no longer be playing home-and-home matches upon different systems. The constitution of the Association provides for an annual meeting to be held at the commencement of the football season every year, and at these meetings it will be always possible to alter. amend, or introduce rules, as may seem desirable. The permanent good of such a society cannot fail to be great.

(J. D. CARTWRIGHT.)

Appendix 7: The Laws of the Game (1871)

1. The maximum length of the ground shall be 200 yards, the maximum breadth shall be 100 yards; the length and breadth shall be marked off with flags; and the goals shall be upright posts, 8 yards apart, with a tape across them, 8 feet from the ground.

2. The winners of the toss shall have the choice of goals. The game shall be commenced by a place-kick from the centre of the ground by the side losing the toss; the other side shall not approach within 10 yards of the ball until it is kicked off.

3. After a goal is won the losing side shall kick-off, and goals shall be changed. In the event, however, of no goal having fallen to either party at the lapse of half the allotted time, ends shall then be changed.

4. A goal shall be won when the ball passes between the goal-posts under the tape, not being thrown, knocked on, or carried.

5. When the ball is in touch, the first player who touches it shall throw it from the point on the boundary line where it left the ground, in a direction at right angles with the boundary line, to a distance of at least six yards, and it shall not be in play until it shall have touched the ground, and the player throwing it in shall not play it until it has been played by another player.

6. When a player has kicked the ball, any one of the same side who is nearer to the opponents' goal-line is out of play, and may not touch the ball himself nor in any way whatever prevent any other player from doing so until the ball has been played, unless there are at least three of his opponents between him and their own goal; but no player is out of play when the ball is kicked from behind the goal-line.

7. When the ball is kicked behind the goal-line, it must be kicked off by the side behind whose goal it went within six yards from the limit of their goal. The side who thus kick the ball are entitled to a fair kick-off in whatever way they please without any obstruction, the opposite side not being able to approach within six yards of the ball.

8. No player shall carry or knock on the ball; and handling the ball, under any pretence whatever, shall be prohibited, except in the case of the goal-keeper, who shall be allowed to use his hands for the protection of his goal.

9. Neither tripping nor hacking shall be allowed, and no player shall use his hands to hold or push his adversary, nor charge him from behind.

10. A player shall not throw the ball nor pass it to another.

11. No player shall take the ball from the ground with his hands while it is in play under any pretence whatever.

12. No player shall wear projecting nails, iron plates, or gutta percha on the soles or heels of his boots.

Definition of Terms:
A **Place-Kick** is a kick at the ball while on the ground, in any position which the kicker may choose to place it.
Hacking is kicking an adversary intentionally.
Tripping is throwing an adversary by the use of the legs.
Knocking on is when a player strikes or propels the ball with his hands or arms.

Holding includes the obstruction of a player by the hand or any part of the arm below the elbow.

Touch is that part of the field, on either side of the ground, which is beyond the line of flags.

Mem. — Handling is understood to be playing the ball with the hand or arm.

Includes amendments as agreed at the Meeting of the Football Association, Freemasons Tavern, Monday 27ᵗʰ February 1871.

Connect with Ian Chester:

email: ianchesteri@btinternet.com
twitter: @Ian20583404
Facebook: Ian Chester
Instagram: chesfox77
Linked-In: Ian Chester

If you have in anyway enjoyed this book, and feel so inclined, please would you be so kind as to leave a review on the Amazon or Goodreads website. As a self-published author, online reviews are like gold dust and open the door to the larger audiences accessible by the major publishers.

Many thanks in advance.

Ian Chester,
Warwickshire,
England.

Appendix 8: 1871-72 FA Cup - Round by Round

FOOTBALL ASSOCIATION CHALLENGE CUP - RESULTS 1871/72

Round 1

Sat 11th November 1871 — *Hitchin Cricket Ground*	
Hitchin	0
Crystal Palace	0
Sat 11th November 1871 — *York Road, Maidenhead*	
Maidenhead United	2
Marlow FC	0
Harrow Chequers	WD
Wanderers	
Sat 11th November 1871 — *West Ham Park*	
Upton Park	0
Clapham Rovers	3
Queens Park	BYE
Donington School	BYE
Royal Engineers	WD
Reigate Priory	
Sat 11th November 1871 — *Limes Field, Barnes*	
Barnes FC	2
Civil Service	0
Hampstead Heathens	BYE

Round 2

Sat 16th December 1871 — *Crystal Palace Cricket Ground*	
Crystal Palace	3
Maidenhead United	0
Sat 16th December 1871 K.O 3 p.m. — *Clapham Common*	
Wanderers	1
Clapham Rovers	0
Queens Park	
Donington School	WD
Sat 23rd December 1871 — *Barnes*	
Royal Engineers	5
Hitchin	0
Wed 10th January 1872 — *Oval*	
Barnes FC	1
Hampstead Heathens	1

Replay — Sat 06/01/1872, *Barnes*: Barnes 0 / Barnes FC 0

Round 3

Sat 20th January 1872 — *Clapham Common*	
Crystal Palace	0
Wanderers	0
Queens Park	BYE
Sat 27th January 1872 — *Queen Lines, Chatham*	
Royal Engineers	3
Hampstead Heathens	0

Semi Final

Mon 4th March 1872 — *Oval*	
Wanderers	0
Queens Park	0
Sat 17th February 1872 — *Oval*	
Royal Engineers	0
Crystal Palace	0

Replay

Queens Park	WD
Sat 09/03/1872 — *Oval*	
Royal Engineers	3
Crystal Palace	0

FINAL

Sat 16th March 1872 — *Oval*	
Wanderers	1
Royal Engineers	0

Appendix 9: Anniversary programmes 1922, 1972, 2022?

	**50th Anniversary** **Sat. 29th April 1922** **PRESTON NORTH END (0)** Versus **HUDDERSFELD TOWN (1)** Scorer: Billy Smith (pen.) Stamford Bridge Attendance : 53,000
	**Centenary Year** **Sat. 6th May 1972** **ARSENAL (0)** Versus **LEEDS UTD (1)** Scorer: Allan Clarke Wembley Stadium Attendance : 100,000 Referee: David Smith
	**150th Anniversary** **Sat.14th May 2022** **??????? (-)** Versus **??????? (-)** Scorer: xxx xxxx Wembley Stadium Attendance : 90,000

BIBLIOGRAPHY:

General:
England's Oldest Football Clubs 1815-1889 – Martin Westby - 2020
The Father of Modern Sport - Keith Booth - The Parrs Wood Press 2002.
The FA Cup – The Complete Story – Guy Lloyd & Nick Holt – Aurum Press Ltd 2005
The Rules of Association Football 1863 – Bodleian Library, University of Oxford 2006
100 years of the FA Cup – Tony Pawson -William Heinemann Ltd. 1972
First Elevens: the birth of international football. Andy Mitchell Media 2012
The WOW Factor – John Blythe Smart – Blythe Smart Publications 2003
Cup Final Extra – Martin Tyler – The Hamlyn Publishing Group Ltd 1981
Official Illustrated History of the FA Cup, Bryon Butler, Headline Book Publishing 1998
The Oval – Souvenir Guidebook – Scala Arts & Heritage Publishers 2018
The First FA Cup - Don Gillan – 2nd Edition 2017
Football Firsts – Tony Matthews – Arcturus Publishing Ltd 2006
The Victorian Football Miscellany- Paul Brown – Goalposts 2013
The early FA Cup Finals & the Southern Amateurs – Keith Warsop – Tony Brown 2004
England's First football Captain, Cuthbert Ottaway 1850-1878 – Michael Southwick 2009
Beastly Fury 'The Strange birth of British Football' Richard Sanders, Bantam Books 2009
History of British Football – Percy Young – Stanley Paul 1969
Puddings, Bullies and Squashes: Early Public School Football Codes – Malcom Tozer –
Independent Publishing Network – October 2020

Crystal Palace Club:
Palace at the Palace – A History of the Crystal Palace and its Football Club, 1851-1915 –
Peter Manning – PowerLaw Ltd 2018
The first Crystal Palace Football Club 1861-1876 – Stuart Hibberd 2021

Sheffield Football Club:
Celebrating 150 years of the World's First Football Club – Heart Ltd 2007
Sheffield Football Club (Oldest in the World) 1857–1957, Fred Walters 1957
From Sheffield With Love – Brendan Murphy – Sports Books Ltd 2007
Sheffield Football a History – Keith Farnsworth – The Hallamshire Press 1995
A History of Sheffield Football 1857-1889 – Marin Westby – 2018

Queen's Park Football Club:
History of the Queen's Park Football Club 1867-1917 – Richard Robinson 1920
– PM Publications 2016

Maidenhead Football Club:
One For Sorrow, Two For Joy – Flowprint Ltd 2011

Royal Engineers:
Foot Soldiers – Nick Collins – Pitch Publishing 2020

The Wanderers:
The Wanderers FC 'Five times FA Cup winners' – Rob Cavallini – Dog N' Duck
Publications 2005

Other Books by Ian Chester

At twelve minutes past three on 28th June 1919, the leaders of the 'Big Four' Allied powers met in the Palace of Versailles in France, to sign a Treaty which would bring down the final curtain on the First World War. Ten hours later, at one o'clock in the morning, a new battle commenced as 67 riders met at the Parc de Princes in Paris, to set off on the second longest Tour de France in history.

Exactly 100 years to the day, let's follow in their footsteps, witnessing every excruciating pedal turn of the 5,560km route. Let's struggle through the bloody battlefields of the Somme, land on the Normandy beaches and bumble along the Brittany Coast. Let's climb the perilous Pyrenees, get swept away by the Marseille Mistral and celebrate the 100th birthday of the 'maillot jaune' outside the Cafe de l'Ascenseur in Grenoble. We'll visit France's long-lost sisters of Alsace & Lorraine, before coming face to face with the mud and blood of the poppy fields of Flanders. Finally, we pedal on to the Party in the Parc in Gay Paris.

This is the story of those brave men, newly returned from the Great War, cycling through the night, often in horrendous conditions, on fixed wheel bikes, all to win the now coveted yellow jersey.

Travel with me and discover the story of
The Green-Toothed Witch and The Yellow Canary.

Available on Amazon in paperback and Kindle or for a signed copy email the author direct at ianchesteri@btinternet.com.

Printed in Great Britain
by Amazon